ALAN HAYNES was born in Surrey and educated at Sutton County Grammar School and University College, Cardiff, where he took an honours degree. After several years of teaching history and English in London he did post-graduate research at the Institute of Historical Research, London University.

This is the first book Mr Haynes has written, but he has contributed many articles and book reviews to *History Today*. He is currently working on a biography of Robert Cecil, 1st Earl of Salisbury.

THE WHITE BEAR

ALAN HAYNES

THE WHITE BEAR

*Robert Dudley, The Elizabethan
Earl of Leicester*

PETER OWEN · LONDON

ISBN 0 7206 0672 1

PETER OWEN PUBLISHERS
73 Kenway Road London SW5 0RE

First published 1987
©Alan Haynes 1987

Photoset and printed in Great Britain by
WBC Print Barton Manor St Philips Bristol

To my mother
and in memory of my father

Contents

Contents

Illustrations

Power consisteth chieflye in three things,
that is, in riches, in public authoritie,
and in pryvate estimacion.

Thomas Blundeville

Introduction

In his biography of Robert Dudley, the Earl of Leicester, published in 1721, Samuel Jebb wrote: 'I have neither endeavoured to advance his merits, nor extenuate his faults. I have strove to do justice to his character, where I thought him injured, and have not been wanting to lay open his irregularities where the charge has been founded upon a just evidence.' The pity is that since then so few who have written about Leicester have approached their subject with such a reasonable framework for what they wanted to achieve. Most have been content to rework previous efforts so that errors and much fanciful claptrap have solidified into a bogus picture of the man. At best he has been regarded as a meddlesome courtier, extravagantly indulged by a besotted monarch; a man lamentably inferior in all the skills of government to William Cecil (Lord Burghley). The picture of Leicester can be even darker, making him corruptly inefficient, stupid, and vindictive towards his enemies.

Exploding this florid mutation of the truth about the man requires a thoroughly detailed examination of all aspects of his life. This book places Leicester as a pivotal figure in Elizabethan England. He achieved his grand position despite the taint of treason he inherited from his able but luckless grandfather, Edmund Dudley, and from his gifted father, John, Duke of Northumberland, both men being executed by previous Tudor monarchs. After spiritedly resisting the accession of Mary Tudor to the throne, Robert Dudley spent some months of great anxiety in the Tower of London, and was fortunate to escape the block. On his release early in 1555 he and his surviving two brothers had to reconstruct as best they could their shattered court careers, and they did so by brief but successful military service in the armies of the Queen's consort, Philip of Spain.

Their fortunes improved even more dramatically when Queen Mary died and her younger sister Elizabeth came to the throne. She was about the same age as Robert, and he was swiftly marked out for her particular favour, partly no doubt because he was tall, dark and handsome. He became her Master of the Horse, an important court position, and then a Knight of the Garter. To help maintain his brilliant style Elizabeth granted him estates and trading privileges. The post-succession euphoria was only partly dissipated when in September 1560 his wife, Lady Amye Dudley, died in odd circumstances that invited speculation then as they still do today. Given the special regard Elizabeth had shown the young lord, it is hardly surprising that his enemies quickly seized upon the demise of Amye to imagine a murder that had freed him for pursuit of the Crown matrimonial. The extreme and persistent lack of evidence for such a melodramatic notion scarcely matters to those who prefer titillating fictions to facts. Moreover, they overlook another factor, that the particular circumstances of Amye's death made his marriage to Elizabeth even less practicable, as Dudley would surely have been the first to note. But in October 1562, when Elizabeth was dangerously ill with smallpox, the depth of her attachment to him was underscored when the proposal was made to an aghast privy council that he should be invested with the powers of Lord Protector. This galled the conservative Cecil and dismayed many more, and their chagrin was heightened later in 1564 when Lord Robert became Baron of Denbigh and Earl of Leicester.

He continued to accumulate as bounty from an open-handed Queen a great patchwork of manors, houses, estates, castles, (notably Kenilworth), forests and ecclesiastical properties in England and Wales. Together with his brother Ambrose (made Lord of Ruthin in 1564), Leicester was the leading landowner of North Wales; a hold he consolidated in July 1565 when he was appointed Chamberlain of the County palatine of Chester. In the following year, as confirmation again of his status as a great magnate and favourite, Elizabeth made her first visit to Kenilworth. Yet the most famous and costly visit was not made for another decade.

The scale of Leicester's hospitality to the Queen, foreign dignitaries and his contemporaries at court was always notable. It needed a substantial income beyond even that to be had from the gifts of pensions and estates, so that in the 1560s and 1570s the earl became by necessity a venture capitalist with investments in a range of speculative business activities, which won him the respect (if not always the admiration) of the merchant community in London.

One of his great interests was the saltpetre trade at a time when English supplies, essential for the manufacture of gunpowder, were desperately restricted. When a sample of the coveted material was sent from Morocco to England by an English trader, tests were carried out at the armoury at Kenilworth. After a decade of irregular trading in Morocco, Leicester became the key figure in the Barbary Company, although its actual trading profits were minimal. Much more important as a prop to his conspicuous consumption (which in itself generated work for hundreds in town and country) was the Sweet Wine Farm, a monopoly that he subleased to the Customs officer of London, Thomas Smyth, for a clear and reliable profit. Leicester was inclined to scatter investments because, like many of his aristocratic contemporaries living on incomes gnawed by inflation, he always needed large sums of money. The risks were high, but the possibilities attracted the gambler in him.

It was in late August 1572, as Elizabeth again visited Kenilworth, that news reached the court from Walsingham, England's ambassador in France, of the massacre of St Bartholomew's Eve. This was a savage culmination, especially in Paris, of sectarian strife in France, and was regarded with dismay and horror in England. Leicester's personal revulsion at the calamity that had befallen the Huguenots was partly due to his religious sympathies and previous contacts with them, and partly because his nephew, Philip Sidney, was in the capital during the murder and mayhem. Happily the young man was able to reach the sanctuary of the English embassy before departing for Germany.

In the period after the massacre Burghley's central position on the privy council as the spokesman for moderate policies was strengthened by the support he received from the Lord Keeper,

Nicholas Bacon. Yet it was Burghley who, with the Queen's approval, promoted Walsingham to the council, and it must have been an uncomfortable jolt when the dour administrator soon shifted his political allegiance to Leicester. The Spanish ambassador wrote to Philip II that, of the seventeen councillors, 'the business really depends upon the Queen, Leicester, Walsingham and Cecil'. There is no reason to doubt this claim, and the records show that the great courtier Leicester was a most conscientious attender at council meetings, quite equalling his old rival, Burghley. Of unfathomable importance for the direction of policy was the intense daily familiarity of the Queen and her councillors, so many of them linked by blood and marriage.

For most of his life Leicester cannily anticipated (and exploited) the Queen's moods; it was part of his armoury as her leading courtier and confidant. To maintain his extraordinary position sometimes required a tactful dissimulation, especially in sexual matters, since Elizabeth's jealousy of any rivals for his affection was intense. Yet in one tantalizing respect he was most unlike his philoprogenitive father: from apparently numerous affairs only one woman is unequivocally recorded as having born him a son, albeit illegitimate, and until the birth of his legal son, the hunchback Lord Denbigh, he was without a direct heir. A further calamity for any dynastic ambitions he might have had came in 1584 when the boy died, and since he was without a male heir for so long, it is not surprising that Leicester took a particular interest in the career of Philip Sidney, who was gratifyingly proud of his Dudley ancestry.

By this time Leicester was approaching the zenith of his political career as the champion of armed Protestantism, and he supported with great vigour the resistance of the Dutch rebels against Spanish oppression. The unflagging way he espoused their cause contrasted emphatically with his contempt for clandestine Catholicism in England, which he hoped to see extirpated. As the desperation of the English Catholics grew under pressure from the government, their anger at Leicester found expression in the publication abroad of the anonymous libel known in brief as *Leicester's Commonwealth* (1584). In spite of strenuous efforts, attempts to suppress the distribution of the book in England failed. The target of the venomous calumnies was of course incensed by the text, without his knowing that it would be instrumental in shaping his posthumous reputation.

He was even less fortunate when the well-meaning and lengthily planned intervention he engineered to assist the Dutch revolt ended in fierce recriminations and without an outstanding victory to his credit. His devotion in earnest to the Protestant cause in the years before the Spanish Armada fleet sailed to destruction in 1588 has often been dismissed in a few contemptuous lines that somehow gleefully record his failure. But at first his commitment was unfeigned, and blame for the débâcle can be split between Elizabeth, the various squabbling Dutch factions, and the earl himself. His time in the United Provinces also cost him much in terms of wealth, and the well-being of his family and friends.

Elizabeth usually receives plaudits for employing Burghley so steadfastly, and only bemused, mild scorn for choosing and endlessly protecting Leicester, whose faults likewise she knew. But it is well to remember his many virtues as a brilliant companion, dedicated patron of arts, letters and science, and statesman. While comparatively minor Elizabethan politicians have been the subject of detailed scrutiny and sober biographies, Leicester has until recently (and with one formidable scholarly exception[1]) been virtually ignored by academic historians, perhaps because there has always been the crucial difficulty of giving a coherent biographical shape to a richly complicated life.

With the approach of the 400th anniversary of Leicester's death in 1588, the effort to deal with him seriously seems more than ever worthwhile, especially if this book can correct some of the accreted nonsense still repeated about Leicester. It is now time to replace the old, shallow picture of the man with a bolder, stronger and broadly detailed examination of a remarkable English Renaissance prince.

NOTE

The chapter titles are quotations from various texts relating to the Earl of Leicester and his period. Years have been taken to commence on 1 January not 25 March.

Chapter 1

My Deadly Stroke

During the lifetime of Robert Dudley his many enemies pointed gleefully to the fate of his grandfather and father. Edmund Dudley and John Dudley, Earl of Warwick and later Duke of Northumberland, had both been executed after sustained service to the Tudors. The Dudleys were often reviled for their patent ambition, cupidity and only transient success, and also for what the old lineal aristocracy thought of as their upstart social pretensions. Wealth then was in land, which equalled social dignity: both John Dudley and his brilliant son were defensive about their ancestry. Therefore they used heralds at the College of Arms to add polish to the family line, although their sensitivity to the jibes was unnecessary, since the family had many connections with the landed class.

In the early fourteenth century John de Sutton had married Margaret, the daughter and heiress of Roger Somery, Baron of Dudley, the family having owned Dudley Castle for over a century. Several generations of John de Suttons followed until the one born at the beginning of the fifteenth century. He married Elizabeth Berkeley, daughter of Sir John Berkeley, a connection that paved the way for the famous 'Berkeley Suit', which was fought in and out of the law courts for over eight generations. The second son of this union, called inevitably John, married yet another Elizabeth, this time the wealthy heiress daughter of Thomas (or John) Bramshot of Sussex, and the couple settled in Atherington. A local office holder and several times MP, his son was Edmund, who followed his father into Parliament. This continuity becomes striking only when we note how by the end of the sixteenth century the Dudley line was petering out for want of legitimate sons.

Edmund Dudley was probably born in the early 1460s into a well-positioned family that had moved to the middle rungs of the educated, landed class. His Uncle William, for example, became Bishop of Durham, which was one of the richest sees in the Church, and he was also briefly Chancellor of Oxford University. It is disputed but it is probable that Edmund began his studies there in about 1475, before moving to Gray's Inn to study law.[1] The Inns of Court did more than offer legal training, and not the least aspect of their importance to talented young men of ambition was their proximity to the court. Such a galvanizing opportunity Edmund seized with a gusto that made him the first great achiever and national figure of the Dudley family. He knew very precisely what he aspired to be – a leading member of the ruling administrative class – and he made a formidable start by being appointed to Henry VII's privy council when he was still in his early twenties. Suspicious of the wealthy merchant class, Edmund Dudley made it clear in his political testament, *The Tree of Commonwealth*, completed in his cell in the Tower of London after the death of his royal patron, that his class should educate their children for power, which in turn would allow them to retain their property. This was what he had started to do for his own young sons, born of a second marriage to Elizabeth Grey, the daughter of Edward Grey, Viscount Lisle.

His intentions were, however, cut short by the axe. On 17 August 1510 his neck and ambitions were sundered by order of the young king, Henry VIII. Dudley and his contemporary, Sir Richard Empson, had been promoted by Henry VII because of their financial acumen and guile. They had shared the judicial work of the council in the Star Chamber and in the chamber of the Duchy of Lancaster. Having worked assiduously for the King's profit as well as their own, they had inevitably made enemies in the court and the country. In the royal family, Margaret, Duchess of Richmond and Derby, and the grand-mother of Henry VIII, regarded them with particular scorn. In the country they were detested for their supposed exactions by merchants and landowners alike, both lay and clerical. So Henry VIII, who succeeded his father in April 1509, needed little prompting to gauge the possibility of pleasing several groups without risk or cost. Thus, these living reminders of his father's fiscal prudence (which some called avarice) were done to death.

Robert Dudley was keenly interested in the career of his grandfather, and in 1562 the antiquarian historian and tailor, John Stow, made a copy of *The Tree of Commonwealth* for him. The young aristocrat was equally fascinated and dismayed by the career and fate of his loved father, John Dudley, who had managed to escape from the shadow of attainted obscurity. He was partly fortunate in that his mother had made a beneficial second marriage to Arthur Plantagenet, the illegitimate son of Edward IV, a union that protected the Dudleys from financial ruin after the death of Edmund. Like his father, John Dudley was trained in law, and he learned to use the courts to rebuild the dismembered family landholdings. Eventually, he even wrested Dudley Castle from a dim-witted cousin, John de Sutton, Lord Dudley.[2] Together with Sir Edward Seymour, later Lord Protector, Dudley was knighted after service with the army in France, and from then on he nurtured a court career that expunged the disgrace of his father.

During Henry VIII's diseased decline at the end of his reign, both men moved steadily towards the centre of Henrician government. In a new creation in 1542, Sir John Dudley became Viscount Lisle, which at least kept him in step with Seymour, who was now Earl of Hertford. A recent political biography of Dudley has suggested that before his ennoblement he had virtually no political enemies. Though a privy councillor and a Knight of the Garter, he does not seem to have antagonized anyone – a quite remarkable achievement, since at the same time he had steadily accumulated lands in twenty-six counties in England and Wales.[3] Yet, acutely conscious of his father's fate, he continually made modest disclaimers about his own abilities and training for government. Indeed, it is possible that as the father of a relentlessly growing family he might have preferred the life of a country gentleman if he had not now been firmly meshed by the requirements of court life.

By 1547 John Dudley had five surviving sons and two daughters from thirteen children, and during the reign of Edward VI all reached an age for marriage. Of the boys, Robert was the fifth son born and thus arrived curiously late in the

sequence of births when we remark on his matchless ambitions.
The exact date of his birthday is still disputed. Early in the
seventeenth century Emanuel van Meteren, who knew him
well, implied that he was born in 1525. Modern writers have
usually preferred a later date, with many now settling for 24
June 1532 or 1533 (when his father was Master of the Armoury
at the Tower). Whatever the truth of this minor matter the
Dudley children were raised at court by devoted parents, and
the boys were all close companions of Edward VI. Like their
father as they grew older, John, Ambrose, Henry, Robert and
Guildford were expected to show knightly prowess to match
their book learning. These skills in combat and equitation were
shown in the tilts organized during the young King's reign.[4]
An especially accomplished horseman, Robert became a first-
string jouster, and in June 1552 received his first royal
appointment as Master of the Buckhounds. He succeeded his
brother John in this post, which had a salary of £33. 6s. 8d., and
he also became a gentleman in ordinary of the bedchamber and,
early in 1553, chief carver to the King.

The marriages of these sons and daughters was a matter
requiring reflection by the parents. In 1550, for example, to
signal a reconciliation between Warwick and Edward Seymour,
still Duke of Somerset though not Lord Protector since a coup in
1549, the younger John Dudley (Lord Lisle until he took his
father's title) married Lady Anne Seymour. This was a union
that both families must have seen as significant and advantageous,
the ceremony taking place before the King. The following day it
was actually followed by another wedding that was to
reverberate in history, literature and even myth, though it
attracted much less attention then. This was the union of Lord
Robert Dudley with Amye Robsart, the only daughter of Sir
John and Lady Elizabeth Robsart. They were landowners in
Norfolk, and because of the illegitimacy of her brother Arthur,
Amye was an heiress, a fact that added to her physical charm.
The couple had probably met first in the previous year during
Warwick's short campaign against the rising led by Robert Kett
of Wymondham, a disaffected tenant of the Dudley family. The
motley clutch of protestors who made up his ramshackle force
was swept aside at Dussin's Dale in late August 1549, and
Warwick's victory helped to consolidate his own political power.

To a great extent the husband and bride – Robert and Amye – were dependent on parental bounty. From Robert's father they received Coxford Priory in Norfolk, as well as other lands, and from Sir John a home at Syderstone which he had previously occupied. Probably it was a love match, since for the young lord it was not a remarkable advance in terms of property or social connection. In fact, to enable his son and daughter-in-law to live comfortably, Northumberland (he became a duke in October 1551) scavenged for properties. Robert Dudley and William Glasier (or Glaseor), a strong family supporter, were jointly granted the manor of Knightwick in Worcestershire. Robert was also made a guardian for two years of the deranged Thomas Philpot, and then the manor of Hemsby near Yarmouth was passed to him. Subsequently Robert Dudley became an MP for a Norfolk seat in the Parliament of 1553, when his Uncle Andrew sat for Oxfordshire and his brother-in-law Sir Henry Sidney for Kent.

Then suddenly in the summer of that year the tubercular sickness which afflicted the young King accelerated, and his rapid decline became apparent. Northumberland, whose power in the government was briefly paramount as he 'ambitiously sought to dominate Edward VI's courtiers and councillors', felt hideously exposed, for he was no longer without enemies and his government was still unpopular at home. Indeed, it has been said that perhaps 'no Tudor government ever stood in greater fear of a rebellious commons than did that of the duke of Northumberland in the period 1550-3'.[5] One of the most intriguing aspects of the duke's landholdings was a pronounced geographical shift to favour the north of England, Northumberland intending, it has been suggested, to build a power base that would be a springboard for seizing the Crown. Thus the final stage was to be the dismemberment of the palatine see of Durham 'to obtain the control of its organization and resources for himself'.[6] Yet this crooked self-seeking, of which the duke has repeatedly been accused, is a posthumous reputation foisted on him by his enemies. The problem with this bold, even piratical figure is that he does not chime with the political or even private character of the man, nor indeed with his physical condition. The duke was mercenary but he did not seek to pillage Crown property. Only two weeks after Bishop Cuthbert Tunstall's deprivation Northumberland was bedridden, and it was by an Act of Parliament rather than a personal peremptory command of the ailing duke that the see of Durham was dissolved and then usefully reconstituted as two smaller sees.[7] Northumberland made temporary gains when he received lands from the King 'but never succeeded in establishing himself as prince of the North as charged by his detractors'.[8]

New evidence about Northumberland as Great Master (or Great Steward) of the King's Household, and as Lord President of the Council, suggests that he was a most adept conciliar administrator with a singular eye for political realities, intending 'to restore efficient administration by conciliar government'. It is possible, but according to Dale Hoak unlikely, that the decision to try to exclude the papist Mary Tudor from the throne was taken by her dying brother. It is also possible that Northumberland and his packed council dared not oppose this action for fear of accelerating the crisis that was looming. Indeed the duke may well have had a premonition of the possible miseries that would stem from her reign, but it must have been a guess, and it was with breath-taking imperviousness to the obvious that he married his son Guildford to Lady Jane Grey, who was declared as Edward's heir one week later. This was widely interpreted then and after as a mechanism to bring the young man closer to the throne; a possible preliminary to an attempt to overthrow the dynastic principle and Henry VIII's Act of Succession. It was this marriage that the duke failed to see would demolish any hope that the country would passively accept Jane as Queen. His choice of the 'devise' was based on several potent political and private considerations, in particular the lamentable fate of his own father some forty years before when a new Tudor monarch had come to the throne. Edmund Dudley had been made a scapegoat, and his gifted son, who had risen so much higher, now feared the same end. Northumberland's greatest error was to delay; a strange lethargy (induced perhaps by stomach ulcers) gripped him, and instead of taking decisive action he fumbled and hesitated when Edward VI died in the arms of one of his closest boyhood friends, the duke's son-in-law, Sir Henry Sidney, on 6 July 1553.

The news was kept from the kingdom for three days, and Mary should have been quietly removed to custody in the

Tower. This might have been accomplished by the gendarme force the duke had earlier established, only to disband them when they proved too expensive to maintain. Instead, Robert and Ambrose Dudley were eventually sent from London with several hundred light horse to Hunsdon in Hertfordshire while Mary was already afoot. She had turned from Broxbourne and, via Wetherden in Suffolk and Framlingham in Norfolk, had proceeded to Kenninghall in order to raise her standard. Gathering her forces and proclaiming herself Queen, Mary wrote to the privy council requiring their loyalty. Immediately the Dudley faction of family and friends were on the defensive, and Northumberland in a fatal seizure of nerve sluggishly cast about for a means to outmanoeuvre Mary, following the proclamation of the succession of Lady Jane Grey. The fierce silence of the city of London to this last announcement revealed that the cause was failing, for the Dudleys and the Greys were virtually her only supporters.

However, outside the city Robert Dudley was defiantly acting on his father's first wishes and desperately trying to save the day. On 11 July he moved from Wisbech to King's Lynn, intending to win this key town for his sister-in-law. Given its strategic position, wealth and size, this could have proved crucial – a fact that the town rulers seem to have understood. For a week they wrestled with their instincts and consciences, trying frantically to assess the situation without any real news of what was happening. Exasperated, Robert Dudley finally rode back to the town on Tuesday, 18 July, this time with a larger force, and according to the subsequent indictment he seized the town by force, proclaiming Queen Jane in the market-place.

Then came an even greater shock. On 20 July this victory was utterly dissipated when the baffled and deflated Northumberland announced at Cambridge the succession of Mary Tudor, and on the same day an order was sent by her councillors to the borough assembly of King's Lynn that Robert and his force should be seized. A command was also given that a watch should be kept for the duke who, it was thought, might try to flee abroad. Having failed so conspicuously to back the right horsemen, the town's leading citizens were longing for an opportunity to make amends. Robert Dudley, who had shown real martial spirit, was seized, along with his much reduced following (possibly after a struggle), and guarded by Lord Grey the small contingent was sent to Mary's camp on 21 July.[9] From there it was a journey under guard to the Beauchamp Tower: Northumberland to the gatehouse; Ambrose and Henry to the Nun's Tower; Warwick and Guildford to the middle floor, with Robert below; and Jane Dudley in the deputy lieutenant's house. Sir Andrew Dudley, the Marquess of Northampton, Nicholas Ridley, Bishop of London, and Sir Richard Corbett were also locked up. But other councillors who shuffled guiltily and adopted a muffled Protestantism scuttled to Mary's royal Catholic fold, among them the prudent William Cecil, raised by Northumberland to be the junior Secretary of State, and later Robert Dudley's greatest rival for power and patronage.

In August, Northumberland, the Earl of Warwick and the Marquess of Northampton were tried for treason and condemned, as was inevitable. Yet only the duke went to the block on 22 August, for it seems that at this stage Mary was determined to be responsible and forgiving, and his sons remained in the Tower. On 22 January 1554 Robert was arraigned in the Guildhall, accused of proclaiming Lady Jane as Queen, taking forcible possession of King's Lynn, and seeking the aid of the townsfolk against the rightful Queen. Yet because none of these high misdemeanours was treason without reference to Mary's death, he remained alive after the inevitable verdict of guilty.[10] Naturally his estates as well as those of Amye were forfeited to the Crown, yet nothing more happened. Wives were allowed to visit, so she remained in contact with him, and the brothers seem to have been kept in quite tolerable circumstances. The lieutenant of the Tower was paid on the order of the privy council 6s. 8d. per day to feed each of them and their servants, and although the huge family resources of property and money had fallen to the Crown, Ambrose, for example, had left his own mattress, bed, bolsters and other items, which were all sent to his cell.[11] Even their mother, the duchess, generously received back from the Queen a variety of seized furniture, tapestries and plate.

Virtually nothing is noted about how the brothers passed their time in captivity, although there is a stone carving of Robert's emblem and initials on a wall, and there are two metrical prayers attributed to John and Robert in the Arundel

Harington manuscript (see Appendix B). The notion that he saw much of Princess Elizabeth is in doubt; it is probably a romantic fiction concocted to explain the extraordinary bond of affection that grew between them. The Dudleys presumably spent much time mourning their adored father, while pondering their own possible fates; and they surely read a good deal, for John's books had not been confiscated. In what amounted to a small library he had a number of books in French, which the Dudley children had been taught by a humanist-scholar refugee from France, a friend of Erasmus, Nicolas Bourbon. There were also Italian and Latin items (Northumberland had known Italian), as well as a Greek grammar.[12] In the grim circumstances self-improving secular reading may have been deemed idle and sacred texts especially necessary, notably following the execution of Lady Jane and Guildford in the aftermath of Wyatt's Rebellion. Yet John, Ambrose and Robert again escaped the block, for which they had their indefatigable mother to thank, since she haunted the court as their agent, her pleas and petitions winning thereby the sympathy of several highly placed Spaniards who served Mary's husband, the Catholic Prince Philip of Spain, son of the Emperor Charles V.

Then, remarkably, at some time during the late autumn or winter of 1554 the surviving brothers were released, though John died almost immediately. Stricken by the tumult of her last years, the Duchess of Northumberland died on 22 January 1555, the day that pardons were dated, as issued, for Ambrose and Robert.[13] They were now faced by the daunting task of rebuilding court careers, and they began with the most obvious means open to them – bold exploits of arms in jousting and on the real field of battle. Like many of their contemporaries, they did not find it peculiar that they should serve their Queen's husband.

The Anglo-Spanish tilts arranged by Philip and his advisers after his arrival in mid-1554 were meant to promote harmony between two nations temporarily and uneasily yoked together by nuptial politics. The one surviving score cheque shows evidence of Philip's conciliatory purpose, and it includes the names of Robert, Henry and Ambrose Dudley.[14] Although Mary's Spanish consort left England for Brussels in September 1555, Robert was determined to seek advancement, and he

travelled abroad, possibly for the second time, to join the King's
entourage later in the year. He returned to England when
entrusted with delivering Philip's diplomatic and personal
mail.[15] Then, to try to ensure that the clouds of disgrace lifted
still further from their family, the brothers, along with other
English aristocrats, enlisted in the English force, under the
command of the Earl of Pembroke, which joined Philip's armies
fighting in France, Robert distinguishing himself as leader of an
artillery train at the Battle of St Quentin. Of course it was
advantageous to the Crown that they were using their energies
abroad, and there was always the possibility that they might get
killed, which was indeed the fate of Henry. Following his
brother's death, Robert returned to England and retired to his
estate at Hemsby, which had been restored to him along with his
title of knight. Thus for a short time Sir Robert and Amye were
together.

On 17 November 1558 Mary, half Spanish by birth, died,
unlamented by many of her subjects, who rejected her religion
and hated her consort's nation. Robert Dudley's extraordinary
public career now began, for it was he who rode to the palace of
the Bishops of Ely, Mortons Palace at Hatfield, where Elizabeth
had spent much time as a virtual prisoner, to inform her that she
was now Queen of England. When he was asked about her
conduct in the future, he advised her to take plenty of fresh air
and exercise – advice she took to heart for the rest of her long
reign. Moreover, to prove her deep affection for this surviving
Dudley, she appointed him Master of the Horse, although there
was a brief flurry of rumour that this high post would go to Lord
William Grey.[16] Dudley also seems to have been in charge of the
arrangements for Elizabeth's coronation, a swift recognition of
his passion for elaborate, symbolic display. In June 1559 he
received excellent recompense for his efforts by being created a
Knight of the Garter, an ancient order of chivalry famous for its
ceremonial observances. When in early October Duke John of
Finland arrived to woo Elizabeth as proxy for his brother Prince
Eric, later King Eric XIV of Sweden, it was Lord Robert who
led the guard of honour, and with his dark looks and lean
bearing he made a splendid figure. On 5 November he and Lord
Hunsdon appeared as the challengers in a tourney, and it was
perhaps to mark the success of this occasion that a heraldic

manuscript was compiled to honour Dudley as a prize-winner.[17] It was probably the work of Robert Cooke, a Cambridge MA and skilful herald painter who later prepared an elaborate pedigree for Dudley, his patron.

Now part of the College of Arms manuscript M.6, fos 56-62, the earlier text offers admirable illustrations of the rules of the tiltyard and the procedures of a tournament.[18] Ambrose and Robert are both featured in one line illustration which shows them delivering blows with the lance; their ragged staff emblems make them easy to identify. Furthermore, the impresa shield mounted behind Robert (which presumably he displayed in the early tournaments of the reign) shows a witty mind at work, for the design is of a vine clinging to an obelisk in the garden fashion of the time. The motto underlines the symbolism: *te stante virebo* (you standing I will flourish). To seasoned observers of court activity and manoeuvring for position it was becoming clear that the taint of Dudley treason was to be short-lived. He was a master of sparkling self-promotion, carried off with memorable flair. Courtly entertainments were of course a critical part of Dudley's campaign, and Henry Machyn recorded in his diary that later in November Lord Robert gave a great banquet in honour of Duke John. Shortly afterwards he was appointed to the office of Constable of Windsor Castle.[19]

There were impressive and continuous signs of royal high favour, and it is no wonder that Thomas Chamberlain chose Dudley and the duke as godfathers of his infant son. The youngest Knight of the Garter was not yet a political force, but the unfeigned pleasure of the Queen in his company was so marked that rivals for her attention watched him enviously. The speed of his rise from obscurity made many queasy, and they wished a plague on the name of Dudley. The Queen, however, may well have been impressed by the two preceding generations of skilled administrator politicians, one of whom had trained William Cecil. Of course Robert Dudley was married, but as Alvarez de Quadra, Bishop of Avila and the ambassador of Philip II of Spain, reported with such interest in March 1560, this was not necessarily binding. He suspected that Dudley might leave his wife in pursuit of the Crown matrimonial, and hence that the Queen was only toying with European princes who sought her hand in marriage.

Chapter 2

Grievous and Dangerous Suspicion

It was perhaps inevitable that during the period of her husband's imprisonment Amye Dudley should grow in independence and learn to deal with family matters. When Robert Dudley was released there was comparatively little change in her circumstances, for his absence abroad and then his new career at court left his wife more and more to her own devices. Yet she was never totally neglected, and prolonged separation is no proof of antipathy or evil intent. In fact Dudley did pay quite frequent visits to Amye immediately after his appointment as Master of the Horse, but the tantalizing prospect of further advancement shackled him to the court. Constant attendance on the Queen was required of the young courtier, and in the last year of Amye's life he did ignore her as he wooed Elizabeth with gallantry and service. His fidelity to his wife was waning, for he now realized that she was essentially a country woman of limited accomplishments, able to embroider[1] but not to bear him a child. To a man with Dudley's sense of family possibilities this would have been a lamentable shortcoming. It is also reasonable to suppose that she would have found court life tedious and confusing, while her husband sought it as a golden haven from poverty and obscurity. Proud of his elegance and horsemanship, Dudley revelled in the stern scrutiny of the court; it tickled his vanity.

In his absence Amye was expected, like a good country wife, to deal with farming matters. In a letter to Mr Flowerdew, the steward at Sydistone, she ordered him to sell some of the 3,000 sheep on the estate so that small debts could be paid off to the needy. Her separation from Dudley receives only a glancing reference in a letter probably written in 1558 or 1559, and it was sent from her temporary home at Denchworth, several miles from Abingdon and Cumnor where she spent the last months of her life.[2] The house she lived in was that of Mr Hyde, whose wife Alice was the daughter of Sir Thomas Essex of Lambourne in Berkshire. The Hydes had a large family, so it is apparent that Amye had not been thrust into melancholy isolation; while the house and courtyard echoed with the clamour of children, servants and animals, the absence of quiet and privacy may well have been irksome, even if the Dudleys and Hydes were old friends. Some years previously it had been the Duke of Northumberland who had sold the manor of Kingston Lisle near Denchworth to Mr Hyde, and when Amye lived with the Hydes she was both a friend and a guest with complete freedom to do as she pleased. Moreover, if Dudley neglected her by his absence, he saw to it that she was without material wants. The accounts kept by William Chaucy and Richard Ellis, acting as his stewards, show a number of entries dealing with various purchases for Amye.[3] Chaucy's accounts beginning in December 1558 and taken up to the time of her death show expenditure totalling £97. 17s. 2d. This included payments for clothes, hired horses, a trunk saddle and mirror. The dozen horses took her north to Lincolnshire and south to Hampshire, and there were journeys to Suffolk and London. Ellis's account book notes a bill of March 1560 for an embroidered velvet hat costing the substantial sum of £3. 6s. 8d., and a pair of velvet shoes costing £3. The account books at Longleat also suggest that Dudley's neglect of his wife has been overstressed in the past, for there are entries for gaming money that he borrowed from Mr Hyde, William Haynes (his personal servant) and a Mr Aldersey, while visiting Denchworth.

Why Amye then chose to move to Cumnor Place, which was some eleven miles away, is a question never likely to be resolved. Built to resemble a Gothic Oxford quadrangle, Cumnor Place had once been owned by the monastery of Abingdon and was close to a large village, with Oxford within easy riding or even walking distance. However, once again she shared the house, which was owned by Dr William Owen. Mr Hyde's widowed sister, Mrs Odingsell, lived there, as did Mrs Owen, and Anthony Forster (the keeper of Dudley's privy purse) and his wife were also tenants. There were household servants, but Amye also had her own attendants, none of whom were in the house to witness her death or the immediate aftermath on Sunday, 8 September 1560.

The news of her death had to be conveyed to Dudley at Windsor, and so a servant called Bowes was dispatched. At the same time Thomas Blount, a close associate of Dudley's in private and business matters, was travelling towards Oxfordshire, apparently without any knowledge of the fatality. Bowes met Blount at an inn on the road that same evening, and the household servant promptly related all he knew of the day's events. He began by remarking that as usual Abingdon Fair had been held that day, and that Lady Dudley had directed all her servants to go to it. She had wanted Mrs Odingsell to join them, but the lady declined, and after a display of some anger Lady Dudley had agreed that, as she was not a servant, Mrs Odingsell was free to do as she pleased. It was further decided that Mrs Owen should dine with Lady Dudley at about 11 a.m., and so with her servants out of the house she was left alone, although the three other ladies of the house had been about with their servants.

The discovery of Amye Dudley's body on the floor at the foot of a flight of stone stairs was not made by the Dudley servants until they had returned from the fair, and the question remains as to why so much time elapsed before the discovery of the body. But Bowes was in no position to answer the many pressing questions that Blount found forming in his mind, for he too had been out of the house. Blount was well aware of the extreme delicacy of the situation for his master. There had already been rumours of threats to Amye's life and, now she had died, Blount saw it as a grievous coincidence. With this in mind he decided to test local opinion in Abingdon, while Bowes continued to Windsor. On hearing the baleful news, Dudley sent a stunned message to Blount requiring immediate information on the exact circumstances of the tragedy. He noted also that he had sent for John Appleyard, Amye's half-brother.

On the morning of Tuesday, 10 September, Blount went to Cumnor and spoke to Lady Dudley's personal maid, Mrs Pinto. Mrs Pinto claimed that her dead mistress had been distressed by something unrevealed – 'divers times I had heard her pray to

God to deliver her from desperation'. Blount delicately phrased a question about the possibility of suicide. 'No, good Mr Blount' was the reply, 'do not so judge my words. If you should so gather, I am sorry I said so much.' Blount did not press the point, although his question had been perfectly legitimate, since the 'desperation' referred to might have been caused by physical pain or spiritual anguish. Mrs Pinto's swift denial of suicide of course tells us as much about a loyal servant as it does about the circumstances of the death. Lady Dudley's testy attitude to the servants on the day of her death may now also be regarded as evidence of some malaise.

Blount wrote to his master on 11 September, a letter that must have trembled in Dudley's hands as he opened it. Blount rehearsed all that Bowes had said, and all that he (Blount) had seen and heard. He added that even before he reached Cumnor a coroner's jury had been established, and that since his arrival he had come to the conclusion that Lady Dudley had indeed been distressed and perturbed by something before she died. The letter actually reached Dudley at Kew on Thursday, 12 September, and he was not much relieved by the contents. 'Until I hear from you again how the matter falleth out, in very truth I cannot be quiet.' He was, however, pleased that a jury had been assembled, since he wanted (and needed) above all that justice should be seen to be done. Suspicion travels faster than truth, and the country and courts in Europe were agog at the thought that he might be involved in Amye's death. On 17 September a prebendary of Durham, the Revd Thomas Lever, Master of Sherbourne Hospital, wrote what many privately thought in an outspoken letter to Cecil and Sir Francis Knollys: 'Therefore I am moved and boldened by writing to signify unto you, that here in these parts seemeth unto me to be a grievous and dangerous suspicion and muttering to the death of her which was the wife of my Lord Robert Dudley. . . .'[4]

Cecil probably shared these suspicions, for he had no high opinion of the young lord whose 'ambitions had a disintegrating effect on court politics'.[5] For his part, Dudley must have been acutely aware that Amye's death in such odd circumstances had done nothing to promote his advancement, which for the time being had to be halted if Elizabeth was not to outrage court and public opinion in a way that would harm her own popularity.

He decided, therefore, to let the jury get on with its tasks without interference, and the fact that he stayed away has been intrepreted by many historians as indifference. This was far from the case, and it is not hard to imagine that, had he raced to Cumnor, he would have been accused of intimidating the jury, or perhaps of trying to bribe them to suppress vital evidence. Like any Christian of the time he would have shrunk from the notion that his wife had committed suicide, and would have preferred her death to have been at the hand of some villain who could be apprehended and prosecuted for a crime. Even illness was likely to remain within the realm of speculation, since there was no autopsy procedure. Villainy was preferred, 'for, as I would be sorry in my heart any such evil should be committed, so should it well appear to the world my innocency by my dealing in the matter'. Having steeled himself when briefly placed under house arrest at Kew, Dudley wanted his late wife's relatives, particularly Arthur Robsart and John Appleyard, to be available to see and hear the deliberations of the jury.

By Friday, 13 September, Blount had acquired from discreet whisperings the news that they could find 'no presumption of evil'. If it was not suicide or murder, then it must have been accidental death – Blount's relief was almost palpable. Leaving Cumnor the following day to breakfast in Abingdon, he indicated in a letter to Dudley that he expected to meet a juryman there, and he would then wait for instructions while remaining alert for any gleanings or developments. What Blount had clearly not prepared for was a perturbed flurry on the part of his nervous employer, who suddenly lost all calm and wrote directly to the jury, a fact that he revealed only sheepishly to his aide. Nor did Dudley gain from this dangerous intervention, for the man who appears to have been the foreman of the jury, a Mr Smith, told him nothing he did not know already. As far as Smith and the rest of the jury were concerned, Amye Dudley had died in some sort of accident. Since, however, this did not fix guilt on anyone, Dudley seems to have found the verdict wanting, and he even considered the advisability of having a second jury. But the hunt for a culprit was bound to fail, since the admittedly paltry evidence suggests only two possible conclusions. The unlikeliest is that Amye had chosen to throw herself down the flight of stairs. The other is that she had died after a fall perhaps induced by a shock of pain from cancer, which may have caused a spontaneous fracture of her spine.[6] Her irritability was consistent with a physical illness that caused her great distress and which Tudor physicians could not alleviate.

On 17 September, some nine days after Amye's death, the young widower received a letter from his brother-in-law, Henry Hastings, Earl of Huntingdon, which by its construction and tone suggests unmistakably that the family felt no reason to suppose that Amye had died in any way other than naturally: 'Although I am sure you are not without plenty of red deer, yet I am bold to send you half a dozen pies of stag.' Then in a postscript he writes:

> As I ended my letter, I understood by letters the death of my Lady your wife. I doubt not but long before this time you have considered what a happy hour it is, which bringeth man from sorrow to joy, from mortality to immortality, from care and trouble to rest and quietness: and that the Lord above worketh all for the best to them that love him well. . . .[7]

Huntingdon was a pious Puritan and it is inconceivable that he would have suppressed any misgivings about the death if he had felt there was any possibility that Dudley had been directly involved.

Prior to the funeral the body of Amye Dudley lay in state in Gloucester College, Oxford. Then on 22 September 1560 she was buried beneath the choir of St Mary's with pomp and the rituals of mourning. Among those who attended the service were the mayor and corporation of the city. Garter and Clarenceux Kings of Arms, Lancaster Herald and Rouge Croix Pursuivant. The chief Crown mourner was Mrs Norris, the daughter of Mrs Forster's uncle, Lord Williams of Thame; and Mrs Blount was also there, but Dudley, forbidden by custom from being present, remained at court, which went into mourning.[8] It was Richard Ellis who itemized some of the costs: Jasper the joiner was paid £11. 10s. 6d.; William Haynes, who collected the shroud from London, was paid £3. 0s. 6d.; and the total cost of the funeral was £531. 6s. 8d.

Given his vulnerable position at court, and his inheritance of
a name synonymous with danger and illegality, it is understandable that Dudley should have felt apprehensive. As it was, his
wife's death in curious circumstances besmirched his reputation
still further, and if he was not haunted by her ghost, he was at the
very least put to considerable trouble by her half-brother, John
Appleyard. Between 1560 and 1567 Appleyard benefited
substantially from his connection with the young lord. Made
Keeper of the Marshalsea prison, he also obtained a commission
to seize concealed prizes at sea without legal proceedings, and he
later became Porter of Berwick. A debt of £400 was guaranteed
by Dudley, and although we need not assume that such benefits
were aimed to purchase silent acquiescence, Appleyard rather
crassly chose to think they were. Appleyard also developed the
notion that Leicester (as he now was) wanted to shuffle him off
into a remote backwater; treatment Appleyard resented.[9] His
hints and nudging asides were certainly listened to by a
triumvirate of the new Earl of Leicester's enemies. The Duke of
Norfolk, the Earl of Sussex and Sir Thomas Heneage used a
merchant intermediary to meet Appleyard at Hampton Court,
and he was offered £1,000, with more to follow, if he
purposefully maintained his campaign against Leicester. The
result was a spell in prison for the greedy rustic, since Leicester
was furious that Appleyard might have jeopardized his chance
of marrying the Queen. Starving and destitute in the Fleet, on
30 May 1567 Appleyard wrote an abject letter to the privy
council stating unequivocally that he was totally satisfied that
Amye's death had been an accident. Two days later he agreed
that for three years he had been trying to blackmail Leicester on
several counts.[10] His dogged stupidity was such that in May 1570
he led an insurrection in Norfolk aimed at freeing the Duke of
Norfolk from the Tower. He was condemned with three others
later in the same year, and after four years' incarceration in
Norwich Castle he was released to house arrest and apparently
died not long after.[11]

Chapter 3

Sweet Robin

When the drama surrounding the death of his first wife had been dissipated, Dudley was free to marry again. Through all the fierce embarrassment it was the one thought he must have clung to for comfort. Yet the truth was that marriage to Elizabeth was now more remote than ever, and his reputation was always to suffer from the taint of Amye's death. What is more, however close his friendship with the Queen, her inclination was always to remain free from the restraints of marriage. Her own father's hectic sequence of marriages had had a marked effect on her. It was much easier for her to cope with a favourite, since the commitment was not absolute and in theory he was disposable. Dudley provided her with invaluable support in the charade of nuptial politics that she played out on the European stage. If it can be assumed that she felt unease at the notion of marriage and sexual union, she still had to outwit suitors with tact and dignity. She also had to distract her domestic advisers, who longed for her to marry and produce an heir to the throne. As time passed, both Elizabeth and Leicester came to recognize that the idea of their marital union was a courtly extravagance, but by the 1570s it had served its purpose as a political diversion and emotional prop.

In January 1561 it was Dudley who initiated a move to counter the suit of King Eric XIV of Sweden, once it was thought that the Archduke Charles (Karl) could be ignored. Dudley's agent was his brother-in-law, Sir Henry Sidney, who approached the Spanish ambassador, de Quadra. Naturally he was suspicious of anything coming from a source so close to Dudley, but his own patron, the Count of Feria, was married to

Jane Dormer, a relation of Sidney's. The latter spoke powerfully of the Queen's wish to marry Dudley. It therefore seemed desirable that the most powerful king in Europe (whom Dudley had served with acknowledged gallantry) should support this union so that the Englishman would 'serve and obey your Majesty like one of your own vassals'.[1] Sir Henry baited the line further by adding that if Philip II did support the marriage, Elizabeth and her consort would be able to reverse the trends of the religious settlement and restore the Catholic faith in England. Bishop de Quadra was tempted by this proposition but he remained wary, having been tricked by Dudley and Lady Sidney over the Austrian suit. He was also alert to and aware of signs that Dudley was favouring Catholics (though whether this was for reasons of faith or policy he was uncertain). A Catholic gentleman of the bedchamber had been encouraged to serve Dudley, and he showed a marked interest in the spiritual crisis of Sir Thomas Copley. The latter had been converted from zealous Protestant to Catholic, and, according to Fr Persons, Dudley's interest came about when Copley 'took pains to examine certain leaves thereof and finding many falsehoods therein which were inexcusable' in Bishop John Jewel's *Apologia* of 1562.[2] On this crisis in faith Copley conferred with Dudley, who 'willed him that the next time Mr Jewel dined at his table he should take occasion after dinner to propose the same which he did soon after'.[3]

Since the Spanish ambassador showed some distaste for the restoration of Catholicism being used as a diplomatic tool, Dudley avoided this tack in his next meeting with him. Now he simply asked that de Quadra should urge the Queen to marry him, finding nothing improper in this suggestion. De Quadra wisely felt he could not accede to this request, so he allowed himself merely to praise Dudley and advise that the Queen should marry. And he kept his word, in response to which Elizabeth blandly admitted her sincere preference for Dudley, while inquiring what Philip II would think if she chose to marry one of her subjects. The following day Dudley, apparently pleased with the efforts of his ally, repeated the alluring offer of a country reconverted to the Catholic faith. But de Quadra drew back, saying that bargains could not be made over such a matter. To Philip II he wrote:

I am thus cautious with these people because if they are playing false, which is quite possible, I do not wish to give them the opportunity of saying that we offered them your Majesty's favour in return for their changing their religion, as they say similar things to make your Majesty disliked by the heretics here and in Germany.[4]

No doubt de Quadra felt that as an urgent matter of policy Dudley's apparently protective wooing of the Queen should be supported for the sake of the substantial Catholic minority in England. These people were haunted by a conflict of loyalties, and agonized over the divide between the spiritual and secular powers. Without the marriage it seemed increasingly to the ambassador that Elizabeth could be removed from the throne only by force – a dramatic conclusion and one fraught with dangers for European stability. Thus the envoy saw two ways for the future, and the ultra-cautious Philip II, before committing himself either way, wanted strong evidence supplied by Elizabeth and Dudley that they were acting in good faith. In his view a suitable gesture would be to send representatives to the Council of Trent; but this suggestion was resisted by Cecil in council, for he was a reluctant European for most of his career, a moderate isolationist as well as a moderate Protestant. Elizabeth could not exclude him from the dealings with de Quadra, although Dudley was little pleased, and was not even mollified when the Earl of Bedford was sent as an envoy to Catherine de Médicis with the apparent intention of co-ordinating Anglo-French co-operation at the Council. Moreover, this very tentative approach to a Roman strain to English foreign and domestic politics was quickly halted by public antipathy, and a scapegoat was found in Sir Edward Waldegrave's household. Cecil smothered Dudley's purpose at this time by a convenient uncovering of a plot, Waldegrave being a known papist. The embarrassment to de Quadra was substantial, and the proposed visit of a papal nuncio cancelled.[5]

De Quadra was mortified, but it was his task to haunt the court, and on St John's Day, 1561, he sat with the Queen and Dudley in the State barge watching fireworks over the Thames at Greenwich. Teasingly asked if he would then marry them, he replied sternly and seriously 'that if they listened to me they could extricate themselves from the tyranny of the councillors who had taken possession of the queen and her affairs. . . . I enlarged on this point somewhat, because I see that unless Robert and the queen are estranged from this gang of heretics they will continue as heretofore. . . ."[6] As for Dudley's position, it was clear that he had achieved nothing concrete in terms of policy at this point and had even been severely disappointed when the Queen sliced up the patent that would have made him an earl. However, he had established by charm and wilful ingenuity that his intention was to become a permanent feature of the political landscape, and that he had to be accepted by councillors and courtiers alike. Furthermore, his initiative had given a lead to Pope Pius IV, who hoped to maintain channels of communication with the English court.

Papal hopes for a restoration of Catholicism in England were certainly raised by the arrival in Rome at the end of 1563 of Thomas Sackville. The young visitor indicated that he and his father, Sir Richard Sackville, were representatives of Roman sympathizers, and that he would personally carry a message from Rome to London. But beyond this offer little happened, as Thomas fell from favour in England. Even so, in 1564 Pius did summon the ex-Bishop of St Asaph to Rome, apparently with the intention of making Goldwell the papal nuncio to England if the approach through Sackville properly advanced.

When nothing happened, Pius chose to support the planned activities of Gurone Bertano, Antonio Bruschetto and his son, Sebastian. Of Genoese parentage, Antonio Bruschetto was one of the many Italian immigrants to England who had settled and married an Englishwoman.[7] Sebastian, however, was still attracted to Rome and went there in 1560 for further study. Bertano decided to employ him, and in 1563 an offer was made to Cecil for the supply of news from the papal court. By the following year Bertano had developed the idea of secret negotiations between London and Rome, and had managed to gain the attention of the Pope. Late in the year Sebastian Bruschetto was entrusted with an eloquent letter of appeal from the Pope to Cecil which begged for his co-operation in the restoration of Catholicism. When Bruschetto had arrived safely in England, his reward was to be taken into the service of the newly ennobled Leicester with a salary of 200 crowns per annum (then about £30). On 4 December he wrote with unwarranted enthusiasm and optimism to Bertano, who was now in Rome, that the ardently desired change of attitude by the government in England was about to take place. Bertano replied in kind, and in the summer of 1565 wrote to Bruschetto that the papal offer of military aid to Elizabeth was still open, once the change to Rome had been accomplished. Bribes may also have been paid to Cecil and Leicester, but this is not certain, although when Leicester read Bruschetto's correspondence he remarked on the difficulty of achieving anything and the necessity for absolute secrecy. When Pius died in December 1565, all these exchanges lapsed.

Elizabeth and her advisers also had continuous and parallel interests of great importance in Scotland and France, geographical proximity making them more important than Rome. In the former country John Knox's Calvinistic fervour had helped to sweep away Catholic rulers in a revolution that the Protestant lords had seized hold of with the aid of English troops. In France the defeat of the French troops who had fought in Scotland, and the increasing rivalry of Catholics and Huguenots, led Cecil to hope that the Protestant forces led by Antoine, King of Navarre, and his brother, Louis de Bourbon, Prince de Condé, with their ally Admiral Coligny, might reinforce England's position as an emerging Protestant power. To help with this endeavour, Cecil judged that Dudley's connection with Spain had to be severed and his position of indulged intimacy with the Queen breached. Having found his target, Cecil worked with the usual means of bribery, and de Quadra's secretary was persuaded to lay bare his employer's private thoughts and recommendations to Madrid. Then, when the growth of religious factions in France led to the collapse of Catherine de Médicis's policy of political pageantry, Cecil was quick to spot a possible advantage to England, and Elizabeth and Dudley assessed with varying degrees of enthusiasm the possibility of active intervention in French domestic affairs.

In May 1562 Cecil's policy led Dudley to establish contacts with the Prince de Condé, and Henry Sidney was sent to France for talks. At the same time Dudley's loyal supporters, Henry Killigrew, Edward Horsey and Thomas Leighton, all began work for him in France, and the importance of this new interest of Dudley's increased when Sir Nicholas Throckmorton (the English ambassador in France) became an unexpected ally of the Dudley coterie. Hitherto Throckmorton had been scathingly critical of the Queen's favourite, but a reconciliation was brilliantly effected by the efforts of the Earl of Bedford. As usual in the sixteenth century this new weight to the group was secured by a personal link when Dudley became godfather to the youngest Throckmorton son.

Even so, many of the leading courtiers and magnates regarded the rise of Dudley with distaste and apprehension. They can scarcely have been comforted by the revival of the title of Earl of Warwick, which was conferred on Ambrose Dudley in December 1561, and their dismay can only have been heightened in the following year when he was appointed general of the Newhaven (Le Havre) expedition. Of course it was his brother who had led demands for intervention in France, voicing the hopes of Protestant activists, and uniquely in her reign Elizabeth mildly agreed to the plan for a modest force to be sent to the Continent. Her easy response to Dudley's pressure may have been due to her desire to appease him over something, allied to a nagging sense of loss that all English men and women felt about the French capture of Calais in 1557. The result was that in July and August the privy council sent out a stream of directives as an agreement was made with Condé that he should receive 140,000 crowns in aid, and that in return he should hand over Le Havre in anticipation of the greater prize of Calais. It was to be the Earl of Warwick who led the small English army that boosted the effort.

The Newhaven expedition of 1562-3 gives an alarming insight into the strains and distortions that resulted from an antiquated military system which needed a complete overhaul. Individuals in the force behaved with exemplary courage. There was William Whittingham, chaplain to Ambrose Dudley and the army, who preached in his corselet, and when the plague broke out distinguished himself 'in going to visit, instruct and comfort . . . so many soldiers dying and dead in one great room'.[8] He even uncovered a plot to set fire to the supply ships in the harbour, but his efforts came to naught when Warwick was wounded, and Elizabeth suffered a crippling bout of nervous parsimony. The small army was disastrously reduced by the plague, and, having achieved nothing, ruefully returned to London. The direct consequence was that the plague then killed many in the city and the south of England, including the unfortunate de Quadra.

Yet despite this sobering reverse Robert Dudley remained high in the Queen's favour, and he was drawn even closer to the centre of administrative and executive power when Elizabeth was struck down by a dangerous bout of smallpox in October 1562. Although her fevered demand that Dudley be made Lord Protector of the Kingdom was rejected by a stunned privy council, he did join that body on 20 October in a striking political advance that Cecil longed to neutralize.

Chapter 4

The Queen Is in Love

The alarm caused by the disfigurement and nearly fatal sickness of Elizabeth was greatest at court. Nursed through it by Dudley's sister Mary, who sacrificed her own appearance in order to offer this dangerous service, the Queen was fortunate and recovered her health. Perhaps the most powerful effect of the Queen's illness was that it highlighted the pressing necessity for a marriage that would secure the kingdom, at a time when the convalescent was psychologically and physically stricken. From her childhood she had seen love, marriage and death as immutably linked; distress and fear did not pass with her recovery. What she felt now was a huge debt to the Dudleys. For the sake of her country could she subdue her terrors and perhaps marry Robert?

Certainly he continued to hope that she would, and his campaign to win her was both public and private. Though Amye's death had brought further odium to his name, and his ancestry was already suspect, he did not slacken his attentions. And the favour shown to him by the Queen, who was at this point besotted by him, shocked and distressed many of his contemporaries. Agitated by her gratitude towards and infatuation with this handsome courtier, a growing band of his enemies hoped to manoeuvre his fall from royal favour before Elizabeth had submitted to his extravagant courtship. He was, of course, equally alert to any opportunity to stress his cause, and so even an event as apparently insignificant as the Christmas festivities of the Inner Temple in 1561-2 was yoked in. The description of drama, compliment and allegory comes from Henry Machyn, and the festivities involved Dudley because the Inner Temple wished to acknowledge gracefully a service he had done them in a dispute over the control of Lyons Inn.[1] In this struggle the Middle Temple had enlisted the weighty aid of Sir Robert Catlin, Lord Chief Justice, and Sir James Dyer, Lord Chief Justice of Common Pleas, to put their case. Despite the weight of judicial expertise Dudley had intervened and persuaded Elizabeth to confirm the rights of the Inner Temple. To show their gratitude the leading figures of the Inner Temple declared that in litigation involving Lord Robert they would not plead for anyone opposing him in court. And as a further mark of their esteem they chose him to be their Christmas Prince, Pallaphilos, while various revels offices were taken by Temple officers: Richard Onslow, Roger Manwood and Anthony Stapleton. Important lawyers and firm Protestants, their choice of Dudley underlines their indifference to his individual acts of kindness to Catholics. If they were aware of his contacts with Philip II, they cannot have regarded them as important – simply a matter of political convenience to be thrown over when necessary, and not evidence of a spiritual inclination to Rome.[2]

The elaborate strands of allegory and political symbolism that constitute a major part of the festive revels have been identified by modern scholarship. This is a task made all the more difficult because in his *Accedens of Armoury* the Tudor author, Gerald Legh, writes as if the court of Pallaphilos (embodied by Dudley) existed. Distinguishing reality and illusion becomes a teasing and interpretive exercise, although it does provide evidence of pre-Shakespearian dramatic ambitions. Before the appearance of Pallaphilos, who serves Pallas, Legh tells the myth of Pallas, Perseus and the Medusa. Then the revels King of Arms relates the allegorical story of Lady Bewty and Desire, which later reappeared in the famous festivities at Kenilworth in 1575. The theme of wooing and the desirable inevitability of matrimony is emphasized in both; Perseus not only saved Andromeda, he also married her. As all this proceeds in dialogue it was probably acted by the Templars, who immediately recognized that Pallaphilos-Desire-Dudley would not attain the blissful state of marriage without tribulations and some testing of his virtues. Dubbed a knight in the court of Honour, Desire then moves to the Temple of Pallas where the goddess then gives him permission to wed Lady Bewty. The whole symbolic performance ended with Pallaphilos creating twenty-four knights in the order of Pegasus, which for the Master of the Horse at the real court could hardly be more appropriate.

On 18 January 1562 the Templars performed before Elizabeth, Dudley and many of this real court a play by Thomas Sackville and Thomas Norton, *Gorboduc*, which again was an entertainment wrapped in political allegory. The play deals with a disputed succession, civil disobedience and the calamity that threatens when ruler and advisers act separately. All of which was in marked contrast to the harmonious spirit of unity found in the revels, and the alarming tone was deliberate, since Dudley 'had everything to gain from this striking contrast in the two entertainments and hence was prepared to take to court a play which might be interpreted as favourable to the succession claims of Catherine Grey'.[3] Apart from the Catholic claimant to the English throne, Mary Queen of Scots, there was also Lady Catherine, the surviving sister of Lady Jane Grey. Her attraction to some in the event of Elizabeth's death was her Protestant faith, not her intelligence, when in the months before the production of *Gorboduc* her pregnancy became obvious, and her secret wedding to the Earl of Hertford was revealed. Elizabeth was enraged at the dynastic considerations this raised – Hertford being a Seymour – and the bride was sent to the Tower. Beforehand the distraught young woman had approached Dudley and asked him to defend her from the Queen's wrath, which she so rightly anticipated.

Since Cecil at this time probably supported Catherine Grey, Dudley's intervention on her behalf was made unlikely. Yet by appearing to favour her Dudley won the good opinion of her friends at court, and in any case if he wooed Elizabeth successfully her claim became irrelevant. Although Elizabeth resisted all his blandishments, he was a skilful manipulator of the dream-world of court pageantry and nuptial politics, and maintained a lively interest in the marriage plans of Mary Queen of Scots.

Mary Stuart was the great grand-daughter of Henry VII, and she made no attempt to disguise her ambitions towards a throne that Catholic Europe regarded as usurped by an illegitimate intruder. Married to the young Dauphin of France, François, when Elizabeth came to the throne, Mary quartered her arms with the arms of England, and in her the Pope had an excellent candidate if the English throne fell vacant through the efforts of the King of France or Spain. The danger to the Tudor dynasty increased when Henri II of France died and François took his place.

However, two events removed the immediate threat to Elizabeth: the successful revolt of the Protestant Scottish lords who drove out Mary of Guise, hitherto the Regent of Scotland (and Mary Stuart's mother), in 1560; and the unexpected death of François in the following year. Suddenly the house of Guise slipped from the pinnacle of power in France and Scotland, the country to which the young widow returned, although in her view it was now under the control of heretics supported from England. She held out against the signing of the Treaty of Edinburgh principally because it called on her to acknowledge Elizabeth's claim to the English throne, and to abstain from pressing her own claim. As long as Elizabeth remained unmarried and childless, the future prospects of the Stuart line were enhanced. But it was necessary for this young and pretty widow to curb her natural instincts, and this she found desperately hard. Nor was she neglected by possible suitors, including some who played intermittent court to Elizabeth: the Archduke Charles; the Earl of Arran; Don Carlos, the neurotic and unstable son of Philip II; the indefatigable Eric XIV of Sweden; Lord Darnley; and even Lord Robert Dudley.

In the highest political circles in England, France and Scotland there was some unanimity of purpose about the fate of this headstrong young woman – a desire to see her married and curbed. Moray chose to work in tandem with Catherine de Médicis for a betrothal to Lord Darnley. Elizabeth, however, rejected the notion of a marriage between royal cousins, although she made no statement in public of her disapproval. Cecil also wanted to prevent the marriage to Darnley, a personable youth with enough Tudor blood and Scottish support to make him acceptable to Mary. Dudley, playing his own hand, seems to have supported the general drift, since in his estimation it might provoke Elizabeth into marrying him in a spontaneous combustion of passion and jealous emulation. He was also aware of the anxiety in the country and in Parliament that Elizabeth should wed, following her bout of smallpox. Perhaps it was fortunate for him that he was saved from the embarrassment of having to pay formal suit to Mary.

When Mary's envoy arrived in London to advocate her claim to the English throne, both Maitland of Lethington and his royal superior viewed attempts to marry her to a Protestant as a means of alienating English Catholics from her cause. Elizabeth rejected their resistance with an amused exclamation that her royal cousin should marry Dudley, whom she (Elizabeth) would choose if she allowed herself the luxury of wedlock. The Scottish envoy swallowed his mirth at the suggestion, but Mary seems to have responded tartly with an ambiguous quip about the 'horsemaster'. It was in further banter with Maitland that Elizabeth made the impish suggestion that, if Ambrose Dudley had shared his brother's charm and good looks, both women could have shared the brothers between them.

Lord Darnley arrived in Scotland when deadlock over Leicester's position had been reached. After much bickering and evasion in several capitals it was actually Mary who seized the initiative with the connivance of Darnley's mother and the secret encouragement of Leicester. On 25 July 1565 Mary and Darnley were married. Ironically this seems to have coincided with a shift in the opinion of Cecil, for he viewed Leicester as a real impediment to marriage negotiations with European princes on Elizabeth's behalf. Certainly the new earl was hoping that Elizabeth would succumb to his wooing, and he told the new Spanish ambassador, Guzman de Silva, of his ambition. He discounted any notion of her marrying Charles IX of France, and he was convinced that any revived negotiations with the Archduke Charles would flounder on the question of religion. What he had overlooked was the stubborn aversion of the Earl of Sussex who, together with Cecil, the Duke of Norfolk and de Silva, favoured the Habsburg marriage. The situation was further muddied by the continued efforts of Eric XIV, who sent Elizabeth gifts of sables, as well as an impoverished royal visitor, Princess Cecilia, the pregnant wife of the Margrave of Baden.

Before she arrived in England the Margravine had been in contact with Leicester. His reputation had spread across Europe and so she wrote complimentary letters and sent him presents she could ill afford. Evidently when he met her he was charmed, and as Master of the Horse arranged lodgings for her party at Bedford House in the Strand, much to the annoyance of the Earl of Bedford. The Queen also enjoyed Cecilia's company, and shortly after Cecilia's son was born he was christened in the Whitehall Palace chapel. In October the Queen dined with Cecilia, and during the gathering Richard Edwardes, Master of the Children of the Chapel Royal, announced a tournament to be held between four stranger knights who had arrived for the wedding of Ambrose Dudley and Bedford's daughter, Lady Anne Russell. Leicester was of course a participant.

The marriage ceremony was held on 11 November, at which Leicester gave the bride away and maybe reflected on his great ambition. It was also in the mind of Philip II, who came closer than most to understanding the true depth of feeling that existed between Elizabeth and her favourite. In October 1565 the King had written to de Silva:

> The archduke's suit is now quite at an end[4] . . . you will, therefore, say no more about it. . . . Let me know the result of the Swedish negotiations, although no doubt they will end like the rest; and, after all, she will either not marry or else marry Robert, to whom she has always been so much attached . . . [for] the queen is in love with Robert. . . .[5]

As for the marriage of the Queen of Scots, let us take the story on, for it was proving an extraordinarily uneven and explosive match. The political situation in Scotland was also in some turmoil, for Elizabeth was giving secret aid to the Protestant opposition to the royal Catholic faction. This she thought less expensive than the open policy advocated by Leicester and Sir Nicholas Throckmorton, and probably less dangerous. In March 1566 Darnley was instrumental in the murder of his wife's private secretary, an Italian musician called David Riccio, but he then exposed the conspiracy, and Mary escaped to give birth to her son in June 1566. In February the following year some sort of resolution to this personal crisis came with the murder of Darnley: Mary's insouciant response was to elope with the probable murderer, the Earl of Bothwell, recently and so conveniently divorced. This example of what many Scots regarded as continental lasciviousness so enraged the Scottish lords (and Mary's Catholic allies), that they seized the initiative by imprisoning her in Lochleven Castle. Elizabeth's reaction was one of angry dismay. She was probably genuinely affronted at this treatment of royalty, and it was said that she considered a declaration of war on Scotland to secure Mary's release. Cecil was far more exercised by the fate of the baby James Stuart, when the rebels forced Mary to abdicate her crown in his favour. Although Mary eventually escaped from custody, her husband had been driven into exile in Denmark, and her imbecile gratification of a whim had cost her a throne without advancing her claim to another. Even her own child was now secured by her enemies under the regency of the Earl of Moray. After the defeat of her supporters at Langside in May 1568, Mary Queen of Scots fled to England to infect English politics with her petulant demands and arrogant plottings. How fortunate for Leicester that he had been rejected by her as a possible husband. Now his only concern was where she could be housed in safe preventive detention.

Chapter 5

The Lamentable Tragedy

Philip II had shown great acumen in his assessment of the whims of Elizabeth that sometimes took on the status of policy. He understood her better than most of his diplomatic representatives, and quickly realized that Leicester was the only authentic candidate for her hand. But he did overlook her capacity for artful procrastination, so that the distant archduke and ever-present earl were teased, rebuffed and placated as was necessary. Leicester found this disturbing, and became jealous of an apparent rival, Thomas Heneage, who was made a gentleman of the privy chamber in 1560, and was a lively, good-hearted companion to Elizabeth. De Silva regarded him more sceptically, while Cecil, Nicholas Bacon and the Earl of Sussex all pressed the ambassador to advance the cause of the archduke. Their case was emphasized by the Duke of Norfolk, who claimed that in the event of Elizabeth's death a marriage would prevent the calamity of a disputed succession. After his interview with her, Norfolk met Leicester and promptly upbraided him for preventing the marriage that the whole country wanted.

Just how aggrieved and unsettled the country was can be assessed from the attitude of the House of Commons in 1566. Meeting again in September after the Easter prorogation they were in a flurry, for during the summer Mary Queen of Scots had given birth to her son, and their attitude of bemused envy was matched outside Parliament by merchants, lawyers, the clergy and scholars. Pressure on Elizabeth was often necessarily oblique, as in the subsidy debate, when, much to her displeasure, the surveyor-general for victualling the navy,

Edward Baeshe, was accused of purloining funds. The Commons also took the risky line that the subsidy would certainly be available when the marriage question was settled satisfactorily. As Elizabeth told de Silva, the sum being mentioned was £250,000.

It is clear from the irritability of Leicester with Heneage, whom Leicester threatened to beat, and Sussex, with whom he sought a duel, that tempers at the court and in council were fiercely strained. Collective agitation led to wrangling and fits of withdrawn sulking. In the autumn Leicester resolved to side with his rivals in order to present a temporarily united front to Elizabeth, and only the tactful and aged Winchester refused to join them. Elizabeth interviewed the lords individually and either denounced them as little less than seditious, like Norfolk, or humiliated them by referring to their personal misfortunes. One of her targets was the Marquess of Northampton, who was involved in a marital dispute that hinged on his bigamy. Leicester himself was stormily rebuked and the meeting ended with the Queen walking out and threatening to arrest the lot of them.

Her anger, however, was matched by her resourcefulness, and by a judicious blend of push and pull, as well as a disclaimer that she had intended to violate the rights of her House of Commons, they were persuaded to pass the subsidy bill, and to drop for the time being the question of the succession. Her breach with Leicester remained only as she lingered over the inevitable reconciliation, as if to remind him that he was still her subject. It was not until the following spring, when Leicester led the opposition to further marriage negotiations with the Emperor Maximilian II on behalf of the archduke, that she impishly renewed their intimate friendship. It was now decided to send the Earl of Sussex to Vienna with the Garter insignia for the Emperor. The Duke of Norfolk and de Silva naturally approved of the plan, and Cecil and Nicholas Bacon also discreetly promoted it. But Sussex then found to his chagrin that the Queen's position on the marriage negotiations veered about so much that, having been refused permission to leave the court, he now requested a defined proposition which he could put before Maximilian. Before he set out for Vienna in June 1567 it was agreed that two crucial principles had to be negotiated: the question of money and the question of religion. A husband who was a Catholic would be able to worship as such in private, but his public observances would have to conform to the practices of the Church of England.

Sussex spent months in Vienna earnestly negotiating, clinging to the view that a satisfactory solution for both sides could be reached. Indeed he clung to this notion long after his aides had jettisoned the whole conception, and only reluctantly would he follow suit, blaming Leicester as Sussex sought his recall to London. If the proposal for a Habsburg-Tudor marriage was not utterly extinguished, Leicester and his faction saw they had nothing further to fear, and England's most immediate threats, Mary Queen of Scots and Philip II, were too embroiled in their own problems for the time being to present a serious challenge to the Elizabethan state. As the unchastened Queen of Scots was harried by her enemies, so a monarch of far greater consequence and power found the stability of his northern European lands compromised by the revolt that began in the United Provinces. This uprising against Spanish domination was to drain men and monies from his taxable resources on a huge and ultimately disastrous scale. Moreover, the presence of a large Spanish army under the command of the Duke of Alva was very unsettling to both France and England. The prospect that one day it might be used in support of Mary was deeply disturbing, and it was her arrival in England that helped to precipitate the domestic crisis of 1569-72. It was de Silva's fanatical successor, de Spes, who organized contacts between Mary and the Catholic magnates of England. Their natural leader was the Duke of Norfolk, whose privileged position allowed him some licensed indiscretions as his motives and actions became even more confused. The suggestion flew about that he would be a suitable candidate for her hand, even as the York-Westminster conference of October 1568 was set up to examine Mary's complicity in murder.

The haunting vision of marriage was planted in Norfolk's mind by the wily Maitland of Lethington, and the duke's slender intelligence seized upon it, despite Elizabeth's fierce antipathy to such wayward thinking. She let it be known that anyone foolish enough to be involved 'shall be ipso facto adjudged as traitorous and shall suffer death'. Yet Norfolk dallied with the notion and Cecil's secret service soon became aware of his thinking. To her credit Elizabeth asked him his intentions, but taxed by her he was unable to answer clearly. Norfolk's aggrieved shifts of mood and intention did nothing to endear him to the patient Cecil, and the break came with the flurries surrounding the seizure of Genoese gold loaned to Philip II. This happy windfall came to England when the fleet carrying the specie to the Spanish armies was harried into English ports by sea-scavengers in the Channel. When the Queen realized the provenance of the loot and its destination, it was quickly and legally transformed into a loan to her. Benedetto Spinola seems to have had a hand in arousing public opinion against the Spanish claim to it by denouncing Spanish ill-treatment of John Hawkins. Since it is unlikely he would have committed himself without prompting, we may surely suspect Leicester's hand in the business. Whoever was behind it Alva reacted, by seizing English goods and banning trade, to which Cecil replied in kind.

This action disturbed Cecil's opponents, since they argued that it brought much closer the prospect of bankruptcy for the country. Undisturbed by the betrayal implicit in their actions, they began negotiations with Spain, de Spes accepting the intervention of the Florentine merchant Roberto Ridolfi. To win Spanish aid they offered public recognition of Mary as Elizabeth's heir, and a substantial element of control of the ruling Queen's freedom. Above all they enthused about England's reversion to Rome. Happily for Cecil, Alva did not accept the ill-conceived notions at face value; something tangible was necessary before commitment to a landing. Elizabeth remained grimly impervious to the jostling of the courtiers who were poised to act against her and Cecil, but could not bring themselves to do so. The French ambassador Fénelon wrote that the crisis came to a head on 22 February, when the Queen seized the initiative and flung a cloak of regal protection around Cecil. Thus he remained in office, and mustering all his acute political sense decided to seek a reconciliation with the estranged duke. It was hoped the noxious marriage plan would now be put aside, and Cecil even managed to find a suitable replacement for the duke, the youngest of his wife's sisters and recently widowed. But Howard pride was too exalted and the duke stayed aloof from these blandishments, without having the nerve to broach the matter with Elizabeth. Instead he approached Leicester, and at Oatlands early in August dangled before the earl the bait of a union with the Queen.

After the court had continued on its summer progress to Sir William More's house at Loseley in Surrey, Leicester did very tentatively hint at these notions to Elizabeth. Again she gave the duke the opportunity to discuss the marriage conundrum calmly and privately with her, but he let the chance pass. Perhaps it was simply exasperation at this rebuff that led to Leicester's diplomatic sickness, which brought the Queen to his bedside at Lord Pembroke's house at Titchfield. Leicester now revealed all, giving ammunition to the Queen when she upbraided Norfolk for his disloyalty. The duke, thoroughly discountenanced, retired to London and then to Kenninghall. This petulance led many to think that he was about to launch himself on his greatest act of folly, and Elizabeth ended her progress at Windsor. She ordered military preparations and the removal of Mary from unfortified Wingfield to fortified Tutbury. Elizabeth's agent in this manoeuvre was the Earl of Huntingdon, who undertook his commission with alacrity. Mary protested vigorously at the impropriety of being placed in the power of a man with his own claim to the English throne through direct descent from George, Duke of Clarence.

Yet none of this significant activity inhibited the duke and his militant allies, the Earls of Northumberland and Westmorland. With their rising in the north of England, the duke was seized and imprisoned in the Tower in October 1569. By an irony that Leicester would have savoured in quiet reflection, the man who had hitherto been one of the duke's mentors, the Earl of Sussex, found himself as Lord President of the Council of the North, and thus responsible for dealing with the revolt. This was one of the last examples in English history of temperamental vassals seeking in a concerted way to throw off the restraints of royal government, and it is clear that economic forces were as much behind it as religious ones. Northumberland in particular was deeply resentful of the new Tudor nobility, and the loss of a rich copper mine to Elizabeth and the Company of Mines Royal, behind which were Leicester and Cecil.

After a brief flurry of success in which the rebels drove out the Bishop Palatine of Durham, Pilkington, the revolt failed from an utter lack of organization. There was no dominating martial

figure to lead it, and the march south was so ineffective that it
stopped of its own accord at Clifford Moor, where it should have
begun. The earls now fled as fugitives to the border country
where government controls were very weak, and 600 of their
followers were executed, only one of whom, an old Marian
called Plombtree, was actually a priest. Elizabeth then sent
Huntingdon to replace the Earl of Sussex, whose half-brother,
Egremont Radcliffe, had embarrassingly defected to the rebels.

'The government beat the rebels because no beating was
required.' Yet their defeat enabled Elizabeth to shrug off the
papal bull of February 1570, 'Regnans in Excelsis', by which
Pius V excommunicated her and declared her claim to the
throne to be falsely based. Even the sailing of a Spanish fleet
through the Channel that summer did not prevent her from
releasing Norfolk. Yet the blemish of failure did not inhibit
Ridolfi, who resumed his meddling, and in 1571 the duke was
rearrested. Despite procrastination Elizabeth eventually decided
that the turbulence created by Norfolk was intolerable and he
had to die. He was executed on 2 June 1572, in part at least a
substitute for Mary, who was still cloaked by a sisterly
protectiveness which, astonishingly, remained for many years.

Leicester's surprise at the execution did nothing to soothe the
outrage of the Howard family who felt betrayed by the earl's
guile. They placed the blame for another family calamity on
him, while in the duke's territorial heartland William Shuckforth
of Shyngham, Norfolk, complained that 'my lord Leicester hath
such a hold as never was in England'. Roger Baker of
Wethersfield, who tended cattle, was even more dangerously
outspoken, for he boldly claimed that Leicester was a knave and
a villain 'and it were a good deed he were hanged'.[1] This was an
audacious thought, with which many at court might secretly
have sympathized, but none had the temerity to give voice to it
during the following years when Leicester became an extremely
hard-working privy councillor.

As the domestic dramas receded, Leicester turned to pay
increasing attention to affairs abroad, particularly the fate of
international Protestantism when confronted by a fierce Catholic
reaction, most notably in France. When the clumsy intervention
of a Huguenot army in the United Provinces was bloodily
repulsed by the Duke of Alva, King Charles IX of France was

driven back into the arms of the Catholic Guise faction. It was this group, with the connivance of Catherine de Médicis, that instigated the violent and barbarous assaults on the Huguenots in August 1572. Leicester's revulsion and anger at the massacre of St Bartholomew's eve was only heightened by the presence in Paris of his nephew Philip Sidney, who like other members of the foreign Protestant community was forced to take refuge in the English embassy in Paris. England's ambassador, Walsingham, wrote to the Queen reporting the massacre, and when his report arrived at Kenilworth in late August 1572, the court went into mourning. The great fear was that it was simply a prelude to an international holocaust of Protestants. In France, however, Catherine de Médicis found danger in an overplayed hand, and she now tried to revive plans for a marriage between Elizabeth and one of her sons, the Duke of Alençon. He, from a mixture of policy and half-conviction, condemned the murders, while his plan to escape to England was several times postponed. In fact, it was through him that Elizabeth was able to help the beleaguered Huguenots, by claiming that if he became her consort he would have freedom to worship as a Catholic in private. In return she required the rulers of France to give fair terms to their oppressed minority. The result was that Charles IX signed a treaty in July 1573 declaring a general amnesty, and offering certain concessions on acts of worship.

In the gloomy aftermath of the massacre Burghley once again re-emerged as the leading statesman of the privy council. It was under his patronage that Walsingham was recalled from France to join that body, and he probably envisaged Walsingham as a judicious counterweight to Leicester. But it is clear that however hard Burghley and Leicester tussled for mastery over policy in the council and at the Queen's side, when required to do so they could work together without public signs of acrimony. In the 1570s Bernardino de Mendoza, who replaced the disgraced de Spes as Spain's ambassador, wrote: '. . . there are seventeen councillors . . . [but] the bulk of the business really depends upon the queen, Leicester, Walsingham and Cecil'.[2] Of the favourite he wrote that 'Leicester, whose spirit is Walsingham, is so highly favoured by the queen, notwithstanding his bad character, that he centres in his hands and those of his friends most of the business of the country'.[3]

An examination of these friends shows a network of relation-
ships which turned it into a family cabal: Warwick, Bedford,
Knollys and Walsingham. For fifteen years after the appointment
of the latter all newcomers to the privy council, save for Lord
Hunsdon, were identified as sympathetic to the earl: Dr Thomas
Wilson, married to the daughter of Sir Richard Empson; Sir
Thomas Bromley; Sir Christopher Hatton; and perhaps more
ambiguously, Lord Howard of Effingham. Howard managed
with a controlled deftness to keep a foot in both camps: Hunsdon
was his father-in-law, but his links with Leicester were
maintained through his elder sister, Douglass, who became
Lady Sheffield. Her extra-marital affair with Leicester was a
passionate, if somewhat one-sided, connection. To avoid
enraging the Queen Leicester tried to keep the affair secret,
even when Lord Sheffield died, either from chagrin, or, as
whispers had it, from poison administered on Leicester's behalf.
In May 1573 Gilbert Talbot, savouring the gossip as always,
wrote to his father, the Earl of Shrewsbury: 'There are two
sisters now in the court that are very far in love with him, as they
have long been; my Lady Sheffield and Frances Howard.'[4] It
seems, then, that at some point Leicester and his widowed lover
went through some sort of troth-plighting ceremony, which the
lady rather foolishly held to be binding, and which Leicester
characteristically did not. Then on 7 August 1574 she gave birth
to a son, who was christened Robert, a child who was raised
eventually with his half-brother Edmund, and the earl's wards,
Charles Butler and Thomas Curson.[5]

Leicester must surely have regretted that his first son could
not be made legitimate and therefore could not be his heir. But
he was unwilling to risk any estrangement with Elizabeth after
the alarms surrounding his links with Norfolk; it might well have
fractured the established peace and amity, and thus the renewed
flow of profitable leases and appointments. He was instead
much more interested in marriages for his nephews Philip and
Robert Sidney to the late duke's nieces. But their mother,
Katherine, Lady Berkeley, fiercely declined the offer and so
provoked Leicester's sustained enmity. With her family involved
in litigation with the Crown over valuable landholdings, her
alienation of the great courtier was a tactical disaster. The earl
strongly pressed the case on behalf of the Crown, and in 1573

Lord Berkeley lost his case. The Queen now took possession of the manors of Symondshall and Wotton, which were then passed on to Leicester and Warwick. The former soon arrived, displaying a crushing cheerfulness, to take possession of his new properties. With a large party of friends and an armed retinue he went first to Michaelwood Lodge, and breezily had some of the surrounding fences smashed before he returned to Wotton to play stoball (a popular Cotswold game resembling a cross between baseball and cricket). After this distraction the party rode to Slimbridge and attempted to invade Rolls Court, but the leaseholder of the Berkeleys defended himself against this high-handed activity, and they rode away.

Some of this activity might have been curbed if in 1565 Leicester had not been pardoned for all offences against statute by unlawful retainers. Moreover, he was licensed at the same time to maintain one hundred for life; in part as status symbols, since they were required to wear the Leicester livery. Others were bodyguards, for although assassination was less common in England than in France or Scotland, the earl was not inclined to take risks. One thug he employed, Tommaso di Vicenzo Sassetti, had been rescued from the gallows and given a pension of £50 per annum. Like all the Italians with court connections Sassetti knew the wealthy Ragusan merchant Nikola Nalješković (indeed he witnessed his will). It would be interesting to know if Leicester exploited this contact and had any business links with this important trader who was based in London.

Chapter 6

So Much Store of Wealth

The passionate attachment of Elizabeth to Leicester did not lead to marriage. Instead her esteem was expressed in an astonishing flow of gifts, often of lands or houses, a generosity that scarcely flagged for almost thirty years. In January 1560 Dudley (as he then was) and Thomas Blount received a grant of lands and the site of Watton Priory in Yorkshire, which they leased to Thomas Hungate for £306 per annum. In April Dudley received a licence to buy 1,000 sarplers of wool for export from London, and in March the following year he obtained the reversion and rent of the house and site of the monastery of Melsa (Meux) in Yorkshire, as well as the reversion and rent of the herbage and pannage of Beverley Park, with a yearly rent of £68. 16s. 8d. There was also the reversion and rent of the site of the manor of Burton Lazars, together with the manor-house, totalling £160. Other minor reversions brought him £17. 5s., a pound of pepper and two hens. In the following year the trickle increased when in April he was granted all his late Uncle Andrew's chattels (but probably not his collection of jewellery), which had been forfeited to the Crown. In July he was licensed to export undressed woollen cloths despite strict controlling legislation. During the six-year term of the licence no one apart from Dudley and the Merchant Adventurers would be allowed to engage in such trade, and he even obtained a private spot in customs-houses to aid his efforts. On 22 October he was granted an annuity of £1,000, and Elizabeth agreed that this would lapse only when grants of land to him exceeded in yearly value the same sum.

One of the most striking gifts to follow this annuity was made in June 1563 when Leicester was granted Kenilworth Manor, Castle and park, and thus he acquired a large territorial base in the heart of England. Lands in Surrey that had once belonged to Merton Abbey also passed to him, as did the manor, borough, castle and park of Clifford in Herefordshire, and lands in Rutland. Above all, there was the simultaneous grant of a large area of North Wales when he became Lord of Denbigh. Far from London, this had even more the appearance of a feudal apanage than his holdings in the Midlands. Denbigh's lordship had not passed from royal control before, and the new lord took a most particular interest in his huge acquisition. One of his first acts was to order his cousin, John Dudley of Stoke Newington, William Glasier, MP for St Ives (1563), and John Yerwerth, a lawyer in his service since 1559, together with Thomas Rolfe, to investigate the lands of the lordship with an eye to improving income. This was done in late July and early August, and in 1564 Dr Ellis Price, a follower of the Dudley family since 1550, became Steward of Denbigh. This was an appointment that would soon enmesh Dudley in difficulties with a powerful local landowner, Sir John Salusbury.[1] (Yet Salusbury left £20 in his will to Leicester, and Warwick took the wardship of his son.)

When the surveyors had finished their work they concluded that leasehold rents when revised would bring in some £200, while enclosure would add another £100 per annum. The tenants were not servile and, following the example of the leaseholders in Chirk, invoked the charter of Henry VII. The resistance to Leicester's new demands was led by the more substantial landowners like Salusbury, and the agreement that Leicester and his tenants eventually made (called a composition) was a complex one. A principal feature was that landholders agreed to pay him a fee for the 'confirmation of their liberties'.[2] And in the following section, which was intended to tighten his hold over rents and encroachments, in return for a payment of £333. 6s. 8d. he offered lawful land titles. Excluded from the composition were demesne and leasehold grants dating from the reign of Henry VIII.

Leicester's anxiety that the composition should be put into operation at once was met by further resistance from tenants, and the whole plan went before the Council of the Marches. Since Sir Henry Sidney was President of the Council, the tenants gained nothing, and the decision went against them. Still feeling aggrieved they approached Leicester through his commissioners, again requesting an alteration in the composition that would give them some relief. The commisioners briskly observed that 'the complaints . . . had been feigned'. Apart from the anticipated benefit to Leicester's purse, the composition had promised some dispersement of lands by enfeoffment. But the process which began in 1568 took so long that John Yerwerth wrote to the earl in 1571 that there was some unrest, and that it was suspected that he was deliberately dragging his heels. This administrative lethargy does not in fact seem to have been deliberate, and probably Leicester's representatives in North Wales were simply overworked by this project and other matters that required their attention. However, the situation was certainly not helped by Glasier, who showed distinct signs of prickly eccentricity.[3] When he was replaced by Sir John Hubaud, Constable of Kenilworth, the rate of enfeoffment increased, suggesting that Glasier was the bottleneck.[4]

By 1575 Leicester's reforms in Denbigh had advanced to the point where he was able to look seriously at the transfer to him by Elizabeth of the Forest of Snowdon. In the letters patent there was a controversial proposition: if within ten years Leicester could prove that encroached land had been improperly acquired by stealth or (even) accident from the Crown, in the Forest, Caernarvon, Anglesey and Merioneth, it would pass to him. Of course this was an incentive, and his approach was the same as it had been in Denbigh, his agents proving far more diligent than those previously employed by the Crown. When the commissioners began their work there was a storm of protest. Indeed so great was the fury that a bill of complaint was addressed to Elizabeth, and a group led by Huw Gwyn Bodfel presented it to her at Windsor. Despite her Welsh ancestry she was not prepared to listen, and for their pains the party was promptly clapped into prison. A further Leicestrian commission then angered the Welsh so much that Elizabeth had to stop their activities before a local insurrection broke out.[5] But the earl was fortunate that their resistance was fragmented and he gained an advantage from the fierce rivalry of certain families. Richard Gruffydd, for example, told Leicester's commissioners that his neighbour John ap Howell (John Powell) at Cefn Treflaeth had illegally encroached on coveted wastes in Rhwngdwyfor a dwyfach and Ponyfed. To this Leicester responded with a bill of complaint placed before the Council of the Marches, using William Maurice as his mouthpiece. Maurice gave evidence that Howell (and his father before him) had encroached on 'ffridd', and he also asserted that when he had been foreman of a jury that had previously scrutinized encroachments they had been found proven. At the same time the earl incorporated into this action a declaration that Moris ap Robert ap Howel of Ynysgain had encroached on some forty acres of land in Ynysgain called Y Fign goch. It seems very likely that ap Howel lost his counterclaim when the ubiquitous Maurice contradicted witnesses who said that it was held as part of a Crown lease tenement. Leicester, as a result of winning this action, saw a welcome addition to his income, ap Howel paying rent thereafter.[6]

Accusations that Leicester was predatory and rapacious beyond all measure, Wales groaning under the yoke of his absolutism, are tendentiously exaggerated. Clearly he did make more money from Denbigh, Chirk, Arwystli and Cyfeiliog (whose lord he became in April 1572) than had many before him (the Dudleys had sold the last two named to Henry VIII). Added to Merioneth and Caernarvon his annual rent roll in the early 1580s totalled nearly £1,500, but, as his demands were lawful, it is unreasonable to accuse him of savage exploitation, even if some of his methods of obtaining a verdict in his own favour were suspect.[7] Since inflation, one of the scourges of the Elizabethan age, gnawed away at his income as his financial burdens increased, his demands were not wickedly extortionate. He believed that tenants and landlord shared an interest which should allow both of them to profit, and if some of his tenants behaved as if he were infringing natural justice, it was because their geographical position far from the court had inflated their notions of independence.

Perhaps too Leicester's perpetual absence from Wales rankled. He was fortunate, however, to have the assistance of Sir Henry Sidney, while in the second rank stood Dr Ellis Price, William Gerard, and the Wynn family in Caernarvonshire. Of those who resisted the growth of Leicester's power in North Wales many were minor figures of only parochial importance, but across the ill-defined border, in Herefordshire, Sir James Croft, Comptroller of the Household, was much more prominent. It may have been William Gerard's views on his fellow-councillors of the Marches that helped to sunder the long-standing friendship based on the family link between Croft and Leicester. Certainly Gerard was not impressed by Croft's cousin, Fabian Phillips, appointed as a judge in Wales by Walsingham, but later a protégé of Whitgift. Gerard wrote of Phillips with a sneer that he was a man 'of small experience'.[8] Of Sir Andrew Corbet, Vice-President of the Council during Sidney's absence in Ireland as Lord Deputy, he remarked, 'a very sickly man not able to take the toil of service'.[9] His suggestion that Corbet be replaced by Sir John Hubaud was, however, ignored, and instead the office fell to an increasingly significant figure, John Whitgift, Bishop of Worcester.[10] Another member of the Leicester group was Henry Townshend, a councillor for the Marches from 1576 and puisne judge of Chester in 1578. It was only later that Sir Henry Sidney grew to mistrust him, as a result of his business dealings with Croft and Phillips.[11]

Together with his brother, made Lord of Ruthin in June 1564, Leicester dominated North Wales, and his position was consolidated when he was appointed Chamberlain of the County palatine of Chester. The town was going through a periodic decline, notably in its trade, and the local people hoped that the earl would be able to help stop it. In May 1569, following their appeal to him, he wrote to Sir Hugh Cholmondeley, Sir John Throckmorton, justice of Chester, and other local dignitaries, asking them to meet the mayor and corporation for discussions about how to improve matters. In April 1571, apparently without any great sense of urgency, the commissioners agreed that the town's trade was indeed ailing and they offered the hope that the earl would 'work an honourable and charitable deed to help reform their decay'.[12] He seems to have taken this request rather literally, for work on repairing Chester Castle began in 1577 and was completed in 1582 at a cost of £650.

Towns and boroughs did not always react with humble pleasure to Leicester's attentions. In 1572 he wrote stingingly to Denbigh:

I have been lately advertised how small consideration you have had of the letter I wrote unto you for the nomination of your burgess . . . [and] if you do not on receipt hereof presently revoke the same and appoint such one as I shall nominate, namely Henry Dynne, be ye well assured never to look for any friendship or favour at my hands in any your affairs hereafter.[13]

The tone is that of Leicester at his most puissant and demanding, yet, as has been pointed out, Richard Cavendish, who sat for the borough for many years, was also an agent of the earl's and active in the marriage exchanges between the Duke of Norfolk and Mary Queen of Scots in the period 1568-9.[14] All very odd, but real borough resistance was possible: at Windsor, where Leicester was chief seneschal of the borough, he had generally commanded the choice of MP, but in 1575 the corporation passed a resolution 'that when the Burgesses of the parliament be chosen, a Townsman shall be chosen for one'.[15] In another example the Earl of Sussex and Leicester tussled over the nomination for Maldon in Essex, and when his rival died Leicester confidently expected his nominee, Richard Brown, to be chosen. But the borough spiritedly demurred and chose instead Edward Lewkenor and William Wiseman – probably at the behest of the new Earl of Sussex. Leicester was therefore forced to switch Brown to Lichfield.[16]

In general, his patronage was valued by the individuals marked out for his favour by service or kinship. The prestige Leicester gained escapes definition, but he probably hoped as well that occasionally Parliament might be swayed by these men in the discharge of royal business. The benefit to patron and protégé was such that Burghley commented on Richard Cavendish that he was 'a most perfect devoted creature to your Lordship'.[17] Others who can be identified include: John Yerwerth, MP for Chester in 1563; and Anthony Forster of Cumnor, the chief controller of Leicester's private purse and MP for Abingdon in 1571 and 1572, who was followed in the seat by Richard Beake, the son-in-law of Leicester's friend, Thomas Reade of Barton.

In the Midlands Leicester's connection with Coventry, only a few miles from Kenilworth, went back to 1559 when Richard

Grafton, the antiquarian historian, secured one of the seats. In 1571 a relative of the earl's and sometime sheriff of the town, Henry Goodere, became its MP, while Sir John Hubaud was twice MP for Warwickshire. Leicester's kinsman and servant, Thomas Dudley, also represented the county, having previously (in 1571) been MP for Wallingford, where Leicester was High Steward. Edward Boughton, Sheriff of Warwickshire in 1580, and a servant of the earl, was probably elected under his patronage for a Coventry seat in 1584, the same year that Thomas Digges became a Southampton MP with Thomas Goddard.[18] The town accepted the mathematician and writer somewhat grudgingly at first, apparently unaware that many of his knowledgeable contemporaries held him to be the equal of John Dee and the more junior Thomas Harriot. Both Digges and Goddard were enjoined 'to bear their own charges for the said Parliament and not to charge the town for anything towards the same'. Digges, who had already been MP for Wallingford, spoke frequently in the House, and the town proved less niggardly than their injunction suggests: they sent him a hogshead of wine costing £3. 10s. In the same Parliament the member for Castle Rising was Richard Drake, who may have been the Drake in the earl's service.

There were probably more, and there is some evidence that the 1584 Parliament, for pressing foreign policy reasons, heard many voices and accents, but all spoke the earl's message. Finally, we may note that virtually all the MPs representing North Wales counties and boroughs at this time went on to serve Leicester in the United Provinces when he led his military expedition to aid the Dutch revolutionaries.[19]

Chapter 7

Be Our Stay in This Behalf

Early in his career Dudley disconcerted many by his apparently instinctive ability to hold contrasting views simultaneously. This was a mark of some considerable sophistication, or perhaps a sign that he was still uncertain about the way his career would develop. His flirtation with international Catholicism has been noted, and at home he did not cast off immediately all his Catholic connections. In January 1561 the Rector of Lincoln College, Oxford, was proposed for the post of Dean of Christ Church. Francis Babington was a Dudley protégé, although by this time he was less in favour and had relinquished his personal chaplainship to the young lord. However, the college had no intention of tolerating the appointment of a crypto-papist and their campaign against Babington succeeded, Thomas Sampson being appointed Dean.[1] In 1564 Babington lost all his preferments – a clear indication that Leicester was no longer interested in offering his protective cloak to those who clung to their Romish tendencies.

In the event, Leicester began to move towards an outwardly pious and committed interest in the growth and well-being of native puritanism. Certainly his family connections all suggested that this was the direction he would take. Yet his spiritual affiliations have long been regarded as suspect, and his exhortations to friends and clients about their spiritual lives seen as instances of his hypocrisy. However, there is a key to Leicester's evolving attitudes, and this can be found in his impish, eclectic mind. He had not studied at university or the Inns of Court, but he had been very well educated in a large family by excellent tutors keen for him to apply his natural aptitudes. In 1564 it was Roger Ascham who wrote, chiding him for taking a greater interest in science subjects than was seemly, but the famous John Dee would not have agreed. Like his father and brothers Leicester took an intelligent interest in many subjects, and of course religion was of compulsive interest to Elizabethans, since so much was at stake. For the young earl such matters were given a distinct edge by international political considerations. Catholicism may have attracted him through loyalty to the memory of his father, who had been induced to return to the old faith just before his execution, and it was not uncommon for the adept to change their practice of worship as monarch and circumstances dictated. In our present age of indifference to organized religion this may appear absurd, but in the sixteenth century it showed a reasonable prudence. Moreover, Leicester had served two Catholic monarchs, and only when it became clear with the Elizabethan religious settlement that the Church of England could not be reunited with Rome, did he bother to conform.

Even then his spirit of independence manifested itself. With the Queen and Cecil setting out the shape of the national Church, his natural inclination was to investigate the spiritual fringe. Here it is useful to recall the Puritan influence that was to mould Dudley's response. His brother Ambrose was married for a time to the daughter of a leading Puritan patron, the Earl of Bedford, and his sisters were married to the Earl of Huntingdon and Sir Henry Sidney. The patronage of this Protestant Puritan élite was a notable influence on the Church that re-established itself in the 1560s. The protection of such socially prominent laymen was of great importance to the preacher who wanted to follow his calling. His livelihood and chance of exercising a useful ministry remained wholly precarious until he had found one.[2] He needed a great protector like Cecil or Leicester to overawe a bishop, and the royal favourite would have agreed before very long with the view of Edward Dering that the Church was 'a company called together by the voice of a preacher'.

The death of Cardinal Pole on the very first day of Elizabeth's reign saved much indignation and embarrassment. Sandys noted: 'That good cardinal, that he might not raise any disturbance, or impede the progress of the gospel, departed this life. . . . We have nothing to fear from Pole, for dead men do not bite.' News of the deaths of Mary and her cardinal swept the Continent, and the Marian exiles who had mostly imbibed pure Calvinism soon began to return home. In fact it was their first-hand observation of the methods of the 'best reformed churches' in Europe that was largely responsible for the various religious perturbations that emerged in the Elizabethan period. By the time of their return all the exiles had gone beyond the Prayer Book of 1552, and they had certainly given up the use of vestments, to which many of them were openly opposed.[3]

In their wake came foreign Protestant refugees, especially after the election of Pope Paul IV. One of the first to arrive in England to enjoy the patronage of the Earl of Bedford (himself recently returned from Zurich) was an advocate of religious toleration, Jacopo Aconcio. An accomplished engineer as well as a writer, Aconcio was introduced at court, and he received a Crown pension of £60 per annum at the earl's prompting. Living in London Aconcio shared a house with the Dutch merchant-scholar Emanuel van Meteren, and both attended the Spanish Calvinist church of St Mary Axe, which the congregation had had to refurbish. It had been granted to a group of refugee worshippers headed by the ex-monk Casiodoro de Reina, who attended the Colloquy of Poissy as an observer for Bedford and Throckmorton. The eirenist spirit of this meeting of Catholic and Huguenot leaders in France caused widespread interest in Europe, and the minister of the French Church in London, Nicolas des Gallars, Sieur de Saules, was also there with Beza and William Whittingham. The last named was Bedford's chaplain before his great services at Newhaven.[4]

Aconcio was part of this group without being absorbed by it, and he was just as likely to take his own line on a matter of controversy. For example, when the junior minister of the Dutch Church at Austin Friars, Adrian Haemstede, became involved in a wrangle with Pieter Delemus, the senior pastor, Aconcio sided with Haemstede, while Delemus[5] was supported by des Gallars. Edmund Grindal, who supervised the foreign churches while he was Bishop of London, excommunicated Haemstede, who was banished in September 1560. In the meantime Aconcio continued to worship with the Spanish Calvinists until de Reina, now married, fled abroad after accusations of heterodoxy, sodomy and adultery.[6] These charges were brought against him by Balthazar Sanchez, a Spanish member of the French congregation, and he was not acquitted until many years later by a Church commission. When Reina did finally return to London he had become a Lutheran!

In the national Church those seeking preferment often turned to Cecil and Dudley. Sandys, who had written so sardonically to Bullinger about Pole's demise, became Bishop of Worcester. The first Elizabethan choice for York, Thomas Young, benefited from Dudley's favour, as did Whittingham, who continued to advance through his Dudley connection. The coveted position of Dean of Durham fell to him in July 1563, although it had been previously promised by Elizabeth to Sir Thomas Wilson. Even Whittingham's opposition to the 1559 Prayer Book did not deter her. Another Dudley client was Thomas Wood, who had served Warwick at Newhaven, and had been first to London with the news of the wound he had taken in the leg, and also of his seasickness. For many years Wood was to act as the Puritan conscience and goad to the magnates who gave the movement support, and having settled in Leicestershire under the benevolent eye of the Earl of Huntingdon, he was able to do this without interference. Wood, then, was the pivot 'between the presbyterian organisation in the capital and the strongly puritan country of the Midlands'.[7]

These great Protestant landowners were at one with the returned exiles' desire for the purification from the national Church of every trace of Rome. But at the same time the Act of Uniformity had contained two strife-stirring provisions which deeply dismayed men like John Jewel, who wrote to Peter Martyr that the returned exiles were beginning to feel 'like strangers in our own country'.[8] The first dealt with vestments, which the exiles on the Continent had abandoned, even the simple surplice, and the second maintained the Queen's authority to establish additional ecclesiastical ceremonies.[8] The controversy over vestments continued for years, and in October 1564 government action in the form of a royal decree against those who declined to conform seemed to be threatened.[10] At the end of the month Bishop Pilkington of Durham attempted to build up influential opposition to such a move by writing to

Leicester, whose views by now largely coincided with those of the reformers. And through his relationship with the Queen Leicester was a constant hindrance to Matthew Parker's attempts to establish uniformity and conformity in the Church of England. Pilkington, bemused by the comparative triviality of the argument and the rage it induced, begged Leicester to intervene with some balm that would take the sting from Parker's demands. He reminded the earl of the scarcity of preachers, and warned that extreme pressure for conformity might give offence abroad, where the progress of the English Church was watched with deep interest. Whittingham also wrote to the earl: 'Oh, noble Earl, at least be our stay in this behalf, that we may not lose that liberty which hitherto by the Queen's Majesty's benignity we have enjoyed.'[11]

Apart from his nonconformity in the matter of vestments, for which he was later deprived of the deanery before he capitulated, Whittingham was also denounced for his contempt for relics. It was claimed that tombstones were used for building purposes, beef and salt fish were stored in fonts, and that his wife was allowed to burn a saint's banner to test the claim that it was miraculously immune to fire. Yet the fact remains that like others who accepted high ecclesiastical preferment Whittingham modified his views on vestments under the pressure of official responsibilities. Parker's strenuous defence of vestments and his attacks on backsliders eventually led the dean to concede, as Calvin had done, that outward show need not interfere with the ministry.

Thomas Sampson, on the other hand, refused to conform and so lost his place as Dean of Christ Church, Oxford, for refusing to wear the surplice.[12] With the aid of the Earl of Huntingdon, and with Leicester's approval, he was installed now as Master of Wigston's Hospital in Leicester, where he attacked popish influence. But it was too late to halt the advance of conformity, as Thomas Lever discovered when he wrote to prominent laymen like Cecil and Leicester that they should use their influence to cast out of the Church 'inward papistrie, and outward monuments of the same'.[13] Only the year before he had written that the earl had given many men 'quietness, liberty and comfort to preach the Gospel of Christ'.[14] Men, that is to say, like Laurence Humphrey and Thomas Sampson who, at

Leicester's insistence, had been able to preach at St Paul's Cross to great crowds. To them can be added Christopher Goodman, to whom Leicester gave aid when he was also in dispute with Parker. Since religious dissent might be regarded as treasonable in whatever form it took, the protagonists had to avoid a direct confrontation with the Queen, but Leicester was able to find Goodman a position as Archdeacon of Richmond.

In the early part of the reign six bishops owed their advancement to Leicester, and to be his chaplain was a vital stepping-stone to advancement. When Babington was deprived of all his preferments, Leicester had another of his chaplains, John Bridgewater, appointed Rector of Lincoln College.[15] During his lifetime the earl had twenty chaplains, which was twice as many as had his brother. Thomas Cooper's career as an academic and ecclesiastic was vitally supported by Leicester, and in March 1565 he published his influential *Thesaurus Lingue Romanae et Britannicae* with the Beauchamp-Dudley device of the bear and ragged staff on the title-page. Two years later he became Dean of Christ Church, and Vice-Chancellor of the University. It was only in 1570 that the Queen's wish prevailed and Cooper became Bishop of Lincoln, in which see he remained until translation in 1584 to Winchester.

Not all churchmen who obtained Leicester's interest found his motives simply pious. The Bishop of Ely, Richard Cox, consecrated in December 1559 as a reward for his past support of the Duke of Northumberland, was constantly assailed by a close friend of Dudley's, Roger, Lord North (as well as by the Queen and Sir Christopher Hatton). As a result 'he reluctantly parted with the best lands of his see', and such was his misery that 'he sought to resign and was hectored again to remain, so that he might part with more'.[17] With this in mind John Watson's offer of £200 to Leicester that he might not be made a bishop, becomes less surprising.[18] The evidence suggests that Leicester did very handsomely out of the established Church. For example, the Bishop of Hereford's Cotswold mansion, Prestbury Moat, fell to him, and the collapse of the Church structure would surely have led to an unseemly free-for-all from which he could not guarantee to pluck the richest plums. Those who regard his support of Puritans as calculating and bogus have sometimes suggested that Leicester wanted, like his father, to oversee the dismantling of the Church, since it would bring on to the land market 'the temporalities of bishoprics and cathedral churches'.[19] But as an astute politician and public figure he knew that he benefited from the Elizabethan Church through his crucial relationship with the Queen. It was Leicester who gained most from the statute by which the upper dignitaries of the Church were to be limited in leasing out Church lands, since the procedure for agreeing rents and leases tended to be channelled through the court.[20]

Like that of any Renaissance prince, Leicester's favour depended on reciprocity, and he could be peremptory when a protégé failed to meet his expectations in some aspect of Church policy. Edmund Scambler, Bishop of Peterborough from 1561 at Leicester's prompting, was told a decade later that the Northampton exercises founded by the advanced Puritan Percival Wiburn should be protected, and on behalf of the local gentry he supported the idea of founding other such groups in the Midlands. Scambler nervously defended his own ground and wrote in reply that it was a somewhat disorderly group and Wiburn a constant and perverse nuisance. Leicester's reply was cool and unyielding: argument was stimulating and likely when preaching 'sharply and precisely' in order to obtain 'the reformation of the licentious sort'.[21] Yet in this case the intervention failed and Wiburn was silenced. But the earl maintained his interest in the affairs of the diocese and in 1576 ordered Scambler to cease trying 'to remove my friend Arthur Wake', a radical Puritan, 'from the possession of a hospital that he has in Northampton'.[22]

Chapter 8

Men in Sundry Knowledges

The polemical side of the Puritans also found an outlet in
didactic literature aimed at a wide readership, and even before
Dudley attained his earldom in 1564 his protection was sought by
controversialists. In 1561 Jean Veron, an immigrant Huguenot
preacher, had published a text on free will under his aegis, and
although he and Dudley had not met, they may have done so
later in the decade. The opportunity would have risen when, to
the dismayed incredulity of the Catholic diplomats in London,
Leicester deliberately chose to worship with the French
Protestants. Veron's Calvinist view was followed by another text
printed in London and dedicated to Dudley by Rowland Hill.
The title, *The Lawes and Statutes of Geneva*, stated very clearly its
source of inspiration, and it was prepared in this translation by
the sometime Marian exile, Robert Fill. John Day dedicated to
Dudley an anonymous translation of Peter Martyr's *Commentaries
on Judges*, knowing that Martyr had been in England during the
ascendancy of Northumberland, and had worked on the revision
of the Prayer Book. Day also issued as printer and publisher the
first part of *The Christian Instruction*, a translation of a text by
Calvin's follower, Pierre Viret.[1] In 1565 the Puritan gentleman
Arthur Golding produced the first part of his translation of
Ovid's *Metamorphoses* while he simultaneously translated Calvin's
Offences. Both were dedicated to Leicester, as was a later
translation by Golding of Calvin's sermons on the Book of Job
which by 1584 had sold out in five editions.[2]

With the support of the earl it is not surprising that Golding's
substantial work was noted in official circles. So it was the privy
council that commissioned him to translate an attack by

Bullinger on Pope Pius V. This scorned the denunciation of the Queen as a usurper, and the translation appeared in 1572, with the bear and ragged staff on the reverse of the title-page. The translator already had the patronage of Cecil, for he lived in his house as the attendant of the young Earl of Oxford, so the shift to the patronage of Leicester was particularly notable. The association of the earl with this important piece of Tudor propaganda is significant, for it shows the security of his reputation as a voice of the privy council. Leicester had allowed his religious beliefs and his associations to evolve, condemning the impervious fanatics somewhat in the eirenist spirit of Aconcio, so that for a decade after 1559 it is quite reasonable to see him as a 'politique', although always of a rather ambiguous kind. This remained so until he grasped the political thrust of puritanism, which stiffened with the threat perceived from Spain and the Catholic forces of the Counter-Reformation. Then he forged unequivocal links with the Puritans, whom he supported while serving the Reformed religion of the monarch and the State.

Catholicism may not have been a very potent political force in England because its adherents were harried and baffled by government scrutiny. But it did have a tenacious hold in private, even in the universities, a fact which exercised the collective attention of the privy council. Their delicate task was to excise the Catholics from the two universities, Winchester College and the Inns of Court, without wrecking the teaching of these places of learning. But the total number of university teachers who resigned rather than agreeing to conform to the Elizabethan religious settlement was around 300, and the result was significant. As John Jewel noted with alarm when he was installed as Bishop of Salisbury, 'our universities, and more especially Oxford are most sadly deserted; without learning, without lectures, and without any regard to religion'.[3] This was a serious situation, as many acknowledged, and it was to be transformed by Leicester as a highly interventionist chancellor of the university from 1564 until his death.

In Cambridge, where Burghley was chancellor, this was a period of consolidation, and intervention there was limited to the religious controversies that animated the growing Puritan presence in the colleges.[4] In August 1565 Leicester and Warwick were among a group of distinguished men made honorary MAs. This made it more seemly for Dudley to intervene in the struggle at St John's College between the master, William Whitaker, and a senior fellow, Everard Digby, about whom in a letter to Archbishop Whitgift Dudley had insisted that he had 'very strong and credible informations that this Digby is a very unsound and factitious fellow'.[5] The prelate had already rebuked Whitaker, and to retreat under pressure from a royal favourite in such a matter was clearly unpalatable. Hence, when Dudley cleverly offered him an escape compromise, he chose to give way. It was decided that Digby should be reinstated, but only for a short time 'Whereby neither this Your Grace's action shall be undone and the college shall be disburdened of a lewd fellow which disturbeth the government and hath empoisoned the youth.'[6]

When Elizabeth visited Oxford in 1566, Leicester took a strenuous, proprietorial role in the university's preparations. At the end of August, while the Queen was still at Woodstock, Leicester and Cecil arrived in the city to check the details for her reception. Then on the 31st, in the afternoon, she moved to Wolvercote, to be greeted there with great ceremony by the chancellor, Cecil, and bedels with staves which were handed in submission to her. The four senior academics who attended Leicester were in scarlet robes, including on this occasion Laurence Humphrey, President of Magdalen, whose antipathy to ecclesiastical finery was well known. After the speech of welcome by the Provost of Oriel, and the kissing of hands with the Queen, she took the opportunity to make a witty sally at Humphrey's expense, noting with approval that on this occasion he was wearing robes. Then the party processed to the north gate of the city, where officers of the town delivered up the mace and the mayor spoke. He pleased Elizabeth even more when he handed her a large gilt cup containing £40 in gold, and he distributed gifts among her party. Then the party advanced to Carfax, where Giles Laurence, Regius professor of Greek, made a speech lasting fifteen minutes in that tongue. Not to be outdone, Elizabeth replied in the same language, but her words were scarcely audible because of the stamping and shuffling of the mule train of her coach. Then, having moved to the gate at Christ Church where she was to stay, she had to listen to another speech, this time by the public orator Kingsmill, who managed to irritate her with his Calvinist tone. After a *Te Deum* in Christ Church Cathedral the Queen retired to her rooms in the deanery.

The following day, a Sunday, she again went to a service in the cathedral, but did not attend the Latin play *Marcus Geminus* which was performed in the college hall that evening. The next day the disputations usually so enjoyed by Elizabeth and her contemporaries were postponed, so evidently she was not well. The college had been prepared for a scholarly barrage and was festooned with Latin and Greek texts on placards, so, in order to fill the gap, Leicester and the Spanish ambassador went to some public lectures, and later in the day Elizabeth had recovered enough to attend a play performance. Yet the circumstances for the drama were not the happiest; a barrier had collapsed earlier in the evening, as a result of which three students had been killed and five injured.

On Tuesday afternoon the postponed disputations took place in St Mary's, the earl being seated on the Queen's left. It is possible that both of them reflected with some unease that the remains of Leicester's late wife were buried close by. Then on Elizabeth's final evening in Oxford she saw another play – probably the second part of *Palamon and Arcite* by Richard Edwardes, which is now lost. The following day, having avoided the public business of Convocation, she passed down the high street to the east gate, and from there on to Rycote, the home of Sir Henry Norris.

Several years afterwards Leicester pushed through a measure designed to strengthen the group of university administrators who discussed matters to be placed before Convocation. Also he reversed a statute from his father's time that the deputies of the chancellor should be elected, and the choice now returned to the discretion of the chancellor. Perhaps most importantly he prompted a valuable measure on behalf of the university in 1571 which, by Act of Parliament, invested the senior academics with 'the rights of perpetual succession' and confirmed all other privileges. This meant that the university no longer had to scurry to a new monarch for a new charter. Alongside these measures a reform was agreed that prevented colleges from artificially extending leases at low rentals. But the most contentious aspect of Leicester's long chancellorship was surely his attempt to regulate the religious tone of the university by the administration of the Thirty-nine Articles, together with the requirement that all matriculating students over sixteen years should acknowledge the royal supremacy. This was a provision that actually proved double-edged in a way which Leicester had not intended, for Puritans might also be ensnared by it. An equally interesting measure was that which sought the removal of inept teachers, an idea that might have been suggested to him by the practice of the University of Padua, with its excellent reputation.[7]

The result of all this interest and work was that by the 1580s the university bore 'all the marks of a vigorous society, full of young scholars and youthful divines'. Certainly the number of men graduating from there was increasing, and Leicester noted with pleasure the growing number of students of divinity.[8] However, he does seem to have been rather dismayed by the usual student pranks and unruly behaviour in the town. In January 1583 he complained that 'the disorders, not muttered of, but openly cried upon continually and almost in every place, are such as touch us less than your religion, your lives and conversation, and the whole state of the Universitye, Professions and learning'.[9] Over-elaborate clothes and the tone of some of the sermons delivered by young preachers also disturbed him. However, he was reluctant to intervene in order to rebuke them, until pressure from the Queen and court gave him no other option. The new requirement was that preachers should be licensed only after they had been tested, commended and investigated.[10] But even these curbs did not put an end to the complaints, and in 1584 Leicester had to write again to the university.

The earl's active life at home and at court left him comparatively little time for private scholarship, but he enjoyed the company of scholarly men. In both London and Oxford he was the key figure in a remarkable network of talent which included Jean Hotman (later his secretary), Richard Hakluyt, Thomas Saile, Richard Garth, the Gentili brothers, Antonio de (or del) Corro, Edward Dyer (one of his gentleman secretaries from 1565), Philip Sidney (his nephew) and John Dee. The latter had once tutored the Dudley brothers in science and mathematics, and he remained a friend for many years. On the fringe of the Oxford group was Stephen Parmenius, born in Hungary and now a student at Christ Church. While there he counted the Unton family as his close friends and the younger Hakluyt as his mentor. The Untons and Dudleys were related, and it was Henry Unton whom Leicester knighted during the campaign in the United Provinces.

Leicester's unstinting generosity and support for these men is illustrated by the career of de Corro, Philip Sidney's tutor in Spanish. It was in 1575 that the earl stirred up a controversy over the Spaniard, once a member of the elusive Italian congregation in London and possibly a secret adherent of the Family of Love. De Corro had been born in Spain of Jewish ancestry, had not graduated from Oxford, and could not pay the appropriate fees when Leicester wrote to Oxford's vice-chancellor Humphrey asking for De Corro's admittance as a doctor of divinity. Reader (lecturer) in divinity at the Inner and Middle Temples at £20 per annum, he had been appointed with the approval of Sandys, Leicester and Cecil, after Grindal had gone to York as archbishop. Unfortunately for de Corro his 'thoroughgoing religious toleration cannot have endeared him to the authorities in Oxford'. Moreover, there was a reported shift in his views on predestination and justification, which led to an act of considerable temerity by John Reynolds, President of Corpus Christi. Reynolds was aghast because he saw Leicester's request (so it was couched) as a step towards a major university post for de Corro, so he attacked the earl's intervention in the matter. This left Humphrey in an unenviable position, and his response was an exercise in damage limitation. When he laid down certain strict conditions for the acceptance of the Spaniard Leicester was furious, and on 23 June 1576 the vice-chancellor was relieved of his post.

By way of a postscript on the suitability of de Corro's advancement it may be noted that the benchers of the Inns seem not to have regretted his departure, indicating that he could leave 'without contribution or reward'.[11] So he went to Oxford under a cloud, and when there continued to press the earl for advancement with such tenacity that he neglected his teaching duties. He ended his days as Prebend of Harlesden, being installed in St Paul's in 1582, a second prebend following three years later.

In London the Leicester circle was distinguished by its internationalism and the breadth of its thinking. Among men like Jean Hotman, a Calvinist who turned to eirenism, a religious movement with direct political implications, and Alberico Gentili (later professor of civil law at Oxford), de Corro's opposition to the use of the sword against heretics caused no scandal.[12] Their eirenism 'was essentially an attempt to evade frightening religious antagonisms', which had led to calamities like the civil wars in France. Philip Sidney had a profound interest in eirenism, since he was a friend of the exiled Daniel Rogers, and Justus Lipsius, the neo-Stoic philosopher. Sidney's travels in Central Europe therefore take on a particular interest. In 1573 he was in Austria; the following year Poland (where some must have wistfully eyed him as a possible candidate for the elective Polish throne) and Moravia. In 1575 he was in Prague, and two years later in the same city he was the Queen's representative to the new emperor, Rudolf II, presenting him with Elizabeth's condolences on the death of his father, Maximilian.[13] Sidney had prepared a spirited defence of Protestantism to which his royal contemporary seems to have listened sympathetically, though Sidney did not find him congenial company and reported so to Walsingham. Yet the unquenchable hope remained that these contacts might be a 'first step towards the reunion of all Christians'.[14] The overriding principle behind this may have been spiritual, but one earthly motive was the ominous and continual pressure from the Turks, defeated by Don John of Austria at the Battle of Lepanto in 1571, but still a great threat by land and sea to Christian Europe.

Before his departure Sidney met his uncle, Leicester, Edward Dyer and John Dee at the latter's famous home in Mortlake, close to that of Walsingham in Barnes. Apart from his orthodox teaching and scholarship Dee was also a religious Hermeticist with a vision of the world transformed on the spiritual as well as the intellectual plane. Such a philosophy required a freedom from constraints that neither the authoritarian Puritans nor the Catholic reaction could comfortably accept. It is no wonder that Dee was steadily misunderstood by many of his contemporaries, and that Leicester's interest in his work (other than astrology) was not widely known; 'Dee must be classed with such unorthodox religious thinkers as Pico, Agrippa and Giordano Bruno'.[15] It was in conjunction with his nephew that Leicester probably sponsored the famous visit to Oxford by Bruno (see Appendix A) in 1583, which coincided with the reception by the university of Albrecht Łaski, Palatine of Sieradz in Poland. By some paradox this noted Catholic family had already produced the Protestant reformer Johannes Łaski, who settled in London in the reign of Edward VI and supervised the first church at Austin Friars for foreign Protestant refugees and immigrants. Albrecht Łaski also visited Dee in the company of Philip Sidney, his interest stimulated by an earlier meeting in Leicester's rooms at Greenwich Palace. Since the Polish nobleman was rich enough to support research into alchemy, Dee actually joined his entourage, and with Edward Kelley he moved to Poland for private seances and recondite research. In 1584 they headed for Prague and the court of Rudolf II, which was saturated in esoteric lore. Dee believed in magical forces that held divine creation together, and his hope seems to have been to uncover them for the advancement of man. At a practical level 'he wrote tracts in English specifically for the benefit of the rising middle class of technologists and artisans'. For the great men of the court like Leicester and Sir Henry Sidney the growth of such practical knowledge was intended to promote English wealth and power.[16]

Chapter 9

As Rich as Renowned as Any

In his *Of Nobility* Francis Bacon wrote that 'new nobility is an act of power, but ancient nobility is an act of time'. William Cecil, created Lord Burghley in 1571, was, even more than Leicester, of the new nobility. Elizabeth was sparing in her creation of titles, and Burghley was given the rare honour as a result of his remarkable and extended political services to the Crown. Since he lacked the dignity that sprang from ancient aristocratic lineage, Burghley, like Leicester (who was lord lieutenant of twelve counties), accepted the office of lord lieutenant of a county whenever it was offered, and at court he showed a certain partiality for the lineal aristocracy, whom he flattered when necessary.[1] Like them he acquired estates and a handsome income, although he is said to have modestly declined an earldom on the grounds that it would prove too costly. Leicester, of course, had no such inhibitions and hesitations in his public career, being a man of boundless self-esteem. Probably he enjoyed the snap of antagonism from such aristocratic dinosaurs as the Earl of Sussex and the Duke of Norfolk, whose income from land equalled the entire annual revenue of Scotland. Burghley deferentially held the middle ground, building his fortune slowly for the sake of his family and anticipated future generations. The earl, however, had no legitimate surviving son for many years and chose to plunge into many activities with great verve, showing the spirit of a buccaneer entrepreneur.

It may be said that Leicester was to become the archetypal figure of the new aristocracy of Elizabethan England. Although he too derived a great income from estates and offices, his real income did not match the swift growth of his expenses. There is clear evidence that Leicester had an unremitting taste for the finest things as a conspicuous consumer, and he liked to be generous to his friends and relations. A card player, he lost frequently to the Queen and often had to borrow money.

With an unabashed interest in profits and income needed to maintain his high style and dignity, Leicester built up a series of business connections in commerce and industry that was as unexpected as it was unrivalled. He became a pivotal figure in the commercial expansion that began to boost English investment in industries and shipping at a time when England was poised to become one of the major sea powers of Europe– the springboard for later global expansion on a heroic scale. His enthusiasms and sometimes wayward initiatives did not always chime with the more sober notions of merchants. Their primary concern was to make money and retain it; his was to make money and spend it in conspicuous consumption. Yet whatever the strains in his dealings with these men, there is no doubt that Leicester played a vital role in the alliance of the new aristocracy with the leading merchants. In Thomas Heywood's drama-pageant *If You Know Not Me, You Know Nobody* (part II), written to extol the building of that temple of early modern capitalism, the Royal Exchange, Leicester appears as a character and is sympathetically treated.[2]

However, the earl and his associates on the privy council with their increasing domination during the 1570s did more than simply seek private riches. The concern to develop (in so far as an insufficient technology and resources would allow) new industries helped to give employment to a landless working class created by the enclosures of the fifteenth and early sixteenth centuries, the dispersal of the feudal bands of the old nobility, and the closure and pillaging of the monasteries and abbeys of the old faith. Now the growth of towns, and especially London, created a demand for ever-growing supplies of fresh food. This in turn led to a revival of arable farming (hitherto somewhat neglected) which absorbed many of the rural unemployed, much to government relief. The social consequences for Elizabethan England are not hard to distinguish, for 'that mass of social discontent which had threatened all the upper classes with revolution and had strengthened Tudor absolutism by creating a desire for strong government, was eliminated'.[3] At the same time the inexorable price rises of the sixteenth century, from which those with something to sell actually benefited, continually sapped those dependent on moribund incomes from fees and rents – the gentry, nobles and monarch.

The sometimes suspicious rivalry of Burghley and Leicester in council did not prevent them from entering into business dealings together when there was an opportunity, however slender, to make money. One of the vital commodities that England still imported from France was salt, and because of the import costs and the fluctuating supplies from a country periodically involved in fierce domestic strife, Burghley was anxious to promote a substantial English salt industry. Francis Berty, Tommaso Baroncelli (Leicester's Antwerp agent) and Jasper Seler began the difficult task of trying to set up this operation when the climate made natural evaporation spasmodic. The Queen's expectations in the patent of white salt rather than cheaper bay salt also caused problems. After several reissues of the patent, the licences to make bay salt were transferred to Leicester, Pembroke, Norfolk, Burghley, Bacon and Knollys, a representative clutch of councillors, and other co-partners. There were many schemes to improve salt supplies, but imports remained crucial, and the Huguenots in France continued to use salt as a bargaining weapon in their dealings with Elizabeth.[4]

England's leading statesman and her leading courtier were also linked by their financial interest in both the Mines Royal and the Mineral and Battery Works. The Company or Society of Mines Royal was founded towards the end of 1564 after several attempts to lure German mining experts to England. The agreement between Thomas Thurland, Master of the Savoy, and Daniel Hochstetter, gave the latter the right 'to search, dig, try, roast, and melt all manner of mines and ores of gold, silver, copper, and quick-silver' in the north-east, north-west and south-west of England, as well as Wales. Hochstetter was then the agent of the German company David Haug and Hans Langnauer of Augsburg, which was allotted eleven principal shares in the new enterprise. Others assigned shares for which they paid £1,200 each, and which meant no more than the right to participate in the monopoly, were Leicester and Burghley, with two shares each. As time passed, both men seem to have encouraged their various business associates to acquire fractional shares out of the original division of twenty-four. Benedetto Spinola had two shares, and in February 1566 John Dudley of Stoke Newington (whose grandfather was the brother of Leicester's great-grandfather) acquired a quarter share. William Patten, who was at that time a follower of Burghley, had half of one share, and by Christmas 1566 Leicester had fractionally reduced his holding by transfers to Thomas Smyth, John Tamworth and Matthew Field. In the following year the Earl of Pembroke joined the investors, probably at Leicester's prompting, but a decade later the list of shareholders was virtually unchanged. Despite the fact that the company proved something of a financial burden, even in 1580 when it was reconstructed the names of the shareholders remained much the same.

Promoting trade abroad always interested Leicester. In 1573 he was approached by a number of merchants still trading with the Iberian peninsula who complained of heavy losses from the confiscation and sale of their goods. Getting the £8,000 they claimed was a difficult matter, hence the deputation that arrived at Leicester House to see the great man. They wanted particularly to appoint their own agents to divide the compensation, replacing Crown officials. As they said, the Staplers and Merchant Company already had this concession 'which they lacked only because they were not a recognised company'. On consideration he was impressed by their arguments, and wrote to Burghley that he thought their solution a reasonable one. In July the earl set up a visit by Thomas Wilferd, who eventually became president of the Spanish Company, to Burghley, and when the charter of the company was granted some four years after the initial approaches to the earl, Walsingham, Sir Thomas Gresham and Leicester became honorary members. They were joined by Sir James Croft and Sir Henry Cobham.[5]

Occasionally Leicester's multiplicity of business interests led to both sides in a dispute seeking his favourable attention. In July 1565 the earl became Chamberlain of Chester when, as noted earlier, the town was suffering a bad patch through contracting trade and prosperity. The townspeople turned to him in the hope that through interest and direction he would be able to arrest this stagnation, and he certainly listened. However, he was not immediately able to achieve anything helpful. Then in the 1570s a number of Chester merchants who had joined the Spanish Company decided to try to establish a monopoly of Spanish trade for members of the company called the 'mere' merchants. Their rivals, the 'merchant retailers', used charters to support their principal claim of rights, and the situation was exacerbated in the next decade by the 'mere' merchants obtaining a licence to export calfskins. As the dispute grew more heated, the privy council intervened to investigate the claims of both sides, while the town fathers again approached Leicester. The mayor boldly pointed out that the town had accepted Robert Dodd as his choice for the post of sword-bearer, and that he had also been made a freeman of the town. But it is unlikely that these urgings achieved anything significant.

These parochial wrangles were not of critical importance to Leicester's own income. But the activities of Thomas Sutton, the controller of the greatest private fortune of the age, certainly were. Sutton laid the basis of his wealth by wrenching from Richard Cox, Bishop of Ely, the splendid manors of Littlebury and Hadstock, and giving the advowsons to Ambrose Dudley. This connection led to an appointment in the north of England following the scandal and death of John Bennett, Master of Ordnance. This was a key position near a still turbulent border, which had the particular advantage of being as far from London and royal scrutiny as it was possible to be. Sutton remained in the north from 1568 to 1581, and while there was both needed and hated as an extremely careful and exacting money-lender to the financially improvident gentry.

Sutton also became involved in the aftermath of the revolt of the Northern Earls, and the squabbling over the vastly rich coal-bearing lands of the Earl of Westmorland, from whom they were forfeit. Bishop Pilkington of Durham, having failed in his martial duties as the Count Palatine, was in a poor position to claim these riches as a reward. Moreover, it was known at court that he was idle, a nepotist, and married, so that each of his daughters received a large dowry when she found a husband. Nor was he the only one to look covetously on the coal deposits: the merchants of Newcastle were just as anxious to control them. Yet when Pilkington died in January 1576 it was not Richard Barnes, the new bishop, nor the merchants who benefited, for

Leicester contrived that the lease of the mines should go to Sutton.

The 'Grand Lease' (as it was called) of the manors of Whickham and Gateshead in Northumberland was an enormous prize. There seems little doubt that as a result of its assignation Leicester gained financially, but as with so many areas of his business life the evidence is missing. Thomas Sutton's lease was for seventy-nine years, and in 1582 it was exchanged for a ninety-year lease. Yet opposed by implacable merchants in the north, his plans for profitable exploitation wrecked, Sutton sold the lease in 1583 to Henry Anderson and William Selby.[6] Because Sutton was not a freeman of Newcastle, charter and custom excluded him from the Elizabethan equivalent of a merchants' closed shop, and despite various ruses to win admission he failed in all his plans. Hence the sale for a few thousand pounds of a lease which, a few years later, was worth £50,000.[7] Sutton left the north deeply chagrined and returned to London, where he maintained the Dudley connection by his marriage to the widow of John Dudley of Stoke Newington, who had bought the lease of that manor from an insolvent William Patten, who owed the Queen £7,928. 7s.

As early as 1571 Leicester became a member of the Muscovy Company, founded in 1555. Yet he and Walsingham lent support to Jerome Horsey when the latter encountered problems in his dealings with the group.[8] Horsey wrote that he had 'received great honour, countenance and particular letters of grace' from the earl, who was a close friend of the trader's relative, Sir Edward Horsey, Captain of the Isle of Wight. Jerome Horsey also noted that Leicester had received from him 'rich furs, white gerfalcons, white bears'.[9]

At the same time Leicester, who was a generous patron of Italians in England, had business links with Acerbo Velutelli. Velutelli was a Florentine with whom the Queen also had financial dealings, and in 1575, at the earl's request, she granted the Italian a patent of monopoly for the import of currants. On the strength of this, Velutelli levied a charge of 5s. 6d. on every hundredweight of currants imported. So long as the trade was in mainly Venetian hands, no complaint was raised. But when an embargo on English ships in Spain forced English merchants to seek new outlets, and they directed their attention to the currant trade, they complained that Velutelli's licence money put them at a disadvantage with the Venetian merchants, because they had to pay Venetian export dues in addition to the English import charges. Their petition for relief succeeded and Velutelli was ordered to levy his licence money on foreigners only. In response to this activity Venetian merchants induced their government to raise the tariff on exports and imports, and negotiations between the two governments came to nothing. Then, in 1582 or the following year, Velutelli's patent was revoked, and a monopoly for the import of currants, sweet wines and oil was granted to Edward Cordell, Edward Homborn, Paul Bayning and others for a period of six years. This was the origin of the Venetian Company, which was later amalgamated with the Levant Company. It seems likely that the names on the monopoly were Leicester's nominees.[10]

Parallel with his abiding interest in trade, Leicester was also involved in the periodic attempts of the government to rationalize and strengthen the administration of the customs. Theoretically the customs tariffs should have raised substantial sums for the government, and in the previous reign attempts had been made by the Marquess of Winchester to raise rates and reduce the number of goods escaping duties. Then in 1564 and 1565 new regulations were devised for the collection of customs revenue, and a *Book of Orders and Instructions* was issued to officials. Unfortunately, finding efficient agents to carry out these precise formulations was not easy, and as a result Elizabeth's councillors decided to adopt a new policy with an ancient history – the farm. Two London businessmen, Henry Smith and James Morley, a mercer and an ironmonger respectively, offered a new scheme for collecting customs on woollen cloths and wines for import and export. In September 1567 at Nicholas Bacon's home, Gorhambury, Elizabeth accepted the idea and it was put into operation. Smith and Morley were given six years to operate the scheme, and the rent paid by them to the Crown was fixed by means of an average being taken of the net customs, minus expenses, during the six-year period.

By the following year Morley, whose instinct for making money was exceptionally well developed, reported to Burghley that the scheme was running effectively. However, his mistake was that he failed to pacify numerous corrupt officials and he had not won the crucial endorsement of Leicester. In August 1568 the earl, using nominees, decided to bid for the farm of wine imports, raising his offer above Morley's rent, while his rivals bid for the wool prize. The result was that in September the Morley–Smith farm was suspended and passed to the earl's nominees. At Michaelmas 1568 Thomas Neale and Henry Godlinge were granted the farm for an annual rent of £9,051. 4s. 5d., and in 1571 this lease was passed to Francis Robinson for seven years. In September 1573 the sweet wine imposition was raised and given to Robinson for seven years at £2,000 per annum, and by December the plum had fallen into Leicester's hands. Several years later Leicester gave up the sweet wine farm 'for a new lease in his own name of both imposition and the customs and subsidy on sweet wines', to run for a decade at a rent of £2,728. 16s. 7½d., which he then promptly subleased to the Customs officer of London, Thomas Smyth, for £3,500. The latter's financial links with the earl were numerous and obscure, although, as we have already seen, both were shareholders in the Company of Mines Royal.

For a decade before these complicated arrangements, which surely benefited individuals but not the Crown, Smyth had been collecting duties for the port of Southampton, and it is possible that from 1574 he did so in a sharing arrangement with Leicester. Prior to this the earl had asked the town corporation 'to grant him a farm of their penalties under the Act of 1571 for six years from Michaelmas 1573', which would have coincided with the transfer of the Robinson farm.[11] The dignitaries of the town decided to submit their case to Leicester, requesting that he should either drop the idea or pay the corporation a fair rent. The unhappily named John Crook arrived in London accompanied by two aides with a Christmas present for the earl of fourteen pounds of marmalade, which cost £1. 5s. 9d. The result is uncertain, and the involvement of Smyth adds to the complexities.[12]

Chapter 10

Trade and Voyage

Leicester's remorseless pursuit of wealth went far beyond national boundaries. His involvement in the trade with Morocco, however, was sustained for reasons beyond the financial: it was a matter of State security. This exotic trading connection may seem unlikely (a Christian power trading with an Islamic country), but there were particular reasons for it.

There had been an English trading presence in Morocco for years before Elizabeth's reign. It was centred on the ports of Agadir and Safi, the principal export being sugar: the English then (as now) were all too partial to the commodity. In return English merchants, to the dismay of the Portuguese, supplied the Moroccans with pikes, lances, armour, and the metal necessary for the manufacture of cannons and naval stores. In so doing they were blithely ignoring the papal injunction on the sale of such materials to the enemies of Christendom. Thus, when the Portuguese were driven from Agadir in 1541, they blamed English and French merchants for arming their enemies so effectively. Elizabeth knew the trade was lucrative if morally dubious, and despite the irritation it caused Philip II she held back from trying to prevent it by government decree. However, in the late spring of 1574, in order to avoid open conflict with Spain, she did agree to ban English traders from venturing farther south than Cape Blanco, thus effectively ending the Guinea trade. She declared also that the trade in weapons to Morocco would cease, as the Portuguese ambassador Giraldi had expressly requested it, but then did nothing to enforce the ban.

In 1577 the ambassador reported that exports of arms were

still reaching Morocco, though the trade was now being carried out by Hansa ships using English mariners. Shortly afterwards Edmund Hogan (or Huggins) appeared before the privy council charged with exporting arms, Giraldi claiming that Hogan's agent, John Williams, had sold thirty barrels of cannon-balls to Moulay Muhammad al Muttawakkil, Shārif of Morocco until he was driven from that position by his uncle, Moulay 'Abd al-Malik, ruler under Turkish suzerainty.[1] Now the munitions were sold for saltpetre (potassium nitrate) as well as sugar. The ambassador also alleged that other English traders were now selling oars and artillery in the country. Yet since at this time both the Queen and the privy council were keenly interested in the saltpetre supplies, it is very likely that Hogan was left unpunished for his opportunism. Within a month he had drawn up a memorandum asking that the ban on the export of arms be lifted.

This document usefully reveals that five years previously Williams had been sent to Hamburg to buy saltpetre, but had found the price too high. He therefore moved on to Lübeck and Danzig, but again was frustrated in his search and returned with only some thin cloth that aroused no interest among buyers in England. Hogan shunted him off to Morocco in the hope of unloading this apparently useless purchase in a warmer climate. It was then that Williams made the delightful discovery that natural saltpetre was in plentiful supply – the problem was to get it to England. This required direct dealings with Moulay Muhammad, who finally agreed that Hogan should receive his supplies if in return he would export ammunition for the Shārif's artillery. A sample of the saltpetre was sent to England, and Burghley sent it on to Kenilworth for scrutiny by Leicester and Warwick, the Master of Ordnance.

What caused this sudden need for saltpetre supplies? The answer lay in the quantities required (for the manufacture of gunpowder) by the English army and navy at a time of sustained antagonism against the Catholic powers of Europe and their empires. Hitherto the arquebus had not been favoured in England and the longbow had retained much of its glamour and supremacy. Bowmen were still being recruited at the end of the sixteenth century, and stocks of gunpowder were kept abroad, notably at Antwerp. But these could not be transported without the authority of the ruler in whose territory they were held. In Mary's reign this had been Philip II, a bizarre situation that alarmed patriots in the privy council when Elizabeth replaced her sister. The shortage of saltpetre had to be made up, hence the delight of the Dudley brothers and their aides at the possibility of a firm supply from Morocco. England had no natural deposits, although a German captain had sold a secret recipe for its production to Elizabeth for £300.[2] The process was unsavoury: earth and animal excrement had to be mixed with lime and ashes. The mixture was then exposed to air in dry, cold places – often city cellars – and it was watered periodically with urine. After much turning, the saltpetre crystallized out and the valiant but highly unpopular saltpetre men removed it.

The Shārif received his cannon-balls from England just as he was engaged in the dynastic quarrel with his uncle. The success of the latter led to a review of Anglo-Moroccan contacts, Williams and another merchant, John Bampton, being called before 'Abd al-Malik to discuss the problem of arms supplies. He told them that if they could supply cannon-balls, he would allow them an exclusive right to buy saltpetre or copper. His offer was accepted and the agreement confirmed by letter. Elizabeth was now prepared to risk Spanish ire, for the new Shārif was also to receive a party of English gun-founders. Moreover, with surprising alacrity she sent Edmund Hogan to Morocco to negotiate a secret agreement. For Giraldi's consumption, Hogan's public instructions proclaimed that he should deal only with complaints by English merchants already in the country, and that armaments and materials of war were beyond his scope.

Through Hogan's report, printed by Hakluyt, filter some clues about his activities (as well as his vanity).[3] He sailed for Morocco on 22 April 1577, and arrived at Safi on 21 May, where he waited for the royal summons. When this came he travelled inland and held talks in Spanish with the Shārif, presenting to him Elizabeth's letters, and gifts that included a bass lute. Hogan thought the secret negotiations had been successful, especially when al-Malik offered safe conduct to English shipping and a promise not to enslave Englishmen. But when he promised to send an ambassador to England Elizabeth became nervous at the possible European repercussions. 'We beg', she wrote, 'that for many good reasons you will send him secretly, so that his coming may not be in any way known.' Yet despite all this care Mendoza, the Spanish ambassador, still had his suspicions that something was afoot, and on 3 June 1578 he reported to Philip II that a ship was prepared to depart for Morocco carrying dogs, horses and costumes for the Shārif. Also on board was a certain Julio who, de Mendoza thought, was a Morisco fluent in eight or nine languages. '[He] is closeted for hours every day with Leicester and Walsingham, and sometimes with the queen. I do not know what he is up to, but it is believed he will go in this ship.'

Then came a blow to English plans that could not have been anticipated by anyone. The Shārif had freed himself from Turkish domination, but was killed when fighting the Portuguese at the Battle of Alcazar in August 1578. His brother, Ahmad al-Mansur, now ruled Morocco and he was much less co-operative, bolstered as he was by the tide of Christian gold that poured into the country to ransom Christian captives. In the same month a letter arrived in London for Elizabeth which said sardonically that among the presents he hoped to send her was the corpse of Leicester's footloose friend Thomas Stukeley, killed in the same battle that had witnessed the death of al-Malik.[4]

Elizabeth wanted the agreement made with the dead Shārif to be renewed, but, under pressure from Philip II, al-Mansur declined to do anything, which was the beginning of a sustained hiatus in Anglo-Moroccan relations. It was not until June 1581 that Elizabeth issued a warrant noting that John Symcot, a London merchant with interests in the trade with the Barbary Coast, had offered to import supplies of saltpetre. However, al-Mansur wanted only timber in exchange, not cash or other commodities. Symcot certainly wanted to deal with him and asked for a licence to buy timber in the south of England, a request to which Elizabeth gave her consent. The quantity allowed was 600 tons in exchange for all the saltpetre that Symcot could accumulate. But the problem was that the Shārif required ship timbers, not cut firewood. In October 1581 de Mendoza wrote to his master in Madrid that some Englishmen had gone to Morocco to make final arrangements for the deal, and that because of the amount required (the equivalent of a small forest), additional supplies had been sought in Holland (presumably in the shape of imports from Sweden). By January 1582 the timber was gathered at Bristol, but then Leicester intervened because the whole operation breached his monopoly. The material was now to be sent directly under his charge, but the plan failed when the ship carrying the material was wrecked.

Research on Leicester's dealings with Morocco has shown that he 'was the principal in this timber transaction' and Symcot was his agent.[5] The Bristol part of the story may simply be the fancy of de Mendoza, and it is unlikely that any timber was exported by anyone in the spring of 1582. Another factor was Symcot's financial peril, which required powerful help to keep creditors and city officials at bay. It was Leicester and the privy council who provided this, although on 19 July the Lord Mayor of London, Sir James Harvey, wrote that Symcot did not merit any special treatment as a debtor, and that his suit was fraudulent. This development was not to the earl's liking, so Leicester reiterated that it was necessary to allow Symcot some freedom of action. It was made clear that 'if any-stay be made either of Symcot or his goods, whereby his voyage shall be hindered . . . there will be great negligence found in you and small care of her Majesty's service'.[6] Leicester did not mean to be balked, and Symcot was allowed to go off to Morocco. State and private concerns probably meshed here for the earl, since there was an urgent need for the saltpetre, and he had probably invested money in the voyage as he had in privateering.[7]

After some 400 years it is impossible to discern more than the faintest outline of Symcot's activities in Morocco. But the jostling between traders is apparent, and at the back of it all is the powerful, if dimly discerned, figure of Leicester. Even after Symcot's death Leicester maintained his interest in Moroccan dealings, and Elizabeth wrote to al-Mansur that a letter from Augustine Lane to the earl had pleased her as an indication of the Shārif's friendly interest in Anglo-Moroccan relations. Independent merchants in England had to struggle to maintain a foothold and, not surprisingly, they lost the struggle with Leicester. In 1585 the Barbary Company was formed, but even then he managed to exasperate members, who claimed that he deliberately hindered their work in seeking his own advantage. It was at this time that Henry Roberts was nominated by the company as its representative in Morocco, and he also acted as the Queen's agent, though with virtually nothing to show for it financially.

The charter of the Barbary Company named Leicester, Warwick and sundry other merchants as licensed traders for twelve years, and, while the company had certain powers, it was the earl who seems to have had overriding control of it. In such a position he decided the fate of Anglo-Moroccan trade in conjunction with Moulay Ahmad. Indeed, Barbary Company is a misnomer, since the charter did not give it that name, and more appropriately it should have been called the Leicester Moroccan Company. It was in conjunction with Richard Staper (one of the Levant merchants) and Alexander Avenon that Leicester and his Spanish-speaking aide, Arthur Atey (Principal of St Alban's Hall, Oxford, 1569–81), engaged in dealings in metal and saltpetre and other items. The appointed agent in Morocco was Henry Roberts, chosen by the earl, and he left London in 1585, living in a ghetto in Marrakesh until August 1588. The Leicester cabal within the company put up goods for their own trading, and the earl's investment was valued at £3,000, while the rest staked much smaller amounts. Avenon put up £275 in cash. Part of the accumulated stock was used in repayment of Leicester's debt of £4,000 to the Shārif for the original trading concessions in metal and saltpetre. But when al-Mansur actually removed more metal from the first shipment than the amount to which he was entitled, Leicester was angry, and by bribes and presents costing nearly £100 he recovered 564 hundredweight of iron.[8] Money well spent apparently, for the price the Shārif paid for his tin alone was nearly double the stock price valuation.

Neither Leicester nor Atey was able to spend much time on the day-to-day business of the company, most of the work falling to Avenon and his assistants in London. In Morocco there were soon six factors besides Roberts: three in Marrakesh – Robert Lion, Miles Dickinson and Edmund Manstidge; and three on the coast at Agadir. The evidence is that for trading purposes most of the work was done during the first year of the company. Between June 1585 and the following year sales in Morocco brought in nearly £3,000, mostly from the selling of saffron and cloth. Exports to England were: almonds (sold at a loss of £120. 4s. 2d.); sugar (profitable if refined, but sold at a loss if left unrefined); and gold ducats bought for £252 (but sold at a loss of £43. 4s. to the Master of the Mint, Richard Martin).[9] Furthermore, in accountants' terms the second year was even worse, though more goods were imported to tempt buyers. The indigo on offer was expensive in Morocco, for it was in constant demand by the desert tribes, while the saltpetre now cost so much that English officials again began to hunt for alternative supplies. Yet desultory trading continued, and in 1588, at a time of real crisis for England, the saltpetre actually made a modest profit of £24. 5s. 6d. It was sold to Richard Hill and one of the famous Evelyn family at Godestone. Net losses over four years were a dispiriting £1,689.

Why did the company continue to import goods that failed to make a profit? The general answer seems to be that it had little choice in the matter. The Moroccans bought goods for which they had to pay or find exchange equivalents. Payment in gold seems to have been limited by export restrictions that remained in force despite the obvious problems. Moreover, a rudimentary banking system could not risk bills on Morocco, so goods it had to be. Leicester, being Master of the Horse, would doubtless have liked to import more Barbary horses to improve English bloodstock lines, but he was prevented by the Shārif's ban on anything other than individual horses being sent as gifts to European rulers. It seems that Morocco produced little that was required in English markets, so that Leicester's interest may not have been simply economic. It is possible that he envisaged the country as a potential ally usefully placed to the south of Spain at a time when he anticipated war. An English supply base at Agadir would have been useful, and might have lent itself to the development of trade with West Africa: the thought of a slave-trade was in many minds. Finally, he may also have given support to Emanuel van Meteren, who in pious hope wanted to distribute Bibles in Hebrew in the country where there was a substantial Jewish minority.

Chapter 11

Thou Wilt Be Excellent

In his lifetime Leicester won a deserved reputation for princely generosity and cultivation. Elizabeth seems to have encouraged him to act as a patron in many fields and, more important, she gave him the financial means to gratify his taste. The result was that he was frequently lauded as the Maecenas of her court, for his position gave him a glorious opportunity, which he gratefully seized.

Leicester had considerable advantage over many Elizabethans, which derived from his privileged childhood and his education; books in particular were not expensive novelties, and he was fluent in languages other than English. Hence the copies of his personal library of essential texts for the courtier – Guazzo, Castiglione and Machiavelli, all in Italian, in which he had been tutored by Michelangelo Florio. It was the expectation of Prospero d'Osma that his report on the royal studs written in that language would be read by the earl, for he took the trouble to apologize for his style. Apart from horse-breeding, Leicester had a sustained interest in cartography, navigation and fortification, and at Leicester House there were model ships, instruments of astronomy, land-surveying equipment and compasses. (His father had collected astrolabes.) Unlike some cultivated men of the period (say Thomas Sackville or Ralegh), Leicester did not have the time or the inclination to write more than letters, but these, especially those written from the United Provinces during his many months of campaigning, make excellent reading. They are pithy and eloquent sometimes to the point of desperation, revealing the humanity of the man. Such were the fierce demands on his time that on one occasion he asked Walsingham to 'bear with the faults of my letter, it is so long I cannot peruse it'.

It was part of Leicester's campaign of self-promotion that his company of actors performed at court and around the country. Touring always made the privy council uneasy that they might be spying for the enemy. With the northern rebellion of the earls, and the papal bull of 1570, the government's paranoia grew even more pronounced, since free-moving companies could not be constantly observed by government agents. As a means of trying to curb this supposed or imagined threat to public safety, a proclamation was issued on 3 January 1572 demanding the control of 'unordinary servants', including players. Tudor governments regarded those who lived by their wits, be they actors or beggars, as potentially seditious. Men without roots and the restraints of the guilds were regarded with deep suspicion, and later in 1572 the government's aim was more clearly stated when these hitherto masterless men were converted by a linguistic sleight of the pen from 'vagabonds' and 'rogues' to men 'whole and mighty in body and able to labour, having not land or master'. Now it was time for the actors to protect themselves, and their nervous response was to rush to secure a permanent sponsor at court. Leicester's men now sought his aid, if not his purse:

> May it please your honour to understand that for as much as there is a certain Proclamation out for the reviving of a statute as touching retainers, as your Lordship knoweth better than we can inform you . . . for avoiding all inconvenience that may grow by reason of the said statute, [we] are bold to trouble your Lordship with this our suit, humbly desiring your honour that, as you have always been our great lord and master, you will now vouchsafe to retain us at this present as your household servants and daily waiters – not that we mean to crave any further stipend.[1]

To show that the company he supported was not made up of unlawful retainers, or rogues and vagabonds who could be punished, the earl had his servant-actors perform again at court during the Christmas season of 1572–3. Now they were rivals to those of the Earl of Sussex, soon to be appointed Lord

Chamberlain, to the considerable irritation of Leicester. The office was an important one, since the incumbent dealt with court ceremonies, the Queen's private accommodations, her travel and wardrobe. The office-holder also had access to State funds, which was important to both men.[2] The attention of the great magnates and other lesser grandees played a part in the tendency of actors' companies to become more professional. That they had an audience and thrived once the issue of their status had been satisfied is obvious from the opening some four years later of James Burbage's public theatre, called with admirable simplicity 'The Theatre'.

The rivalry of Leicester and Sussex seems to have given the adult companies a boost at a time when the boy companies were particularly popular. The Children of Paul's, under the expert tutelage of Sebastian Westcott, won many friends at court, and their master was able to attract the beneficent attention of the Queen and Leicester. Both protected him from attacks caused by his Catholicism, and even after he was excommunicated by Grindal, this protection continued. In a letter to Cecil written in August 1563, the bishop recalled Dudley's earnest inquiries on Westcott's behalf, hoping that a decision would be delayed or averted. Delayed it was, and the bishop wrote to Dudley that Westcott had until 1 October to adjust his beliefs: 'I am contented because your Lordship writeth so earnestly for him.' Since Grindal must have been aware of the Queen's partiality in the case, Westcott remained in his mastership. However, by the mid-1570s, with increasing pressure on recusants, even Westcott was to spend some time in the Marshalsea 'to which Aylmer confined both catholics and protestant non-conformists with fine impartiality'.[3] The Children of Paul's were primarily choristers, and acting, though important, was secondary. At Merchant Taylors' School, where a protégé of the earl's was headmaster, acting was part of the curriculum, and in the decade after 1572 Richard Mulcaster's troupe visited the court at least eight times.[4]

Like Mulcaster, the Master of the Children of the Chapel Royal, William Hunnis, also found Leicester's influence useful when he lost his place to Richard Ferrant, already Master of the Children of Windsor Chapel. Hunnis opened a campaign to retrieve his lost post, and in 1578 published a metrical rendering of the whole book of Genesis dedicated to the earl – the famous 'Hive Full of Hunny' appearing with the bear and ragged staff on the reverse of the title-page.[5] By 1581 Hunnis had triumphed and Leicester had to write on his behalf to Sir William More, who had complained that the rooms he had hired out in Blackfriars to Ferrant in 1576 were not being used for teaching but for the performance of plays. Leicester replied that Hunnis was preparing and rehearsing the children in order to divert and please the Queen, which was answer enough. The family connection continued when Robert Hunnis entered Leicester's service.

Despite his interest in the boys' companies, Leicester showed no particular interest in education at the pre-university level. In contrast, Cecil gave help to his old schools in Grantham and Stamford, as well as an annuity to Westminster School. The earl, having been privately tutored, had no such loyalties, but both men took an interest in admired teachers like Camden, Savile and William Malim. In March 1572 Leicester received from the latter the dedication of a slender volume called *The true Report of all the success of Famagusta*, translated from Italian for the benefit of a wider reading public. Presumably it was boredom or ambition that took Malim away from Eton, where he was headmaster from 1561. Three years later he had arrived in Constantinople apparently funded by the earl, and perhaps also engaged in a mission for the Queen and privy council. There he stayed for eight months, and at the end of that time he returned to England with a knowledge of Turkish and other languages, which made him a rare commodity in Elizabethan England. However, it was John Drusius whom Leicester asked the university to support as a lecturer in Syriac.

The earl's influence was also used to advance John Harmar, who in 1588 became headmaster of Winchester after a distinguished academic career. In 1579 Harmar had produced a translation of Calvin's *Sermons upon the Ten Commandments*, which was well received by a public apparently eager to have another doctrinal work on their shelves. After receiving his MA in 1582, Harmar was given funds by the earl for travel abroad and, having attended lectures by Beza, produced a translation of Beza's *Sermons upon the Canticle of Canticles*, which was published in Oxford by Joseph Barnes. It was at Leicester's behest that

Harmar was appointed Regius professor of Greek at Oxford in 1585, and two years later was made proctor of the university.

Barnes the printer and the university owed much to the earl, who proved a vigorous chancellor. The debt was acknowledged in the 'Carmina Gratulatoria', a sheet produced by Barnes to celebrate Leicester's visit to the town in 1585. The first book from his press was John Case's *Speculum Moralium*, written by a fellow of St John's and dedicated to Leicester. Most of the books that Barnes produced had religious issues under scrutiny, and after Case other academics whom Leicester took up had books published in Oxford. De Corro's Latin paraphrase of Ecclesiastes appeared in 1579, and the dedication of the English translation in 1586 was to Lady Mary Dudley. Her brother certainly had a general interest in printing, for, apart from Barnes, he offered support to John Day, Rowland Hill, John Harrison and James Rowbotham.[6]

The library that Leicester acquired is of particular interest, and of the ninety or so books identified as his, many were standard works, including a nine-volume edition of Erasmus printed in Basle in 1540, and the Aldine Aristotle in six volumes now in the Lambeth Palace Library. Leicester's books also included a number of historical works in Italian, possibly acquired as a collection and all bound in about 1560: Machiavelli, Sabellico, Trissino and Pietro Martiri Vermigli. Perhaps they were a gift from Aconcio. Four bindings called the 'Cartouche' group are of texts in Greek: *Josephus*; *Philo Judaeus; Eusebius* and *Ecclesiasticae Historiae* – all in the Lambeth Palace Library. The bindings nearly all carry the bear and ragged staff device, with a crescent to indicate the cadency of the second son.[7] The Henry Davis Gift in the British Museum also has a binding done for Leicester, dating from 1574. It is of Asser's *Aelfredi Regis Gestae* and is in brown calf, blocked in gold with corner-pieces and signed ED. There is also a sunken panel of pinched velvet and a brown calf centre-piece containing the Dudley emblem in a sunk medallion.

Like any great magnate of the Elizabethan period with several houses to maintain even when he was not personally in residence, Leicester was a prodigious consumer of luxury goods. His accounts and inventories show an endless stream of purchases from embroidered bed-hangings, cushions, tapestries, furniture and plate, to precious items given as New Year gifts to Elizabeth. In 1573, for example, he gave her a fan of white feathers set in a gold handle decorated with emeralds, diamonds and rubies, 'and on each side a white bear and two pearls hanging a lion ramping with a white muzzled bear at his feet'.[8] In the following year he gave her a doublet of white satin embroidered with gold thread and decorated with diamonds and rubies. Later gifts included a gold chain elaborately knotted with twelve little gold cinquefoils set with diamonds, and a porringer of bloodstone with two gold handles fashioned as snakes. In 1585 he gave her a sable skin with the head and feet of gold, diamonds and rubies.

When Leicester required something particularly fine or rare his agents had to make strenuous efforts to obtain the sought-after item. In the early 1570s he wrote to Anthony Forster:

> I willed Ellis to speak to you and Mr. Spinola again for that I perceived that he hath word from Flanders that I cannot have such hangings thence as I looked for, for my dining chamber at Kenilworth yet he thought there would be very good to be had at this present in London and as good cheap as in Flanders. Palmer's wife told me at Hatfield that she was offered very good for 15/- or 16/- an ell. In any wise deal with Mr. Spinola hereabout, for [he] is able to get such stuff better cheap than any man. And I am sure he will do his best for me. And though I cannot have them so deep as I would yet if they be large of wideness and 12 or 13 feet high it shall suffice. . . .[9]

How many privy councillors today would worry about such things?

Apart from the palace of Whitehall, where he had rooms, and his great mansion at the east end of the Strand, Leicester also had a provincial court in his territorial heartland in the Midlands. Kenilworth Castle in Warwickshire was close to his brother Ambrose's castle at Warwick, but it was isolated from the court, so he spent relatively little time there. He clearly preferred his out-of-London retreat at Wanstead, a rambling courtyard house purchased from the heirs of Lord Chancellor

Rich in 1567. It was a transaction requiring a good deal of documentation to secure his title: a licence of alienation (not difficult for him to obtain, since he had a ten-year lease from that year of the Office of Alienations, a department in Chancery responsible for collecting fines on the transfer of lands held 'in capite'); a lease and a re-lease; a fine and a recovery; an indenture of bargain and sale, and a bond for performance of covenants.[10]

Kenilworth was old even when he acquired it from the Queen as a property suitable for a great favourite. Originally a stone fortress built in the late twelfth century to replace the first structure of earth and timber, it had evolved and grown considerably in scale. Its essential function was to house the Queen and court when they were on progress, and to make it comfortable Leicester embarked on a sequence of alterations to increase space and comfort. In this respect he was like many of his wealthy contemporaries: in 1571–2 Burghley spent £2,700 on Theobalds in Hertfordshire, and between 1567 and 1578 he averaged £1,000 per annum on his schemes. Norfolk at Kenninghall, Hatton in Holdenby, and Sir John Thynne at Longleat, undertook huge building projects, the latter showing a concern that was close to monomania. Sir John devoted his life to Longleat, which precluded him from sustaining a career at court.

Kenilworth had actually been acquired for the Dudleys by Leicester's father, but had reverted to the Crown. Now, in about 1570, the earl began the alterations, and since he had no time to supervise, he placed William Spicer in charge to buy stone and timber, hire labourers, and negotiate fees and wages. Originally from Nunnery in Wiltshire, Spicer had the experience Leicester sought, since he had once worked for Thynne, but after arguments and friction with his employer he took himself off, having pocketed some of Thynne's rents.[11] His working relationship with Leicester was much more to his taste, and he saw his career prospects improve dramatically. As an indication of Leicester's satisfaction, Spicer received the lease of the manor of Long Itchington, not far from Kenilworth. This he would return to the earl if he received an important post in the Queen's Works. In 1584 Spicer succeeded Rowland Johnson at Berwick without any indication that he was required to live there, but he was appointed Surveyor of the Royal Works only some years after Leicester's death. In the meantime, in conjunction with the earl, Spicer helped to create a Gothic-Renaissance palace, which today is no more than a handsome ruin.

One of the first decisions at Kenilworth was to insert new windows in the old keep, and it would be interesting to know if the glass came from the newly founded glass manufactory of Jean Carré, the holder of the first patent to make glass in Elizabethan England. Then the north entrance was levelled and a great new gatehouse was erected, a solid red sandstone building with four octagonal towers and a porch that bears the carved letters R.D. New stables were also built, and with the extra space caused by the removal of the north entrance Leicester was able to remodel the gardens. Within the huge wall that separated the castle and the lake was a high path overlooking the garden; twelve feet wide, it was embellished with sculptures and obelisks. There were two arbours of scented trees and intertwined flowers, and beyond them parterres with wild strawberries and 'caves' filled with exotic birds imported from France, Africa and the Canary Islands.[12]

Much of the timber used in the castle and the stables came from the surrounding estate. Very likely it was Spicer who suggested an interesting method of seasoning it quickly. Cut timber was reduced to pieces of a manageable size, which were immersed in water to remove any acidity or sap. These were then dried in special ovens. The success of the method is self-evident, since the roof and timber framing of the stables have survived.

Leicester's London homes had included a house in Sything Lane and, later, lodgings at Durham Place in the Strand. But his rise in status required a larger settling and he chose as his metropolitan palace the former Exeter House, which had belonged to the Bishops of Exeter and also required alterations.[13] A rambling mansion of some fifty-two rooms, it had twenty tenements and a gatehouse facing St Clement Danes, the front of Leicester House extending from Arundel House on the west side for nearly 350 feet. It was some 200 feet deep, and beyond it there was a terrace and garden extending to the Thames and Exeter Steps, where presumably Leicester kept his river-boat. The garden was very large, and, apart from formal flower-beds and walks, there was a shrubbery and a small orchard. One of the other amenities was a tennis-court, for the earl enjoyed the game and a good panting sweat, especially when he could take money from his opponents. In the south-east corner of the garden was the banqueting house, and in May 1575 Leicester wrote to Burghley: 'I have to thank your Lordship also very heartily . . . that your Lordship is pleased to help me that I may have some stone toward the making of a little banquet house in my garden.'[14] In fact, what Burghley had done was to instruct the Purveyor of the Queen's Works, Henry Hawthorne, to supply the stone.[15]

To cover the walls of all the properties he acquired, Leicester bought great quantities of carpets and wall-hangings. Also on display were the many paintings he had collected, including a substantial number of Spanish pictures left in England after the departure of Queen Mary's consort, Philip II. Of the 200 or so pictures in his collection, some two-thirds were portraits, and among those displayed at Kenilworth were two full-length portraits of the earl.[16] One of these showed him in armour (see plate 1); the other showed him in russet silk or satin, as do two other surviving pictures, one in the National Portrait Gallery and the other in the Wallace Collection. There was also a portrait, which has since disappeared, which showed him dressed in black, perhaps copying the style of a Spanish grandee. More portraits of the Queen and Burghley survive than of Leicester: however, there are more portrait *types* of him than of any other Elizabethan nobleman, which suggests that he was active as a patron of painters.[17] Certainly the Italian artist Federico Zuccaro was lured to England for six months by the earl, who probably used the wealthy Antwerp banker Tommaso Baroncelli to make the offer. Arriving in March 1575, Zuccaro produced two full-length portraits of Elizabeth and Leicester, which were surely displayed during the Kenilworth festivities. Unfortunately they are also missing, presumed destroyed, and Zuccaro returned to Italy without having changed the style of portrait painting in England. All that has survived are the preparatory sketches which are now in the British Museum.[18]

In England the greatest skill in portrait painting at this time was to be found in the works of certain miniaturists, and in 1570 or 1571 Elizabeth made the emerging Nicholas Hilliard her official goldsmith and miniature painter. Leicester too was a patron of the artist, who named several of his children after members of the Dudley family. Three certain portrait miniatures by him of the earl have survived. One dated 1576 is in the National Portrait Gallery, and two are in private collections. The finest of the three (plate 2) has emerged only recently from benign neglect by experts, to be recognized as an earlier picture than that in the National Portrait Gallery. Painted with great finesse after 1571 and before 1576, it may have been a gift from Leicester to his sister Mary, Lady Sidney.[19]

From a decade later two fine larger portraits have survived: William Segar (Portcullis Pursuivant at the College of Arms where Leicester was Deputy Earl Marshal) produced a picture of the ageing white-haired earl, which is now in Hatfield House. And J. van Ravesteyn completed a head and shoulders study that subtly hints at the perturbations of the earl during his time in the Low Countries, and which is now in the Rijksmuseum, Amsterdam (plate 4).

The loss of the armour portrait from Kenilworth is particularly irksome because it might have given some clues to Leicester's dealings with the great continental armourer Eliseus Libaerts of Antwerp. In March 1576 Libaerts arrived in England with samples for his prospective client. He carried with him a letter from Baroncelli, and also a sporting arquebus that the earl had ordered from the banker not long before.[20] Leicester would have been impressed by the masterful technique of the armourer, but he may also have been confounded by the extremely high cost of such remarkable workmanship which splendidly united utility and artistic ingenuity. There are pictures that suggest the earl did actually own armour with mannerist-type strapwork, but his regular source for such equipment was the Royal Armoury at Greenwich.[21] The suit of armour now in the Tower of London (Inv. No. II. 81) was made there, probably for the Kenilworth festivities, since what has survived is armour for the tilt. The left side of the helmet is without vent-holes, or 'breaths', so as to protect the face from splinters from the opponent's lance, and the tournament was such a specialized event that the armourer could ignore the usual field requirements of good ventilation and upper body mobility.[22] Indeed, the earl's complete garniture probably had lighter and more open alternative pieces to make it possible to wear the suit on a real battlefield, a visual hint of which appears in the unattributed portrait of Leicester at Parham Park.

Chapter 12

A Convenient House

The refashioning of Kenilworth gave useful employment to local skilled men for years. But the Dudley brothers also began to plan an act of charity that would give direct aid to the poor and indigent: the building of a hospital or home of rest. In September 1571 Leicester, Warwick and other notables and their ladies visited the town of Warwick, and the leading citizens there began angling for the building of the hospital in the town rather than in Kenilworth. They knew from their representatives in Parliament, John Fisher and Edward Aglionby, that the earl had obtained the necessary Act of Parliament for such an undertaking to begin, and they were anxious to benefit from it. When the town bailiff and the leading citizens heard of the proposed visit of the brothers, they decided at a meeting held on 25 September 'that a yoke of good oxen should be prepared and bestowed on the said Lords at their coming'. But having settled for this useful present, they made a miscalculation that was to cost the town dear. Instead of meeting the great party with due deference outside the town, they decided to stay put, 'being ready in the town to offer welcome to the said Lords with their present'.

The following day two members of the corporation purchased the oxen from one of the town's leading citizens, John Butler, who was well acquainted with the earl. It was on his perhaps not disinterested advice that the bailiff and townsmen further decided to postpone greeting the illustrious visitors until the day after their arrival. Common sense should have alerted them to the probability that a man of Leicester's lofty temperament would regard any delay as a slight – and so it proved. The earl had expected all the town dignitaries to attend him and his party outside the town limits for a dignified entry into Warwick. But when he arrived on 27 September he found his presence scarcely noted, so he rode off to Kenilworth, as the unfortuate bailiff and corporation found the next day when they went to John Fisher's house, where Leicester had intended to stop. In some trepidation they waited his return, and their discomfiture was increased when in mid-afternoon they were upbraided by Leicester's servants for treating the earl so casually. Leicester's return to the town merely increased their unease, for he now totally ignored them.

Shocked and distressed, the miserable townsmen turned again to John Butler for advice. He seems to have prevailed upon Sir John Hubaud and Thomas Dudley to make a supplication to the earl on the town's behalf. All this has the air of being a performance, as does Leicester's gracious acceptance of the apologies. The following day was the feast of St Michael and, since Leicester was a Knight of the Order of St Michael of France, the day was observed with a procession and prayers. The bailiff, burgesses, Leicester's retinue, local gentry, friends and the Dragon Pursuivant and Clarenceux King of Arms from the College of Arms walked before him to St Mary's. He was dressed in white velvet shoes, silk stockings, a doublet of silver, and a jerkin of white velvet decorated with gold thread and precious stones. His cloak or robe was of white satin embroidered with gold thread, and the final touch was a black velvet cap with a high white plume. After prayers and ceremony Leicester returned to the priory where he was staying and gave a dinner, but he sat by himself in splendid isolation.

His departure from the town was set for 2 October, and, having learned a lesson in tact, the bailiff arrived at Fisher's residence to offer humble service to the earl when he next came to the town. The earl's response was affable, and as the party rode out he remarked on a building that would be 'a convenient house for to make an hospital for certain poor people'. The one that he singled out was clearly not ideal, but John Fisher instantly said that the town would be delighted to hand over not only a building for such a purpose, but also a chapel and outbuildings if the earl required them. Butler then gilded the offer by saying that such an arrangement would save 500 marks.

Naturally Leicester pounced, urging that they should stop to view the place immediately. Thus, without the prior knowledge of the corporation who might have resisted Butler's plan, the earl was brought to the old Guildhall, where the leading citizens had met for many years. The earl dismounted and followed his guide to view the building, and having seen it and the chapel, was immediately taken by Butler's apparently spontaneous suggestion that here indeed was what Leicester required. The earl was so pleased with events that he commissioned William Spicer, his mason-architect, to survey and report on the buildings as soon as possible.

Within two or three days of Leicester's departure, Spicer was shown over the old buildings by the ubiquitous Butler. The former then wrote to the earl to commend the choice, provided that the entire cluster of buildings were made available. The meeting hall, school and chapel were probably some 200 years old, having once belonged to the guilds of Holy Trinity and St George, and in the early part of the sixteenth century had housed the grammar school. Leicester was pleased with the report and promptly wrote to Butler that he required all the buildings, although these would scarcely accommodate his overall plan. Butler responded as was required, and at a meeting of the burgesses on Saturday, 27 October, it was agreed that the earl should have all the properties he required without payment. Their only proviso was that he should be asked to persuade his brother and the Queen that some of the wastelands on the outskirts of the town should be handed over to the corporation for the building of new houses and a school. They also requested that, since Leicester had timber holdings in Staffordshire, he should provide some timber for the buildings. Butler was to put this request in private, while Fisher delivered their letter.

Early in November, having met in prayer, the burgesses signed the letter to Leicester, and it was handed to Fisher for delivery. Since he had to make the journey to London soon afterwards, it reached the earl on 9 November, but he was busy in attendance on the Queen, and the private conversation that Fisher sought was postponed. Then on 27 November, when he managed to speak to the earl at Greenwich, he found he had grown cool over the whole matter, 'saving that as touching timber he would give some to serve their purposes'. However, this did not discourage the burgesses who, with a commendable devotion to duty in the festive season, decided on 26 December 1571 to send the deed of gift to Leicester 'for his New Year's gift'.[1] Although the hospital was founded in late 1571 or early 1572, its 'Ordinances, Statutes and Rules' were not completed until November 1585 on the eve of Leicester's departure to the United Provinces, which occurred shortly before the installation of Thomas Cartwright as master, appointed to succeed Ralph Griffin, who combined his mastership with a scripture lectureship founded by Leicester, and worth £50 per annum.[2] The ceremony was conducted in front of the twelve brethren, who wore their handsome blue gowns with the insignia of the bear and ragged staff on the sleeve. This costume is still worn on Sundays and special occasions by the residents of the finely restored buildings. Piety was even expressed decoratively in the architecture of the hospital, for the gateposts were entwined with scriptural texts, and others were scattered about the building.

This private charitable act was only a tiny amelioration of great social problems. Leicester of course knew this, for, even if he retreated to the grand comforts at Kenilworth or Wanstead, he was still deluged with petitions and begging letters from the high-born and lowly in Elizabethan society. It is clear he had a social conscience, though his enemies and later historians have been at pains to deny it. Yet as Chamberlain of Chester he wrote to the mayor and justices of the peace in the town to alleviate the suffering of those placed in the town gaol. He had, after all, some experience of imprisonment, even if he had not starved, and so he wrote asking that the matter might be given 'good consideration'. Yet he was also a realist and, unlike Sutton, his business associate, he did not hoard money, as he admitted; nor did he plan to spend it on one huge project as his brother-in-law, the Earl of Huntingdon, had once done when he sought the Queen's permission to sell all his estates so as to raise an army to aid the Huguenots in France. Leicester employed his wealth for public and private works, serving his own and parochial interests together wherever they were compatible, with the continuous aim of increasing his influence and enhancing his reputation. The hospital scheme and the church built in Denbigh were also partly the result of his faltering domestic circumstances. By 1575 he was a middle-aged man with only one young illegitimate son who could not claim the Dudley patrimony. Moreover, his brother Warwick was childless, and his Sidney nephews not yet impoverished, so Leicester was willing to undertake public works, whereas Burghley, who had a family and an heir, preferred to lavish his fortune on the mansions of Theobalds and Burghley House.

Leicester wanted to build the church in Denbigh for two particular reasons. By its position between the castle and the town it would replace the structurally unsound castle chapel, and furthermore it would act as a parish church for an area that was without one. The notion coincided with the translation of Edmund Grindal to Canterbury, and the view has been expressed that the building of the church was an element of Grindal's desire 'to mould the episcopacy to reform': the church would offer a building free from Catholic imagery and planning.[3] The momentum of change in the Church of England was now more pronounced, but there was still an urgent need, as the prince and primate agreed, for reforming and articulate preachers. They noted that one of the continuing effects of the Reformation was the lowering of society's esteem for the clergy, who were still less learned than was desirable. Early in the reign, of 160 clergy in the archdeaconry of London, forty-two had no knowledge of Latin, thirteen no classical learning at all, and only three knew any Greek.[4] The situation in Wales was no better, for the comparative poverty of the Church and its livings attracted only mediocre men. Leicester's intention with his church in Denbigh was that it should be a great pulpit. To set the tone, William Morgan was made rector of the parish in 1575, with encouragement to translate the Old Testament into Welsh. His translation appeared in 1588.[5]

The proportions of the church were handsome: 168 feet east to west, and 72 feet across. It was large enough for a cathedral rather than simply a parish church, and indeed it has been suggested that ultimately it was intended to replace St Asaph's Cathedral, for the initials of the Bishop of St Asaph's (Richard Hughes) appear on the stone of dedication. Its size certainly made it a great rarity in post-Reformation England, and it was especially notable in a period that saw more emphasis on shipbuilding than ecclesiastical building of any merit or scale.

The interior had classical detailing, while the exterior was a late flourish of Gothic. Just how much of this boldly conceived building was finished between the laying of the stone of dedication in 1578 and Leicester's departure for the United Provinces in 1585 is not clear. Perhaps the roof was in place, but military affairs made such heavy demands on Leicester's purse that it could not be completed properly, and today like Kenilworth it is a ruin. What remains is testimony to Leicester's solicitude and 'to a brief flowering of the puritan fervour'.[6]

Yet, even so, it was not stern enough for the Puritan Thomas Wood who, remote from court, offered Leicester and other Puritan lords detailed admonitions on matters of doctrine and organization. Wood was especially ardent in seeking to protect the 'prophesyings' – that is, meetings of ordinary people of Puritan persuasion who gathered to air their views and interpret the Scriptures in free association. These meetings were detested by Elizabeth, and in 1576 the Southam group in south Warwickshire, under the moderation of the radical Puritan John Oxenbridge, was disbanded by Bishop Bentham of Coventry and Lichfield. This presented Leicester with a problem, for he manifestly could not change the Queen's mind on the matter, and he was sure to lose some credit with the Puritans. His only success was to intervene on behalf of the justices of the peace who had hitherto protected the 'prophesyings', and he was now criticized for failing to protect the meeting rigorously enough.

Some went even further and, remarkably, accused him of conniving at the elimination of Southam. Wood wrote to the Dudley brothers that ordinary people were scandalized by this, as well as rumours of a most disreputable kind about Leicester's private conduct. Despite Wood's rebuke, Warwick and Leicester remained cool and unexcited in their replies, neither bothering to refute the allegations at length. Warwick simply noted that he was 'all flesh and blood and frail of nature', and Leicester echoed him.[7] As he remarked, apparently unabashed, his behaviour was particularly scrutinized because of his social prominence: 'I may fall many ways and have more witnesses thereof than others who perhaps be no saints neither.'[8] Moreover, whatever the opinions of the advanced Puritans, Leicester was not frantic to remove the traditional powers of the bishops over their flocks. When he intervened to protect individuals, he did so not to promote Presbyterianism as such, but to allow new voices to invigorate and stir the established but still callow spiritual offspring of Henry VIII and Archbishop Cranmer. Though the sincerity of his Puritanism is no longer questioned by most historians, there is no doubt that Leicester 'was too committed economically and politically to the existing system to accept wholeheartedly the challenge posed by presbyterianism'.[9] Nor could he swallow the carping zeal of the extreme Puritans, when what primarily appealed to him in the late 1570s was their violent rebuttals of Catholic propaganda. One of the Puritan polemicists who benefited from Leicester's attentions was Meredith Hanmer, who concentrated his attacks on the Jesuits while holding a number of incumbencies within the Anglican Church. Altogether much rougher was Anthony Munday, a literary journeyman who had written a pamphlet in 1580 on the portent-filled earthquake of April that year.[9] Between 1581 and 1584 he wrote intemperate attacks on Catholicism and provided evidence against Campion and other Jesuit missionaries prior to their executions.

Ironically, even as he supported in various ways these literary hacks, Leicester made a disastrous and uncharacteristic error when Grindal died in 1583. Since the Church had been leaderless since 1577, when the Queen had decided to suspend Grindal from his office for supporting Puritan principles of conscience, she now decided to elevate John Whitgift, Bishop of Worcester, to Canterbury. It seems that Leicester accepted this appointment without demur when he should have been more alert to the possible consequences. Whitgift, once Master of Trinity College, Cambridge, had already clashed in the early 1570s with Thomas Cartwright, on the latter's appointment as Lady Margaret professor of divinity, and had then helped to manoeuvre him into exile in Geneva.

Whitgift now became the most effective instrument that Elizabeth could have chosen to enforce and defend the notion of the established Church. In May 1584 the ex officio oath administered in the Court of High Commission was revived to bring Puritans and recusants to heel. But the secrecy of the Catholics was strikingly contrasted with the defiant openness of the Puritans. The latter needed to air their consciences, and this

1 Robert Dudley, Earl of Leicester *c.* 1575

2 Queen Elizabeth I playing the lute

3 The Earl of Leicester, from a miniature by Nicholas Hilliard

4 The Earl of Leicester in his later years, from a portrait by J.A. van Ravesteyn

cost them dear as Whitgift sought the strict enforcement of his Eleven Articles. The spirituality of laity in groups like the 'prophesyings' was attacked; the Bishop's Bible was to replace the Geneva translation, with its dangerous notation, the services in the Prayer Book were to be given unaltered and the sacraments administered. Enforcing these and other requirements for an orderly national Church led to the excoriation of the new archbishop by his opponents, even as censorship was administered more rigorously. Yet the Puritan presses continued to print tracts, and the privy council was deluged with furious petitions as Whitgift sternly ignored the clamour.

Chapter 13

The Lake, the Lodge, the Lord

At Kenilworth Leicester had no reason to build a church, for the village already had one, but he did have to consider the future of the castle's chapel and, since it was awkwardly placed, he had it pulled down and replaced by stables. These had another ecclesiastical element in them, since the stone that was used came from the demolished Kenilworth Abbey. By 1575 the rebuilding at the castle, which had transformed it into a luxurious retreat, was so far advanced that Leicester could contemplate with pleasure a third visit by the Queen and court during the summer.

The midsummer progresses were an essential part of the continuing courtship of Elizabeth and her countrymen and women, a sixteenth-century equivalent of today's royal walkabout, with its amazing revelation that even queens have legs. Released from affairs of state, and away from the fetid city in summer, the Queen and the court descended on small towns and the country houses of wealthy subjects for days and weeks of civic welcomes, tableaux, plays, hunting, dancing, music and cards. What Elizabeth contrived in these creaking perambulations round the Midlands, East Anglia and south-east of England was remarkable, for the remote, even exotic, Queen was transformed into the beloved red-headed daughter of Henry VIII, a diseased despot whom folk-memory held in awe and affection by simply forgetting his more odious characteristics.

From Easter 1575 Leicester became more and more concerned with the arrangements for the Queen's reception at Kenilworth. The entire visit was to be a huge diversion set about with courtly and domestic rituals. After years of teasing deliberation the Queen remained free, and so Leicester took the opportunity to test again his abilities as an impresario and suitor. Aware that he was now middle-aged, his waistline thickening, and his hair turning silver, the earl now sought to hold time at bay – literally, as we shall see.

When letters were sent to the Sheriffs of Oxfordshire and Warwickshire to levy 300 quarters of wheat each for delivery to the castle, Leicester also alerted writers and performers to begin preparing masques and 'shewes'. George Gascoigne, educated at Cambridge and the Middle Temple, once a soldier of fortune and now a journeyman of letters, was commissioned by Leicester to write commendatory verses for 'The Noble Art of Venery', and also masques. William Hunnis, Master of the Children of the Chapel Royal, was also alerted, since the company customarily accompanied the Queen on progress, and other actors to appear before her were Leicester's Men, led by James Burbage.

Since the castle itself was a symbol of royal bounty, the earl was uninhibited about the scale of the festivities and the demands on his purse. Fourteen earls and seventeen barons with their wives were lodged there, together with foreign ambassadors and privy councillors. These guests were waited on by numerous liveried servants as well as Leicester's entourage of gentlemen clad in velvet. Early in July Elizabeth and her companions arrived at Long Itchington, where they dined with the earl in a vast tent, and then, as the warm summer evening darkened, the huge royal party rode slowly to the castle.

It was about eight o'clock that a horse carrying the Queen and led by the earl arrived at Kenilworth Park, to be greeted by a sibyl. Then the party moved through the Brayes and tilt-yard, built between the lake and lower pool, crossing a short bridge on which were seven pairs of poles decorated with the bounty of the gods. There were also Latin verses of welcome on an ornate placard, devised by William Patten, a minor antiquarian writer and Teller of the Exchequer until 1568. The first serious student of Armenian in England, he had relinquished his post, his estates and position because of debts.[1] It was only his access to Burghley and Leicester that allowed him somewhat to retrieve his situation. He is of greater interest than might otherwise be the case, since Robert Laneham's *Letter* of 1575, the chief source of details of the festivities, has been convincingly ascribed to him.[2] Despite the title this was written anonymously, and its satire and wit led to the suppression of the first edition within a few days of publication. Indeed, on 10 September Patten wrote to Burghley a letter of apology which clearly suggests that he was the author and that Robert Langham, Keeper of the Council Chamber, had been embarrassed by the squib.[3]

Having crossed the bridge, the porter of the castle appeared mumbling crossly about the interruption of his sleep in a way that beguilingly resembles the response of the porter in *Macbeth*:

What stir, what coil is here? come back, hold, whither now?
No one so stout to stir, what harrying have we here. . . ?
What dainty darling's here? Oh God, a peerless pearl. . . .

He then offered his club and keys to the Queen in homage, and she signified her gracious acceptance. We may note that the porter was John Badger of Christ Church, Oxford, and he had actually written the lines. Trumpets now sounded from the gatehouse where the real trumpeters were concealed, so that the sound appeared to come from six huge figures, each eight feet tall and symbolizing the heroic stature of man in King Arthur's time. Then Elizabeth moved on to meet the Lady of the Lake, who appeared to rehearse her life following the extinction of the fraternity of the Round Table. Surrounded by her aquatic entourage the Lady claimed that, after the death of King Arthur, she had immersed herself in the Kenilworth lake, but chose this propitious moment to reappear, since this third visit of the Queen was a guarantee of future peace. The verses written by George Ferrers end:

Pass on, Madam, you need no longer stand;
The Lake, the Lodge, the Lord are yours to command.

Elizabeth's response sparkled with humour: 'We had thought indeed the Lake had been ours, and do you call it yours now? Well, we will herein commune more with you hereafter.' Finally, following more Latin verses by Mulcaster and Patten, she retired to her suite of rooms before the gunfire salute and fireworks that were supposed to signal the pleasure of Jupiter at receiving a royal guest.

The following day, Sunday, the Queen and her party attended divine service at the local church in the morning. In the afternoon there was music and dancing, followed by fireworks supplied by an Italian firework-maker. The day after that was hot, and the Queen did not venture out to hunt until five o'clock, returning at about nine by torchlight through the woods. As the hunting party did so George Gascoigne in the costume of an *hombre salvagio*, a folk wood spirit, appeared, clutching a small oak sapling, and spouting relentless doggerel that punned laboriously on the name Dudley. Then in a bold attempt to introduce some drama into his texts he flamboyantly broke the small tree he was holding over his thigh and hurled it aside. This barely missed the Queen's horse and the animal shied. She retained her seat, however, and indicated that she was not upset; indeed, she was probably secretly pleased at this equestrian display before Leicester, who was noted for his vanity about his own skill in manège.

A week later, some days of wet and windy weather cleared and again, after morning service, the afternoon was spent in the walled tilt-yard, a raised area linking Mortimer's Tower and the Gallery Tower. From this position Elizabeth and Leicester watched the rustic entertainments of bride-ale, burlesque, morris dancing and tilting at the quintain. The first of these was an irreverent mocking of the marriage ceremony, while the last was a parody of courtly behaviour, full of sexual implications. A rider, perhaps on a cart-horse, and without stirrups and boots, tried to break the quintain (a board mounted on a transverse bar) with his lance. If his aim was less than perfect he would be knocked from his horse, or perhaps the shoulders of a friend. Laneham noted: 'The bridegroom had first course at the quintain and broke his spear . . . his mare in his manage did a little stumble, that much ado had his manhood to sit in the saddle. . . .' After this amusement came a presentation by men of Coventry led by Captain Cox of a hock-tide sword dance, and a representation of an encounter between Danes and Saxons was incomplete when supper was served before a play by Leicester's Men.

With the return of fine weather the Queen again went

hunting late in the afternoon of the following day, and as the party returned Triton appeared on a 'mermaid' with an eighteen-foot tail. When his speech was delivered Arion appeared 'riding aloft upon his old friend the dolphin that from head to tail was four and twenty feet long'. This time Henry Goldingham, who played Arion, delivered his verses to music issuing from the dolphin's stomach, where six instrumentalists were hidden. Yet even before completing them he removed his mask and revealed his true self, much to Elizabeth's amusement.

Later that evening Elizabeth knighted Thomas Cecil (Burghley's son), Henry Cobham, Thomas Stanhope, Arthur Bassett and the Catholic Thomas Tresham. Then she took part in a faith-healing activity known as curing the king's evil or scrofula, a tubercular condition of the neck glands. By the sixteenth century any inflammation or sore could be included in the cases attended by the Queen, and on that evening she laid hands on nine of the afflicted, curing 'only by handling and prayers'.[4] Apart from the relief of those suffering, this ritual brought Elizabeth great prestige, for in English eyes it confirmed her legitimate claim to the throne (something denied by the Pope), since it was a curative power obtained only by lawful inheritance.

The earl's attention to comfort and entertainment was well received, and when Cox and the Coventry men were brought back to complete their performance they were rewarded by the Queen with two buck deer and five marks. Yet the following day, 20 July, something unexpected and unexplained happened and an entertainment by Gascoigne was cancelled. Possibly Elizabeth was tired, or she anticipated with a certain horror another piece of nuptial propaganda. Or is it possible that she sensed a growing bond of affection between her favourite and Lettice Knollys, Countess of Essex? Whatever the cause, a supper to be held in a pavilion at Wedgnock Park, some three miles from the castle, was cancelled when it appeared that the court might be leaving at short notice.

However, the Queen remained for another week, hunting to the last minute until the farewell appearance of Gascoigne dressed as Sylvanus. In a charming if rather worn conceit he suggested that the recent rain 'was nothing else but the very flowing tears of the gods, who melted into moan for your hasty departure'. He alluded then to the fate of Deep-desire and Due-desert, changed by Zabeta into the holly and laurel. Deep-desire is clearly Leicester, who as a gesture to make clear his constancy was still pressing his suit, and it was at this point that the party encountered a strategically placed holly bush. A voice (surely that of George Ferrers whose family crest was of a holly bush) now spoke of the mournful agonies of gods, goddesses, nymphs and satyrs at Elizabeth's coming departure. By this he linked 'Leicester's old allegory of Desire with his Olympian fiction'.[5]

The Kenilworth festivities were elaborately contrived, ephemeral, and to modern taste faintly ridiculous – the romanticism absurdly inflated and the calculating flattery of the Queen debased by long usage. But they were held for a twofold purpose: first, to display Leicester's great wealth and position; and second, to hint strongly at his claim to reciprocal loyalty from the adored Queen. Like any favourite Leicester needed reassurance, for his youthful glamour had faded with age and what now bound him to the Queen was a warm familiarity. So he wanted the festivities to suggest both the effortless permanence of the reign and the ageless permanence of a relationship which, in its unlikely fashion, had lasted many years. Like most Englishmen of the late sixteenth century he had renounced the adoration of a heavenly Virgin, only to replace her with a secular version. Elizabeth was both a woman and a symbol, and to underline this extraordinary status a timeless moment was created at Kenilworth – literally so, for, when she arrived, the hands of the castle's great clock were fixed.

What did it all cost? There are no detailed accounts, though Laneham's *Letter* ends with fulsome praise of Leicester's calculated extravagance. A special expense would have been for the obligatory parting gift to the sovereign. Her delight in jewellery was well known, and on this occasion it has been suggested that Leicester gave her a covered cup and ewer of crystal mounted in gold.[6] Nor is it certain that he had to bear the entire cost of the visit, since hosts were able to replenish their pockets from the funds of the Cofferer of the Royal Household, while many of the minor functionaries would have stayed in Warwick. Moreover, it seems very likely that Ambrose Dudley would have assisted his brother with money and supplies, so that the total cost to Leicester would have been about £1,700 for the seventeen days. The notion that he poured out many thousands of pounds is absurd, for Elizabeth's visit to Burghley the same year for two weeks was meticulously reckoned to have cost £340. 17*s.* 4*d.*[7] Other investigations have shown that Sir Thomas Egerton, over twenty years later, spent some £2,000 to entertain the Queen and her court.[8] It is highly improbable that Leicester, even his heyday before his huge expenditure on the expedition to the Low Countries, could have exceeded such an amount.

Chapter 14

Good Love and Liking

In the years after the death of Amye Dudley, Leicester's public and private behaviour was scrutinized by a court devoted to gossip. Even as he wooed the Queen he acquired a reputation for seducing any available women, whether of high or low birth. The sequence of casual affairs (if that is what it was) eventually ended with a liaison with Lady Douglass Sheffield, who years later claimed in the Star Chamber that she had in fact been married to him and that the child she had born was therefore legitimate. When the younger Robert Dudley tried to prove his birthright he naturally called his mother as a witness, but her testimony proved halting and unreliable. This was not altogether surprising, since thirty years had passed, but her version of events now was that a betrothal to Leicester had taken place two years later at Esher. There had been witnesses, she claimed, including Sir Edward Horsey, but unfortunately they were all dead. Nor could anyone substantiate her claim that Leicester had tried to free himself from his parental responsibilities by offering her an income of £700 per annum, and that when she refused the money he browbeat her with threats of poverty and degradation.[1]

In the opinion of the Star Chamber the evidence cited by the young Dudley and his mother failed to establish their case. The assessors must have noticed that when Leicester finally married Letitia (Lettice) in 1578, Lady Douglass not only remained silent, but that Sir Francis Knollys, who would have had intimate knowledge of his friend and colleague's affairs, allowed his daughter to marry, albeit with two ceremonies. Lady Douglass then proceeded to become the wife of Sir Edward

Stafford, Paulet's successor as ambassador to France in 1583. Did she commit bigamy because she thought Leicester had?

One of the earl's principal concerns in the time after the Kenilworth festivities was that his relationship with Lettice, Countess of Essex (her second husband, Walter Devereux, Earl of Essex, did not die until September 1576), should be kept as secret as possible. He and the red-headed countess knew very well the Queen's capacity for violent, primitive jealousy, and their marriage by one of Leicester's chaplains, Humphrey Tyndall, on 21 September 1578 at Wanstead, was a very subdued affair.[2] There was none of the flourish and finery that might have been expected, so it could well be that the bride was already pregnant.

Apart from the Earl of Pembroke, Ambrose Dudley, Roger, Lord North, Sir Francis Knollys and Richard Knollys, probably only one other courtier was immediately aware of the marriage. Probably Philip Sidney knew of this dangerous match, since he was by now resident at Leicester House in the Strand. Leicester had grown to admire his qualities and serious intelligence, but it was with his other nephew that he had the easy relationship that recalled his own happy childhood. During the Christmas festivities of 1577 Sir Edward Horsey wrote to William Davison: '. . . this day my Lord of Leicester is to return to the court; he has been absent ten days making merry with his nephew, the earl of Pembroke at Wilton'.[3] Leicester's closest male friend, apart from his family, seems to have been Lord North, a contemporary who shared Leicester's interests and amusements; both read widely in Italian and both were patrons of actors' companies. In the summer of 1577 North lost £50 to Leicester at cards, and when North entertained Elizabeth at his Suffolk home, Kirtling, the earl loaned him some musicians to augment the small consort he already employed. Their friendship was sustained for many years, and North was glad to have his court career defended by a brilliant ally. His younger brother Thomas, who translated Plutarch, also gained Leicester's favour. Recommending Thomas North to Burghley, the earl noted that he was 'a very honest gentleman, and hath many good things in him, which are drowned only by poverty'.

Apart from courtier friends, in Leicester's closest circle at this time was Thomas Digges, the Copernican scientist and engineer who had been raised and taught by John Dee after the involvement of his father, Leonard Digges, in Wyatt's Rebellion. In 1579, while Thomas Digges was working on improvements for coastal fortifications, a particular interest of Leicester's, he dedicated to Leicester his treatise, *An Arithmetical Warlike Treatise named Stratioticos*.[4] Several years later Leicester was almost certainly godfather to Dudley Digges, and in 1584 the boy's father was MP for Southampton under the patronage of the earl. Leicester wrote with conviction to Walsingham that he is 'a very wise stout fellow'. Other friends and allies included Sir Francis Jobson, Sir Edward Horsey, and Sir Thomas Leighton, married to Lettice's sister. Walsingham was not his equal in rank, but the earl frequently drank and talked with him on Friday nights.[5]

Among his servants Leicester was generally well regarded and many, like William Haynes, now promoted his gentleman of the bedchamber, profited from his access to the highest in the land, as well as his thoroughly developed sense of good-lordship. Some received material gifts, while others could be pardoned for some misdemeanour at the earl's prompting. At his suit Edward Lynell, George Watson, John Browne, William Harris, Edward Owen, John Hussey and ten others were pardoned for breaking and entering the house of William Willis at Priorsmerton in Warwickshire, and stealing £44 and some plate.[6] A servant who failed to please, however, could not expect to escape lightly. For example, in 1573 Leicester applied to Walsingham for assistance to bring back to England a young man who had left his service and fled to France to the household of the Cardinal de Bourbon. Leicester was incensed by this occurrence and wanted the lad back 'to make him an example unto other our servants not to presume hereafter to abuse their masters'.[7] Walsingham replied that the young man now regretted his flight and wanted to return. But Leicester refused anything so straightforward, and in a rather sinister fashion suggested that after a quiet interval the youth should be seized and bundled back to England.

Apart from servants, Leicester also had a number of wards whom, his enemies contended, he kept in his charge only out of self-interest, since, while they were minors, he could plunder their estates and fortunes. However, being a guardian was not always a route to easy profits, even when one had as many as seven wards at a time, as Leicester had.[8] Getting permission from Burghley, the corrupt Master of the Court of Wards, for monies to be spent repairing the estates of Edward Verney was exceedingly difficult, even when Leicester said if necessary he would spend his own money to preserve the boy's patrimony. Moreover, if his interest in his wards was corrupt, why should Thomas Salusbury, the grandson and heir of Sir John Salusbury, choose to serve Leicester after studying at Trinity College, Oxford? It may have been because his friend Edward Jones, the heir to Plas Cadwgan, was also in Leicester's service, but presumably this alone would not have persuaded him if the earl had pillaged his inheritance. In the event, it was the unfortunate Jones who suffered disastrously from guilt by association when the young Salusbury was arrested in the aftermath of the plottings of his Oxford contemporary, Anthony Babington. Seized at Llewenni, the family home of the Salusburys, Thomas was tried and executed along with Jones on 21 September 1586; both victims of the prevailing anti-Catholic fury of the times.[9]

Despite the baleful image of Leicester so assiduously fostered by his enemies, and too easily accepted as accurate by later historians, Leicester could also tactfully refuse a wardship. In the same month that Salusbury and Jones died, the earl replied to a letter from Hugh Fortescue and Anthony Monck:

> After my hearty commendations, I have received by this bearer your letter in behalf of my young kinsman Robert Bassett, for whose wardship I would have been very glad to have dealt myself to his behalf, as well for his own sake as for his father's [Sir Arthur Bassett's] affection and kindness ever toward me I may not easily forget, if the incredible charge and expenses of this journey [to the Provinces] had not made me unfit and unable at this present to do it. Nevertheless I have according to your request written by this bearer both to my Lord Treasurer and to Mr Ralegh in that behalf. . . .[10]

There is an unabashed honesty about this letter that rings true and sincere. Leicester could be equally attentive with the old as well. In November 1572 he wrote to John Parkhurst, Bishop of Norwich, on behalf of Dr Willoughby, once physician to Queen Anne Boleyn and now impoverished by the loss of his much needed income from several ecclesiastical livings. Having known Willoughby since her childhood, Elizabeth was also angry, and Leicester instructed the bishop to restore the income of the old man or give adequate reasons for his distress. In the following month the bishop rather nervously defended himself, adding that 'I have take order that the old doctor shall be truly answered of such stipend yearly as he hath hitherto enjoyed.'[11] Several years later Leicester intervened in the City of London in a dispute between an old blind man called Philpot who laid a complaint against two other citizens.[12] It would be interesting to know if this was the same Philpot whose guardianship he had been given years before.

As well as heeding the importunings of individuals in all parts of the country who sought his help in a temporary alliance, the earl continued to attract young university trained men to his service. In 1579 Edmund Spenser removed from Rochester to live in Leicester House, hoping for significant employment by the earl. He may have made the move with the tacit encouragement of Philip Sidney, having been introduced to him by Gabriel Harvey who had burrowed into the outer periphery of the Leicester circle at the time of Elizabeth I's visit to Audley End the year before. Harvey had been present for a disputation in Leicester's rooms by scholars drawn from Cambridge, and he briskly set aside his earlier patrons, Sir Thomas Smith and Sir Walter Mildmay, in order to angle for the earl's patronage. This, he dreamed, might take him far beyond a fellowship at Pembroke. His earlier poetic efforts had been noted by Leicester and War-wick, and the former, to whom they had been dedicated, now decided to take up Harvey in a test of his intellectual prowess. But, conceited and ambitious and lacking both tact and an innate sense of proportion, the young man succeeded only in embarrassing the earl before the Queen and court. If Leicester had ever intended to use Harvey on diplomatic missions, the ingratiating posturing rapidly and permanently changed his mind. Above all else the earl valued dignity.

Yet Harvey's vanity was so majestic that he could not see that his chance of even minor posts or employment had vanished, and he went on to publish a Latin text, *Gratulationem Valdinensium*, which in Book III offered extravagant praise of the earl.[13] Harvey's charming ignorance of Leicester's marriage is displayed in the section praising the earl as a potential husband of the Queen, and in all his shameless angling shows the worst aspect of the complex system of patronage. It may have been necessary in a country without a professional administrative class, but it could lead to a demeaning persistence compounded by envy, dissimulation and self-disgust. On the other hand in a privilege-dominated age it could be a useful social adhesive, and as one commentator has put it, 'the only counter-balance to hierarchical privilege for those whose ambition exceeded their birth'.[14] If Harvey, having found a niche, had been content to stay in it, he might have been much happier, and certainly Leicester did not entirely drop him from consideration, having once picked him out. With the end of his fellowship in sight, and without any other income, Harvey begged for an extension, and with Leicester and the Master of Pembroke, William Fulke, on his side he hoped for success. However, even with this formidable backing, the other fellows refused to consider his request, and it was not before December 1578 that he was elected fellow of Trinity Hall. Even so, he was far from content with this appointment, and gnawed by the imperative of advancement he moved now to London to wait on the earl in the company of Edmund Spenser.

Unhappily, neither of the duo thrived by uprooting themselves, and by September 1580 the most coveted position of secretary to Leicester had fallen to Arthur Atey. To swallow this rebuff Harvey retired to academic life, to be subjected to the amused scorn of his contemporaries in the university. The wits seem to have found him so absurd and comic that even his harmless and apparently well-known addiction to annotating books was satirized in a Latin play called *Pedantius*. Probably written by Edward Forset, it was presented at Trinity Hall in early February 1581, and inexorably Harvey's academic career slowed to a halt.[15] In 1585 he was rejected for the mastership of his college, and even his doctorate in civil law from Oxford, probably gained with the very last vestige of Leicester's patient aid, could not advance him further. Embittered and frustrated, he retired eventually to Saffron Walden.

As for Spenser, in October 1579 he wrote to Harvey that he was about to be sent abroad in Leicester's service. But this hope was soon dispelled and the poet may well have rued his friend's advocacy, for he was eventually made secretary to the Lord Deputy of Ireland, Lord Grey de Wilton. Being in Ireland was regarded as tantamount to exile, and certainly Spenser considered his removal from the Leicester circle as a painful demotion. He wrote in 'Virgil's Gnat':

> Wrong'd yet not daring to express my pain
> To you (great Lord) the causer of my care,
> In cloudy tears my cause I thus complain
> Unto yourself, that only privy are.

It has been suggested, on the other hand, that the earl contrived this position for the poet as a reward for service, but as we know that Leicester and Lord Grey, though distantly related, were neither friends nor political allies, this seems improbable. It does seem that Spenser was being rebuked for a slighting reference in the September *Eclogue* to Lord North, the *Shepheardes Calender*, containing lightly disguised material from contemporary life which may also have upset Philip Sidney.

But none of this prevented Spenser from writing about Leicester and his concerns in *The Faerie Queene*. Whatever happened as the work grew and was reshaped, the 'Knight of the White Bear' had an important role in the plan for the work.[16] It has also been suggested that for his King Arthur he may have drawn on some aspects of Leicester's public persona and, when one recalls the conspicuous Arthurian symbolism of the Kenilworth festivities, this seems quite possible. It is true that Arthur is essentially a composite figure of sublime virtue, but when in Book V the policies of the radical group in the privy council are aired, the Belge episode does strongly suggest Leicester's policy in the United Provinces. In writing this national epic, Spenser could hardly miss the opportunity of annexing and reusing Kenilworth imagery to mesh with the later activities of the earl. Where *The Faerie Queene* stands in contrast to the Kenilworth festivities, if a comparison may be made between the two, is in its formal ingenuity and sustained structure; pageantry in the poem is subordinated to literary ends rather than just romantic conceits.

The antiquarian and historical strain in Spenser's work was deeply bound up with a burgeoning sense, both individual and collective, of national promise and an as yet unfulfilled national mission. This crowning sense of identity was not limited to the Leicester circle, the universities or the Inns of Court, although it found significant expression there. It was also felt by John Stow, who benefited from John Dee's immense learning while producing huge volumes of history in the style of the old annalists. Stow's rival for Leicester's attention was the compiler Richard Grafton, who remained loyal to the earl as a propagandist for the Tudors and the reformed religion. According to Thomas Blundeville (he and Aconcio were friends), the earl enthusiastically primed himself with the study of history texts and 'accepted the practical help of the historians in the problems of ruling'.[17] It was the case that what he had learned was very soon to be tested in the most formidable way possible – by the exercise of arms in pursuit of freedom for the United Provinces.

Chapter 15

Infernal Marriages

In the 1560s two great empires struggled for control of the Mediterranean, with the island of Malta as a pivot for their ambitions. The defeat of the Turks did not remove the enormous threat they posed, and Philip II's unease was heightened by events in the Netherlands, where the great hunger of 1565 was followed the next year by serious riots. The revolt of the Dutch against Spanish hegemony was at the outset largely passive and was occasioned by Philip's foreign policy; the contempt shown for local privileges and religious observations; as well as the question of taxation. The slide into armed resistance was largely the responsibility of the provinces of Holland and Zeeland, and the events were closely watched in England and France. French policy was improvised by whoever had the upper hand in the intermittent civil war. The English were slightly less devious, since they had a genuine interest in the fate of their Protestant co-religionists in the Provinces. At the same time English opinion still clung to the view that France was the major enemy, and that French control of Flushing was a tormenting notion to a trading nation. After the death of Charles IX, King Henri III ruled France with the overweening attentions of his mother, Catherine de Médicis, but even she was unable to curb his younger brother François, Duke of Alençon (and from 1574 Duke of Anjou). It was his airily imprecise ambitions that became wildly and improbably entangled in Elizabethan nuptial politics and the fate of the slowly emerging Dutch nation.

For years Elizabeth had to move delicately to avoid antagonizing Spain by openly siding with rebels who in all truth expressed ideas she found repugnant. So when Don Luis de Requesens, Alva's replacement, sent his agent to London for talks, the Dutch cause was seen to wilt. However, centralized Spanish control of the coastal towns of the Provinces (especially Flushing and Middelburg) was an undoubted threat to England, and her nervous equivocation was underlined when Prince William of Orange suffered a series of reverses. He was the foremost leader of the Dutch, yet his powers as stadholder were severely limited, and late in 1574 he threatened to resign unless he was allowed a greater freedom in decision-making.

A year later and it was again Elizabeth who was anxiously trying to define her position, the privy council being called together to debate the direction of English foreign policy. On 9 January 1576 Burghley, Leicester, Walsingham and Bacon met envoys from William, two trusted friends: Paulus Buys and Marnix St Aldegonde. Burghley and Bacon represented the moderate strain of the council, Leicester and Walsingham acting as the spokesmen for the radical activists. Though the latter saw Spain as the gravest threat to the Protestant powers, he had no illusions about the Queen's attitude to intervention in the Provinces, anticipating a policy that he thought would be self-defeating. It was to counter his position that Bacon in turn argued that England was not able to fight a war when aid to the Dutch from other Protestant powers was likely to be meagre, if it came at all. His pragmatic response was simply to increase aid to the Dutch, even through the use of mercenaries, however despised they might be. Burghley apparently had little to add to his satellite's views, except the thought that if a negotiated settlement between the war parties could not be reached, perhaps the best England could hope for was an ensuing stalemate.

At this time Anglo-Dutch relations were not helped by shipping squabbles, acts of piracy being perpetrated by the Sea Beggars, who had seized Brill, a small seaport at the mouth of the Maas, in April 1572, after being banned from English ports in the previous month. But Elizabeth's hint of a friendlier stance in relation to Spain was deplored even by the moderates in the council, and Walsingham and Leicester worked to persuade William to curb these maritime vagrants. English contempt for Spain was heightened when, after the death of Requesens, pay arrears led to a revolt in the Spanish army and the dreadful sacking of Antwerp. Other provinces now joined Holland and Zeeland in the Pacification of Ghent, signed on 8 November 1576. In this agreement all provinces agreed to unite in seeking a settlement from Philip II that would remove their grievances.

In February 1577 Don John of Austria, who had replaced Requesens, gave his consent in the Perpetual Edict to this arrangement. But he was not prepared to see the Dutch make so many significant advances without some attempt to seize the initiative from them. The Pacification was therefore blown apart with the walls of Namur in July, and once again the military position of William of Orange deteriorated.[1] In England the privy council generally took the view that open aid was now unavoidable. Leicester must have seethed with excitement and anticipation as he saw the possibility of military intervention by England. Certainly his supporters envisaged active involvement: Sir Edward Horsey wrote to William Davison, 'I believe before Candlemas or shortly after, you shall see my Lord of Leicester well accompanied in the Low Countries.'

Yet for another eight years Elizabeth teetered on the brink of such commitment. By then Dutch circumstances had changed so dramatically following the assassination of William of Orange that Leicester's position as commander of the English forces and governor of the Provinces was made impossibly complex. But before the Queen would allow her ageing favourite to fight a real war, the covert war had to go on, until by 1578 more peace negotiations with Spain had been started. For both Prince William and Leicester the late years of the 1570s were not a happy time. The earl's position was threatened by the possible exposure of his secret marriage, and the prince now faced a new commander of the Spanish forces, Alessandro Farnese, Duke of Parma, a gifted soldier and diplomat. The result of his attentions was the Union of Arras, which was cunningly intended to lure southern provinces away from their northern allies, who replied with the Union of Utrecht. Parma's tactical skill and political deftness were demonstrated when with slow investment he reconstructed Spanish control in the south, winning towns by blockade, then offering advantageous terms. Conformity to Catholicism was required, but those Protestants who resisted this step were allowed two years of reflection before they were expelled. Then in March 1580 Rennenberg, the stadholder of Friesland, Groningen and Overijsel, made peace with Spain, so that a greater part of the north-eastern provinces fell to Parma.

In England at the same time Burghley was moved to try to revive the idea that Elizabeth should marry the Duke of Anjou. His agent in this endeavour was Edward Stafford, who was in France during May 1578 and who returned to England with the conviction that there would be no opposition from the French court to the link. Burghley seems to have thought that Anjou was simply too dangerous to be left to float from one plot to another, and he developed the conviction that he could be used in English interests. There was some satisfaction to be gained from the thought that this might embroil him with his brother Henri III, while open war with Spain was still avoided. Burghley and Sussex were both of the opinion that, whatever the excesses of Anjou, he could not cost more than secret subsidies to the Dutch and the hopelessly ineffectual prince-mercenary, John-Casimir of the Palatinate, whom Leicester had expansively entertained in February of that year.

The threatened courtship naturally galvanized the earl, Warwick, Bedford, Hatton, Sir Francis Knollys and Walsingham. Especially when in July Elizabeth, while on progress in East Anglia, received Anjou's representatives at Long Melford. De Bacqueville and de Quincey were entertained as lavishly as possible, and then the Queen flung a rebuke at the Lord Chamberlain, Sussex, for not providing enough silver cutlery. When Sussex denied this omission, Elizabeth flew into a tantrum, which amused the Spanish ambassador. The incident is revealing in that it shows some of the strain felt in those uncertain days; Elizabethan tempers were on a short fuse. Leicester for his part seems to have taken the matter of the marriage seriously, deploying his arguments and rather thin resources with the maximum of effect, and snubbing the French, while Elizabeth wanted Anjou to come to England. The general opinion in Europe also seems to have supported the view that Anjou should leave the Provinces. However, in the autumn it was Henri's advisers Rambouillet and L'Aubespine who joined de Bacqueville on a return visit to England. Ironically, they tried to remove Leicester's opposition by a proposal that he should marry a French princess – and this within days of his marriage to Lettice. Anjou in the meantime was becoming alarmed that shortly 'he must ignominiously turn tail again and re-enter France . . . to the tender mercy of his affectionate brother'.[2]

Even so, it was still not Anjou who arrived early in 1579, but a close friend, Jean de Simier, who was to act as proxy for his diminutive master. De Simier cannot have had a very lofty view of marriage, since he had recently discovered the adultery of his own wife with his younger brother, whom he murdered. However, by his exceptional charm and by proffering jewels from Anjou, he disarmed the Queen, whose initial response had been cool. Leicester, knowing Elizabeth and anticipating trouble, sensibly took the view that he should also know his adversary in this elaborate game, so he dined with Simier after a royal audience. The Frenchman seems to have taken his task of proxy gallantry as seriously as anyone could and the French ambassador, Castelnau de la Mauvissière, noted that as expected Elizabeth bloomed under his flattery. Anjou and the Queen now began to exchange letters in French couched in a florid romantic vein, but which of course did nothing to remove the crucial problem of Anjou's Catholicism. Simier took the view that his master should come to England to lavish attentions on Elizabeth since she was susceptible to male gallantry. But at this suggestion she prevaricated, aware as she was of the strained atmosphere that his presence would create in the country, and Mauvissière realistically advised the duke to stay put for the time being.

Burghley in the meantime prepared huge memoranda on the qualities of the match, and in March 1579, after weeks of pondering and anxious reflection, it was settled that Anjou should come to England in April. To soothe Leicester, Henri III wrote that the arrival of his brother would not imperil the earl's place in the kingdom. Leicester wryly retorted that Anjou should land as Parliament went into session, for he would personally spare no effort to stir the Lords and Commons in favour of the union. Indeed, although he meant to sabotage it, Leicester's public efforts were now directed towards welcoming Anjou. He sent Davison to Flanders for expensive materials, velvets, silks and satins, and £400 worth of gold and silver fabric.

The Spanish ambassador reported all these activities to Philip II, even as he urged Elizabeth to break off the negotiations. The ever-sceptical Philip took a wholly relaxed attitude to the matter but, just in case, he continued to hand out bribes to certain privy councillors. When Simier and Rochetaille began making demands that were meant to enhance Anjou's position as consort, the Spanish monarch's anticipations seemed to have been acute, for Elizabeth shied away from the requests. She moved to Leicester's house at Wanstead, and there the French were entertained by a significant piece: Philip Sidney's first public non-academic entertainment, called *The Lady of May*.[3] This piece had a thoroughly conventional theme, setting out the arguments for the active versus the contemplative life. But the show was provocative, since it presented the material in such a way that it became a debate which appealed to the Queen as a gesture that would soothe away the hurts to Leicester's pride.

Elizabeth now wanted the privy council to put their views on marriage to her in writing, but they wisely refused. Instead, during the brief stay at Wanstead, the important core of the council met almost continuously, and when they returned to Whitehall the full council met to concentrate their opposition to the marriage. Only the Earl of Sussex held back, believing that it was not only possible but necessary. On hearing the generally held view Simier stormed off to the Queen, who seemed to be moved but not depressed by the opinion of her closest advisers. Only Anjou managed to keep the whole question alive by moderating his demands and announcing that he was now certainly coming to England. Elizabeth wanted to avoid the possible embarrassment of meetings but eventually agreed that he should do so. He was to come in mid-August, and in the meantime Leicester was sent out to hunt with Mauvissière, and the Queen dined *à deux* with Simier.

It does seem that Leicester was increasingly irritated by the Queen's wild fluctuations of mood and tone about the whole matter. When the time came for the prince to arrive, Leicester plainly asked her not to sign the passport, and when it became clear that Anjou was to be admitted to court, the earl retired to Wanstead for a diplomatic illness that brought the Queen to his bedside. But this reconciliation was short-lived when an attempt was made to assassinate Simier. The intended victim and the furious Queen both suspected that Leicester had been responsible. The Frenchman took his revenge with a gleeful revelation to the Queen that Leicester was married to Lettice. The Queen's dislike of her younger, beautiful rival was unremitting, and tension was further increased when a gun went off as Simier and the Queen were using the State barge on the Thames.

All these arch diplomatic wranglings gave Leicester's Puritan allies additional material for their fiery opposition to the marriage. They pointed out that if, as seemed probable, Henri III died without an heir, Elizabeth would be married to a Catholic monarch and the country yoked to Rome. When Anjou arrived in London the city was poised to explode with resentment, Puritan preachers denouncing the godless French to all who would listen. A pamphlet called *The discovery of a gaping gulf wherein England is like to be swallowed by another French marriage* was written and circulated by John Stubbs, the brother-in-law of Thomas Cartwright, an act of literary temerity that cost him his right hand. At court the duke was scarcely acknowledged and there was great relief when he had to return to France on the death of Bussy d'Amboise in a duel. Even so, some held the view that an Anglo-French alliance of some sort might prevent Philip II from swallowing up Portugal when King Dom Sebastian died. The privy council again went into virtually continuous discussions on 22 October, the minutes being maintained by Burghley.[4] In six days of poring over the problem they reached the conclusion that the flaws in the marriage proposal outweighed any possible advantage. They would not advise in its favour unless the Queen expressly and peremptorily desired them to do so.

This calculated response was given to the Queen by Leicester, Burghley, Lincoln and Sussex, and they had to suffer the inevitable tears and storms. Yet she accepted without a disproportionate display of wrath the attack on the marriage proposal that Philip Sidney eagerly wrote at his uncle's prompting. The hearts of Protestants would be

galled, if not alienated, when they shall see you take a husband, a Frenchman and a papist, in whom, howsoever

fine wits may find further dealings or painted excuses . . .
common people will know . . . he is the son of the Jezebel of
our age; that his brother made oblation of his sister's
marriage, the easier to make massacres of our brethren in
belief. He . . . did sack La Charité and utterly spoil them with
fire and sword! This I say, even at first sight gives occasion to
all truly religious to abhor such a master, and consequently to
diminish much of the hopeful love they long held to you.[5]

The depth of English feelings was perfectly clear to an
experienced observer like Mauvissière. During 1580 he decided
that he must free himself from the taint of his Catholic allies at
the English court, particularly when much anger was generated
by the landing in Ireland of forces led by the ill-fated Dr Sanders
and supported by the Pope, and by the Jesuit missions to
England as well as talk of a continental 'Holy League'.
Mauvissière argued that renewed tensions with Spain would
bring England and France closer. The English Catholics, he
thought, would be only a hindrance, since the government was
poised to reduce their activities by stringent penalties. Leicester
himself was poised to attack the English Catholics during the
Christmas festivities of 1580. His intention was that this should
also ruin the intrigues of the absent Simier, now back in France.
    Leicester's weapon in this battle was the young Edward de
Vere, Earl of Oxford, who had returned from Italy with ideas
that dismayed his friends and enemies alike. Leicester persuaded
Oxford to reveal to Elizabeth the fact that he had been an
intimate of Mauvissière during 1577, and that unspecified
Catholic plotting threatened now to engulf her. When his
revelations were greeted with a certain scepticism, Oxford
offered Charles Arundell, a crypto-Catholic with numerous
court connections, £1,000 to testify that he was indeed speaking
the truth. Arundell refused, but Leicester saw to it that Oxford's
charges were formally presented to the Queen. Warned of the
danger by someone at court (probably Sussex), Arundell and his
Catholic friends took refuge with de Mendoza. But this was only
a temporary retreat and when they gave themselves up they
were placed in the custody of various courtiers. Hatton took
charge of Lord Henry Howard; Arundell, Howard's second
cousin, was held at Sutton in Surrey; while Southwell was

placed with Walsingham. Oxford's revelations seem to have fractured a homosexual Catholic coterie, for Howard and Arundell now reviled Oxford for sexual irregularities, Arundell declaring: 'I will prove him a buggerer, of a boy that is his cook.'[6] Then, having added atheism to Oxford's crimes, he suggested that Leicester and Sidney were targets for assassination as outstanding leaders of the Protestant faction at court.[7] This last plot may have been added to trump Leicester's own allegation that the closet Catholics planned to murder Elizabeth. Even so, after a hearing Howard and Arundell were freed, and Leicester now stalked other Catholics. One who fled abroad to escape his attention was a follower of the Earl of Sussex, Dr William Tresham, of the then famous Catholic family.[8]

In France there had been much bickering about the rank of any new envoy to be sent to England. But on 14 April 1581 some 500 French nobles and dignitaries boarded ship for England, arriving at Dover on the 17th. In the view of the privy council the embassy was pointless, but to gild the lily, large sums of money were spent. A grandstand was erected in the Palace of Westminster; plate was ordered and mercers were required to sell their goods more cheaply, in order to satisfy Elizabeth's vanity. Leicester, as Master of the Horse, and his news officials had to provide transport from Dover, and the French arrived at Gravesend for a parliamentary meeting before barges took them to Somerset House.

On St George's Day the embassy visited Whitehall for a lavish banquet. A specially constructed banqueting hall was covered with painted canvas decorated with fruits and flowers, the ceiling with stars and sunbeams and the royal arms of England and France. Silver and gold cloth draped the walls, and at one end was a dais with a throne set under a silk canopy weighty with seed-pearl roses. To vie with the splendours of the surroundings Elizabeth wore a dress of cloth of gold decorated with diamonds and rubies. When the young Dauphin stepped forward she greeted him with a kiss on the lips, and after several days of courtly diversions he had the wit to ask with whom he was to negotiate. Elizabeth named Leicester, Walsingham, Bedford, Hatton, Sussex and Burghley. From these names we realize that three, possibly four, opposed both the marriage and talks. It was

Leicester who was impresario to Sidney's allegorical triumph, *The Fortress of Perfect Beauty*, presented before the court and guests. This was intended as a not very oblique statement that if Leicester himself could not win the Queen in marriage, neither could a Frenchman. It was expressed with the ritualistic display of Renaissance Neoplatonic imagery. Originally intended for St George's Day, it was finally given on 15–16 May in the tilt-yard at Whitehall. The thematic 'device' was that Sidney, Philip Howard, the Earl of Arundel, Lord Windsor and Fulke Greville were the four foster-children of Desire. They would lay siege to the Fortress of Beauty, defended by faithful knights of the Queen, including the four Knollys brothers. Apparently Leicester's four brothers-in-law even dared to make a reference to their opposition to the marriage proposal in a speech heralding their entry into the tilt.[9]

In Henry Goldwell's *A Brief Declaration of the Shews* it is noted that Sidney wore steely blue armour, gilded and engraved. He was followed into the arena by four spare horses, either draped in cloth of gold embroidered with pearls, or sporting 'gold and silver feathers very richly and cunningly wrought'. The pages riding the horses wore silver coats and silver stockings with matching hats decorated with gold bands and white plumes. Then came thirty gentlemen and four trumpeters all gorgeously dressed.[10] The entertainment offered the large audience was an elaborate mixture of symbolism, jousting and song. It ended on the second day when a boy was sent to the Queen 'being clothed in ash-coloured garments in token of humble submission', and he extended to her an olive branch, claiming that the four foster-children were now subordinated for ever to her royal virtue.

As for Anjou at this time, he was heavily involved in the affairs of the Dutch rebels and aimed to relieve Cambrai, which was besieged by Parma. Desperate to retrieve something from the protracted and apparently pointless talks in England, Anjou suddenly decided to leave the field and he raced across the Channel to England. Among Henri III's official representatives this was an unwelcome appearance at a delicate moment. It was almost equally embarrassing to Elizabeth, who promised money and support for his projected military activities and promptly sent him back to the Provinces. All Europe now knew full well that the marriage was all moonshine.[11]

Yet later in the year Anjou did return to stay with Stafford before riding to Richmond for a private meeting with Elizabeth. With relaxed high confidence Leicester now affected to champion the marriage, and de Mendoza reported to Philip II: 'Leicester leaves nothing undone and in the absence of the Prince Dauphin' (who had returned to France laden with gifts) 'always hands Alençon [*sic*] the napkin, publicly declaring that there seems to be no other way for the queen to secure the tranquillity of England but for her to marry . . . and Walsingham says the same.'[12] The inevitable reversal followed after generous bribes from Henri III, and Leicester with Hatton's connivance reverted to denouncing the proposal to any courtier inclined to listen. Surrounded by people he could not understand with motives he could not fathom, Anjou literally did not know if he was coming or going. He was finally pushed off to the Provinces as a new deputation arrived in England, this time from the States-General. Accompanied by the delighted Leicester, many other gentlemen and a retinue of some 600, the bemused Anjou departed from London. As a mark of his distinction Elizabeth travelled with him as far as Canterbury, and her parting gift to him was a more than generous £25,000 packed in fish barrels. Hunsdon and Leicester also had monies for the Dutch rebels, and the great party sailed to Flushing on 10 February. The earl carried something else besides: a secret request to William of Orange that Anjou should be kept in the Provinces and, even before he sailed, new marriage plans were being constructed around a rich Médicis cousin.

Although Francis Talbot had reported to Shrewsbury that food was scarce in Flanders, and Leicester cautiously took supplies of beef and mutton, on arrival the English mission was greeted with huge celebrations. Elaborate paraphernalia accompanied the entries and progresses, and no doubt the earl was moved and excited by these noisy events. At the centre of it all of course was the unlikely figure of Anjou, who was for the moment lauded as the saviour of the Provinces, and was made Duke of Brabant in a ceremony at Antwerp. Yet the fact remains that Anjou actually became less important even as he accrued titles and honours. The first meeting of William of Orange and Leicester, his natural ally, was much more significant. Indeed the volume recording the entry into Antwerp was almost dedicated to the earl, and in the event it would have been more appropriate, for Anjou swiftly proved that he could not govern – worse, that he was ungovernable. His religion, nationality, limited powers and jealousy of William created endless problems. In January 1583 the Frenchman attempted to lead a coup that would have freed him from the treaty agreement signed in 1581. Its failure 'wiped out whatever residue of trust still existed between him and his Low Countries subjects'.[13] With the collapse of the episode in Antwerp and other towns Anjou retreated to France, where he died in the following year, to the general relief of above all the English. Yet the problems of immediate policy still remained for the Protestant associates, and for England the critical point was the drawing of France into an effective alliance when the French were far from convinced that Spain was a great threat to their interests. The marriage to Anjou would have locked them into the cause; without it they thought it better to stay aloof.

As for Leicester, he and the entourage who had accompanied Anjou were recalled rather speedily to England 'in consequence of the heavy expenses he and those who accompanied him were incurring'.[14] The reason was quite simply that the Queen in pursuit of her foreign policy had poured gold over the French duke: £60,000 in 1581 and 1582.[15] It was a plank of her policy that had manifestly failed, despite her sustained reluctance to note its many deficiences. Perhaps its worst effect was to help to make Leicester's task in the following years harrowingly difficult, for all his committed persistence.

Chapter 16

If Opportunity Offers

Leicester once wrote to the Earl Marshal, the Earl of Shrewsbury, to recommend Humphrey Hales for the vacant post of Bluemantle Pursuivant. Leicester thought him an honest gentleman and 'there is nothing more honourable for you, nor more profitable to the nobility, than to see fit men placed in these offices'.[1] Since then critics have often reflected that the earl's own ability to pick 'fit men' was itself flawed, and that he very often made serious errors. Yet in a public career of thirty years, encompassing so many aspects of Elizabethan life, the failure seems understandable. It was partly a question of time: with so much to do he could not vet every petitioner for office, nor when an appointment was made could he stand at the man's shoulder to oversee his work. Leicester assiduously attended privy council meetings even though the councillors often quietly grumbled that the Queen all too often ignored their deliberations. With his office of Master of the Horse Leicester had learned to delegate functions to his staff. It was left to the surveyor Lewis Stockett to organize repairs and building programmes for the royal stables and barns, but it was Leicester who directed expenditure both in and out of London.[2] This was probably useful preparation for the office of Lord Steward of the Royal Household which passed to him in 1584, probably as consolation for the appointment of Lord Howard as Lord Chamberlain. Previous holders of the stewardship had all treated it as a sinecure, but Leicester felt much could be done to improve on the antiquated 'below stairs' administration that supplied the Elizabethan court with food, drink, fuel and lighting.

As Lord Steward Leicester controlled the board of Green

Cloth, which was comprised of senior administrators of the household, the treasurer and comptroller, who together with the earl were known as the 'white staves' from their wands of office.[3] As his office was coveted, so inevitably were lesser positions eagerly sought after, since they gave the corrupt administrator fine opportunities for advantageous dishonesty. Leicester could not reduce or eliminate, as he might have hoped to do, the worst excesses when his own father-in-law was treasurer and used the office as usual to line his pockets and fill his larder. Knollys seems to have regarded royal supplies as a perquisite of his own, dining one Christmas on the tongues of lambs and does and a boar, all quietly deducted from the royal larders.[4] Sir James Croft, the Comptroller, whom over the years Leicester had grown to dislike, did much the same.

Whatever his immediate difficulties Leicester was a conscientious working member of the board of Green Cloth. He was gratified that Elizabeth had shown confidence in his ability to effect changes that would benefit the Crown. 'It hath pleased her Majesty', he wrote, 'to call me to the place of lord steward within her most honourable house and to give me special charge as principal officer unto whom reformation of such abuses does chiefly appertain to have care thereof'. But it was controlling the purveyors to the household that proved harder than he had anticipated, for they had the greatest direct opportunities for high-handed behaviour in the markets and countryside. Indeed, the most significant cause of the hatred the purveyors aroused was their enforceable right to buy items in large quantities at a substantial discount to the Crown. Parliament on a number of occasions sought to restrict purveyors, and freedom from purveyance was a highly regarded and strenuously maintained local privilege. In 1579, for example, the privy council had written to the JPs in Oxfordshire and Berkshire to remind them that by statute from the reign of Mary the tenants and farmers on land owned by St John's College, Oxford, were exempt from purveyance. Yet in September 1581 Leicester was again forced to intervene because the injunction was not being obeyed, and the farmers were still being harried. It was the earl's intention that the JPs should meet to devise a strategy to protect the tenants.

In an attempt to appease those who felt purveyance to be

unjust, the government did offer composition as an alternative. This was an arrangement whereby counties could confer with the privy council to agree what fixed amounts they had to provide in the way of fish, fowl, beef, butter, cream, eggs and so on. When a composition agreement was made, purveyors were withdrawn, and it was generally hoped that the rancour they caused would disappear. In many counties composition was the preferred method of supply. But in others, where the intrusions of the purveyors were rare, it was found to be equally disadvantageous. Any system of supply was likely to cause great disquiet when the annual quantities required were so huge: for example, Essex compounded for 41,600 pounds of butter and 4 million eggs. Moreover, commodities not covered by compounding, such as rare game birds, were still subject to purveyance. And purveyance was also necessary when the Queen was on progress.

Since the beginning of the reign Burghley had watched household expenses rise alarmingly, whether there was a lord steward or not. Now Leicester, after consulting his colleague, began to search for areas of household administration where costs could be cut. He began in the brewery, which had to supply vast quantities of potable ale and beer, by suggesting that the malt should be purchased more cheaply. Control of the brewery fell to the buttery, and officials of this section of the household made their purchases from a select ring of some sixty London brewers with a monopoly of supplies of royal liquor. It was during the 1570s that complaints began about the quality of beer and ale, and in 1575 Leicester had been most disconcerted when the Queen on progress had found her favourite ale to be unpalatable. In an age of uncertain water supplies the provision of bad beer and ale infuriated her, and Leicester wrote to Burghley at the end of June: 'God be thanked she is very merry. But at her first coming, being a marvellous hot day . . . [there was] not one drop of good drink for her, so ill was she provided for, notwithstanding of her telling of her coming hither.'[5] He went on that 'it had been as good to have drunk Malmsey', which was a heavy, sweet wine from Monemvassia in Greece. 'It did put her very far out of temper, and almost all the company beside.'

For a period following this very minor crisis the household

had undertaken its own brewing at Sion in Middlesex. The operation was controlled by Mr Abingdon, the Cofferer, but it ended when he died in 1582. Shortly afterwards the Master of the Household, Anthony Crane, tried to promote another royal brewing scheme, this time in Puddle Dock, but this also failed and the brewhouse operation was then abandoned in the face of the antagonism of former royal suppliers in London. In 1585, however, Leicester intervened and the royal brewhouse was restarted and remained in operation until March 1588. But Leicester's chief concern at this time was with the forward buying of malt, and the quality of the end-product was little improved. Although he claimed a saving of £1,000, the brewhouse eventually closed, and the household again reverted to using the ring of brewers. It was probably the chronic lack of immediate funds available to the Cofferer that prevented a more successful intervention as malt prices rose.[6]

The Lord Steward was also forced to intervene in the buying of poultry, for which the appetite of the court never seemed to flag. Apart from exotic game reserved for the Queen's table only, the poultry division of the household had to buy chickens for roasting and boiling for courtiers, servants and domestics. Since the numbers were enormous, a bitter rivalry developed between the household's 'fine purveyor', supplying the royal table, and those buying fowls for the general markets of London. John Raymond, the fine purveyor, saw his supplies steadily dwindling, and in 1586 he ordered his deputies to ignore all purchase controls. They were now to seize poultry from the 'higlers', market middlemen, and from city poulterers on their stalls and in their shops. The result was a furious outcry, and Leicester felt obliged to sack the execrated Raymond and his assistants, appointing in his place Henry Windredge and Nicholas Borden.

Possibly Leicester might have achieved more significant domestic reforms if he had not been so preoccupied with the fate of the United Provinces. At a less elevated level he had also certain beneficial personal connections with several of his subordinates. Of these the most powerful and corrupt was John Haynes, Serjeant of the Acatry – that is, of meat purchases. Once again the quantities were prodigious, and with the shift to composition deliveries were made on certain days. Some live animals were quickly slaughtered and salted for the larder; others were kept on the hoof on royal pastures in south-east England, or more immediately on pastures where we now find Tottenham Court Road. It was John Haynes who secured control of the latter and used them for his own stock, and the cattle of nobles whose favour he sought. It seems probable that with his large London mansion full of guests and relations Leicester himself kept stock there. Moreover, one of the meat purveyors who worked under Haynes was called John Dudley. He was sacked with his colleagues in the 1590s when their exactions became too insupportable. The name Dudley may have been a coincidence, though Leicester clearly favoured his own relatives, and a meat purveyor working closely with the Serjeant would have been useful.

It would be interesting to know if household supplies were ever diverted to the expeditions which, like his father, Northumberland, the earl sponsored and into which he put his own funds. Or perhaps he did so only when the Queen had invested in the same voyage. When Martin Frobisher wanted to raise money for his voyage to northern Canada, he aroused interest by claiming to have found the passage to Cathay. Through Edward Dyer, Warwick and Leicester both took shares of £50, but even this modest investment was lost when the ore samples that so excited the mariner turned out to be iron pyrites. Yet on the strength of the optimism engendered by the mirage of gold, Frobisher made further voyages in 1577 and 1578. The investors in the latter (to Baffin Island) certainly did not make a profit, and even the crews were unpaid: Leicester had ventured £202. 10s. and the Queen £1,350.

As early as 1564 Leicester and Cecil had invested in the second slaving voyage of John Hawkins who, having sold his African human cargo, filled his hold with fish, giving the ship an even more pungent smell. He sailed into Plymouth to acclaim, for the shares in the voyage showed a 60 per cent profit. For Leicester it was an indication that venture capital could boost his income, but it was not for years that he could afford to acquire a ship of his own. Originally built for Henry Oughtred by the shipwright Matthew Baker, she was modelled on the *Revenge* and work began on her in about 1578 at Hamble. When completed she usefully doubled as a cargo vessel and a warship, since forty guns could be installed on the upper and lower decks.[7]

At one time the privy council thought of using *Galleon Oughtred* in the Azores, a force seizing Terceira for use as a base for an attack on the Spanish treasure fleet. After that the English fleet would move to the Caribbean and finally sail via the Cape of Good Hope to Calicut on the west coast of India with the intention of establishing an English spice trade. All this was known by Philip II, since de Mendoza was kept informed by Leicester's enemy on the privy council, Sir James Croft. In January 1580 the ambassador wrote to Madrid of another privateer prepared for the earl and ready to sail to the Indies: 'Although I understand the main object to be robbery if opportunity offers, the design is also to aid Drake, if they come across him . . . as Leicester and his party are those who are behind Drake.'[8] In March of the same year de Mendoza noted that the ship had encountered contrary winds which had driven her into port in Ireland. There she was seized by the Earl of Desmond, who ill-treated the crew. 'Leicester is much grieved at this as the ship was well-fitted.' By September the ambassador's pleasure would have been curtailed, for then Drake reached Plymouth at the end of his epic voyage around the world – the first Englishman to achieve this feat.

A chronic lack of funds and diplomatic considerations prevented any advance with the privy council's plan for the *Galleon Oughtred*. But in mid-1581 Leicester began to consider another scheme involving the ship. With the participation of the Muscovy Company, represented by Alderman Richard Martin who hoped to provide the *Mary Edwards*, Leicester now set his hopes on a trading voyage to the Molucca Islands. The cost of promoting the expedition was to be shared, the earl buying *Galleon Oughtred* from her owner for £2,800. Payment of £2,000 in instalments seems to have been agreed, Leicester handing over as a token 'sufficient new and good velvet to make a gown for Oughtred's wife, Lady Elizabeth Courtenay'.[9] The remaining £800 was apparently Oughtred's substantial investment. Others involved were: Drake, for some £700 and the *Bark Francis*; the Earl of Shrewsbury, who planned to send *Bark Talbot*, but who eventually settled for £200; and the Levant Company, which made available the *Edward Bonaventure* as a second ship. Leicester's friends and relations also bought shares according to their means.

The earl now paid for the sheathing of the ship, which was proudly renamed *Galleon Leicester*, and he also met the cost of munitions, provisions and tackle. In October 1581 Frobisher reported to him on the preparations for the voyage and Leicester began considering who should lead the little fleet of ships and pinnaces. Frobisher was the initial choice from the short list, but for reasons that are not clear he decided to withdraw. Here then was a chance for Leicester to prove his ability to choose the fit man, but unfortunately Edward Fenton was selected. Even in the preliminary stages of organizing the command, personal antagonisms threatened the stability of the entire project. For example, Christopher Carleil withdrew because of his resentment at the post given to the untried son of John Hawkins. Less contentiously Leicester also selected two priests and diarists for the expedition: Richard Madox, Fellow of All Souls, and John Walker (once a chaplain to the earl), who got a dispensation to keep his livings while chaplain with the expedition. The important post of physician went to John Banister, a student under William Clowes and known personally to Leicester from the recent excursion to accompany Anjou to the Provinces.

On a misty Saturday at the end of March 1582 Leicester and Walsingham visited the *Edward Bonaventure* to see the state of preparation for what eventually turned into a voyage of piracy. The proclaimed intention was to test the hazards and commercial possibilities of the route to the East Indies, sailing via the Strait of Magellan. But even now Madox and Walker were uneasy at Fenton's antagonism towards those who opposed his apeing of Drake, and the five trade factors were among those buffeted by his irascibility and paranoid delusions. Fenton's decision to cruise Spanish trade routes in order to harry their shipping was highly inappropriate, but was abetted by a Portuguese called Simão Fernandes, a Protestant convert.[10] The whole affair neatly illustrates the contrasting demands of merchants and anti-Spanish gentlemen in preparing and executing such voyages as well as the difficulty of controlling turbulent seamen. Although the Muscovy Company helped with ships and stores through three of its members, little merchant money was invested because the promotion was suspect. Moreover, Leicester's attitude did not convince the merchants who were approached through his secretary Arthur Atey; none of them agreed to invest in what they saw as an unsound venture.[11] Their caution was endorsed when one of the trade factors, Miles Evans, became so angrily disillusioned with the progress of the expedition that he demanded to be left in Guinea. He returned to England in a bark that Fenton had already sold to some Portuguese traders, while the remainder of the little fleet sailed on to slow disintegration and disaster. In trading terms nothing was achieved, and even the plans concocted for piracy proved useless.[12] The venture simply cost lives and money: among those who died was Richard Madox.

Evidently the Strait of Magellan was far too dangerous for shipping, and by choosing that route to the East Indies Fenton was highlighting his nonchalant lack of concern for mercantile matters. There was even less pretence of this when Drake sailed in 1585 to intercept the Spanish treasure fleet, taking *Galleon Leicester* with him. Once again the effort and investment failed to yield anything for those involved, although it did have some significance as a relief for the hard-pressed Dutch, and as a booster for English confidence.

Leicester's interest in exploration and adventuring was in part inspired by cupidity, but less ignoble motives may also be adduced. Certainly profit cannot have been uppermost in his mind when he supported the madcap Thomas Stukely, who could run through fortunes faster than most; and Leicester had known him for years. Promoting these voyages shows a nationalistic strain, and that many were scarcely exploratory in the pure sense. Yet they were proof that English shipbuilding and navigation had improved beyond all measure since the middle of the century, and the veil of caution was being lifted. The new spirit of enterprise stemmed partly from the change in attitude brought about by the theoretical work of John Dee, for all his mystical vapourings an important figure because he was an enthusiast; and partly from the admired Hakluyt, who gave concrete (if sometimes inaccurate) information. Sailors, travellers and promoters at court all consulted them. Furthermore, the self-limiting ordinance that had hitherto prevented English encroachment on Portuguese territory was swept aside in the 1580s when Spain swallowed up Portugal and her empire on the death of King Dom Sebastian.[13] The new order emerging was reflected in the fact that the pretender to the Portuguese throne, Dom Antonio, took refuge in England and became an intimate of the Leicester circle in the English court.

Chapter 17

Gross and Wicked
Heretics

From the mid-1570s until his departure for the United Provinces in 1585 Leicester was the dominant courtier-statesman in England. Burghley lost ground despite the furore over the earl's clandestine marriage to Lettice. It is not then surprising that Leicester developed an overriding sense of his own importance, which individuals and groups had to acknowledge, even if grudgingly. Everyone knew that his proximity to the throne gave him power. Wanting his help for the incorporation of the town of Tewkesbury, of which he was High Steward, the leading citizens presented him with a huge ox, seventeen hands high, which cost £14, and to which the whole town had contributed. The gift worked and they got what they wanted; but this was not always the case, and Sigismondo di Cavalli, the Venetian ambassador to France, commented on one occasion that 'Leicester has given offence to many persons and is generally detested'.

There is no doubt that he was hated by Catholics, and published libels of the earl attacked him for a multiplicity of reasons. One now preserved in State Papers was written in about 1584 by someone disguised behind the initials R.F.[1] It repeats the surprised dismay of many that this offspring of a traitor should now hold an unassailable position in the country, and even his well-known Puritan sympathies are denied, since 'he is of no religion but what brings him gain, like Machiavelli, his master'. The same point is made in the famous and vividly unattractive portrait of the earl in a lengthy diatribe called *The Copy of a Letter written by a Master of Art of Cambridge*, or more familiarly, *Leicester's Commonwealth*. Written as a response to the thwarted French courtship by Anjou of Elizabeth, the authors were also incensed by the earl's involvement in the government persecution of Catholics. Since papists could not attack the Queen without accusations of treason, they transferred whatever guilt they found in her to the ubiquitous earl, whose malevolence in the *Commonwealth* appears almost satanic. His greatest crime was that 'being himself of no religion, [he] feedeth notwithstanding upon our differences in religion to the fatting of himself and ruin of the realm'. Apart from the attack on him, the text also musters arguments about the possible successor to Elizabeth, highlighting the claim of Mary Queen of Scots, and to a lesser extent that of her son James.[2] This was at a time when the mention of the lady could send strong men into paroxysms of bemused disgust: Walsingham called her the 'bosom serpent', and at any given opportunity Leicester would argue for her execution.

Copies of *Leicester's Commonwealth* began to appear in England in the autumn of 1584 after the text had been collated by a group of English lay Catholic exiles in France. Their material came from court gossip, Howard family traditions and very possibly reports by Douglass, Lady Sheffield. They were powerfully aided by the collaboration of a Jesuit priest, Fr Persons, and his name immediately became associated with the book. Later a French translation appeared, but there were no Italian and Latin versions.[3] In any case, the English version did its work and it was Walsingham who wrote to Leicester that the clandestine libel was 'the most malicious thing that was ever penned sithence the beginning of the world'. Having had reports from his spies, the principal secretary confidently ascribed it to Lord Paget, Dr William Tresham (who had fled abroad in 'extreme fear of the cruelty of the earl of Leicester') and Charles Arundell. As we have seen, Arundell had been briefly imprisoned through the efforts of the earl and his unstable henchman, the Earl of Oxford. In the aftermath of the Throckmorton Plot Arundell and Lord Paget had fled to France, and then came the arrests of the Earls of Arundel and Northumberland. The latter was kept in confinement by Sir Thomas Leighton, Leicester's brother-in-law, before being removed to the Tower, where apparently he killed himself in June 1585.

Fr Persons was not the principal author of the libel, yet he organized its distribution from his bases in Rouen and Paris. In September 1584 Ralph Emerson, one of Person's aides, for the second time smuggled copies of the *Commonwealth* into England. But he was swiftly detected, arrested and interrogated before committal to the Counter in Poultry Street.[4] The Lord Mayor of London, Sir Edward Osborne, sent a copy of the libel to Walsingham, who passed it on to the victim. Furious, Leicester sent Richard Hakluyt, chaplain of the English embassy in France, back to Paris in early October with a demand that the ambassador, Sir Edward Stafford, should swiftly identify the culprits. But of course Stafford was no friend of Leicester's: he had married the discarded Lady Sheffield, and his own brother, William Stafford, was accused of treasonable activities. However, of necessity he had to make inquiries, and after these he reported on 29 October that the text had been printed in England, with the additional recommendation that the best policy was simply to ignore it. Leicester would have none of it and, under pressure from the earl, the privy council took the view that this was not merely a personal squib but an attack on the Elizabethan regime.

Walsingham's agents tracked down one consignment, but, like any dissident text today, those that got through found a ready market for wide distribution. Even a proclamation from Elizabeth issued from Hampton Court failed to prevent its secret distribution. The rumour in Paris in January 1585 was that the earl had sent an assassin to murder Arundell, which tied in elegantly with the contents of the libel. There is some evidence that the Arundell family had fallen out of favour beforehand and Thomas Arundell, son of Sir Matthew, claimed much later that 'the credit of my poor house in Leicester's time greatly weakened'.[5]

In April 1585 a copy of the *Commonwealth* actually reached William Shelley of Michelgrove. Two years before, there had been a plan to land an army under the Duke of Guise on the Sussex coast, and Lord Paget's brother had been sent to Petworth to win the support of the principal Catholics of the area. The Earl of Northumberland and the unfortunate Shelley had been spotted as a result of this contact. Yet despite that he was now in the Tower, Shelley was able to pass on his copy when he had finished reading it.[6] In fact the widespread audience that the book secured is confirmed by the official exertions that went into trying to suppress it. Moreover, it was even popular reading at court. On one occasion the Earl of Ormond greeted Sir John Harington (Leicester being close by) with a breezy 'Good Morrow, Mr Reader'. When Leicester asked what so absorbed him, Harington blushed and lied, saying Ariosto.

As James VI of Scotland was induced to denounce the libel in a proclamation from Holyroodhouse, Sir Philip Sidney was agitatedly preparing a defence of his uncle.[7] He was hampered and angered by the fact that the culprit had not been revealed, and his defence was constructed around the claim of the Dudleys to an ancient lineage. Since this item remained in manuscript Leicester probably took the view that its genealogical bias was not particularly helpful when the libel attacked him on so many delicate aspects of his life. He may also have hoped that the culmination of his work during the strained 1580s would erase the memory of the *Commonwealth*. Unfortunately for him, this did not come about, later writers generally regarded it uncritically, and perhaps even with relish. One of the slyest concoctions based on this material is in the Sloane manuscripts at the British Library.[8] The 'News from Heaven and Hell' was sensibly written after Leicester's death (unless cheerfully anticipatory of it), and gleefully records his efforts, dressed in a lawn shirt with personal monogram, beaver hat and baskins, with his steward's staff in his hand, to toil and wheedle his way past St Peter into heaven. Before this 'his Robinship' and 'his barrenship' encounters Sarcotheos, an intermediate demon whom he fatuously trusts to brand Amye Lettice on his forehead. Humiliated and abused by St Peter, Leicester removes himself to the dark kingdom of Tartaria to be perpetually tormented sexually: 'Thus was his paradise turned into his purgatory . . . and his prick of desire into a pillar of fire.'[9]

Much of the material for the short text is drawn from *Leicester's Commonwealth*, and the general depiction of the earl is not charitable. But the tone is different, with a leering humour, and 'there is very little of the personal bitterness found in other libels'.[10] It is matter of regret that reading figures for these defamatory texts do not exist. What is unmistakable is the sense of impotence of the writers, who must have realized that the intense interest in England caused by the revolt of the Dutch would smother their own case. Moreover, the alliance of the great men like Leicester and Walsingham, with their tentacles of power and patronage reaching through the great City merchants and their representatives in Parliament, down to preachers and pamphleteers, meant that the Catholic outsiders were prodded and buffeted into corners. The singularity of the Dutch revolt was that, as an uprising against an anointed king, 'it should not have appealed to the imagination of a self-consciously monarchical society'. Yet there were those in England who felt a kinship with their co-religionists in the United Provinces and wanted active English involvement in the struggle. Haunted by the threat from Spain English men and women began to view that country and her ruler with a mixture of hatred and bravado.[11] Now the Catholic seminarists trained in Europe who secretly flitted into England from the continental seminaries were regarded as political agitators rather than simply priests, and Protestant writers, supported by men like Leicester, were engaged to assail popery. Laurence Humphrey and William Whitaker argued that Catholic missionary activity was indeed treasonable, for the priests supported a pope whose expressed aim was to suborn the people of England from their allegiance. At the same time the government acted to increase the penalties against Catholicism; a convert was now guilty of treason, and a recusant could be fined £20.

The opposition of Leicester and his associates gradually moved on from religious controversy to unrestrained political antagonism. The assault on Spanish power and resources could be pursued anywhere in the world. When Francis Drake returned to Plymouth in 1581 with a shipload of Spanish treasure, Burghley favoured restitution, while Leicester and Walsingham (as statesmen and investors in the enterprise) would have none of that. The unravelling of the Throckmorton conspiracy, with its evidence of Spanish involvement, led to the expulsion of de Mendoza, the ambassador, and now contacts between Spain and England at the official level lapsed. Plots against Elizabeth were frequent, but this one had a special significance because it raised again the issue of legitimate succession to the Queen if she died (which now seemed all too probable) unmarried and childless. Her contemporaries had begun to accept this problem with greater equanimity than they had mustered in the early years of her reign. But Leicester and Burghley again disagreed on a possible successor. With no great enthusiasm Burghley favoured Edward Seymour, the son of Catherine Grey, and he then revised his opinion and moved to support the young James VI of Scotland. Leicester and Walsingham chose to back the Puritan Earl of Huntingdon, with his Plantagenet blood, although Leicester seems to have found his brother-in-law an uncomfortably quaint option, and he began dealing in Scotland for the marriage of his infant son Robert, Lord Denbigh, to Arabella Stuart, who was then being raised by her grandmother, Lady Shrewsbury.

Before Arabella could become Queen of England in succession to Elizabeth, two Stuarts had to die: Mary Queen of Scots and her son. In the early 1580s that regally stupid lady made the first demise altogether more likely by underestimating the enmity of Walsingham. Since Ridolfi's Plot Mary had been kept under guard in Sheffield Castle by the Earl of Shrewsbury, who seems to have taken his duties lightly. However, in April 1585 she was removed to Tutbury and the custody of Sir Amias Paulet, a gentleman of strict Puritan rectitude, and after his grim regime she was moved on to Chartley Manor. Displaying a naïveté that is breath-taking, she had been coaxed into believing that her correspondence was secret, when in fact every latter was read by Walsingham. By 1586, when Leicester was in the United Provinces, Mary had allowed herself to become involved with Anthony Babington, whose scheme to free her made the assassination of Elizabeth imperative. This was a piece of murderous opportunism that Mary eventually accepted, and when she did so Walsingham pounced. Consequently, to the general delight of the country, Babington and his associates went to the block. The boldness with which Elizabeth and Walsingham alone manoeuvred against the plotters was remarkable. One of the would-be killers, Barnewell, came across Elizabeth walking with an unarmed party in Richmond Park, but when he was fiercely scrutinized by her he lost his nerve and withdrew. All this was seen as the inevitable prelude to the execution of Mary after a special commission found her guilty.

The possibility of Elizabeth dying at an assassin's hands had been terrifyingly real, for already two years before William of

Orange had suffered the same fate. This had caused a wave of pained dismay in England, and Leicester had seized the initiative in London from Burghley by devising the Bond of Association (October 1584). Those who took the oath were pledged to kill anyone who came to the throne of England following the assassination of Elizabeth. It was an emotional piece of propaganda, but understandable given the lowering atmosphere that had settled over the country.

It was just a month before William of Orange that the Duke of Anjou had died, so when Henri III refused the Dutch offer of sovereignty, the Provinces were thrown into a constitutional crisis. The situation was aggravated for them by Philip II entering an alliance with the Sainte Union of the Guise family, promising them regular subsidies at a time when the new heir to the throne of France, Henri of Navarre, was a Protestant. This Franco-Spanish link frightened both the Dutch and the English, yet in the rebel territories provincial particularism was flourishing against a common interest, each province and municipal government feverishly seeking its own advantage. Some suggested they should look to Germany, though there Protestants were Lutherans rather than Calvinists.[12] Others were now contemplating Leicester as an appropriate figure to unite the disparate groups: the view taken by Paulus Buys, Advocate of Holland, and a crucial figure in the coming years.

Another crucial figure, Burghley, was not an enthusiastic interventionist, indeed he regarded the notion with deep mistrust, yet by the summer of 1584 even he was advocating the giving of aid to the Dutch. By the autumn of that year he was advising Elizabeth to bring together all Spain's enemies in an alliance, and she now accepted the view that the apparently imminent collapse of the Dutch made foreign intervention vitally necessary. But the thought that the French might take the lion's share of this duty led to the plausible conclusion that after a Franco-Spanish clash England might be judiciously placed to offer mediation. On 21 March 1585 the Dutch agents in London, Ortel and de Griese, met Leicester and then Burghley, who offered them some comfort. After meeting the Queen the Dutch representatives felt sufficiently comforted to report that if the States-General sent a delegation to negotiate with the Queen, things would go better than they had with

France. This was followed by a meeting between William
Davison, English ambassador to the United Provinces, and the
States-General, at which Davison named Flushing, Brill and
Enkhuisen as towns suitable to be handed over as evidence of
Dutch good faith. Anxious for reasonable terms the States-
General might be, but a delegation did not arrive in England
until June 1585, with instructions to offer Elizabeth what had
been rejected by Henri III. Alternatively, there might be a
protectorate of the Provinces, and in any case Elizabeth had to
be persuaded to provide troops to sustain it. The command
would go to a general of superior status in English society;
someone who could become part of the administration of the
Provinces.

The Dutch delegation came to England in late June, and
notable among them were Johan van Oldenbarnevelt, Jacob
Valcke, Paulus Buys (now serving Utrecht) and Hessel Aijsma.
They were introduced at court by Thomas Sackville, Lord
Buckhurst and William Davison, and on 27 June Davison and
Colonel John Norris took them to the house of Sir Thomas
Bromley for talks with the privy council. Much was revealed by
Burghley's opening comments, and it became clear to all that
establishing terms was not going to be easy. Burghley exploited
Elizabeth's fastidious disinclination to assist rebels of any kind
against a ruling monarch, and he gloomily stressed the cost to
English trade. Elizabeth would not accept sovereignty, only a
protectorate, and her support for the cause was at less than white
heat. As for the cautionary towns, the province of Zeeland was
adamant that Flushing should remain in Dutch hands. Meeting
followed meeting during the summer, both sides inclining to
drive as hard a bargain as possible.

It was the siege of Antwerp that pushed them towards a
provisional treaty. According to this treaty, Elizabeth would
supply and pay for 400 cavalry and 4,000 infantry for three
months up to 22 November.[13] As Paulus Buys was to observe,
Burghley controlled the purse-strings, but Leicester and
Walsingham were strongly pro-Dutch and they had to be
cultivated. Hence Buys gave a dinner for the earl, during
which the broad outlines of Anglo-Dutch co-operation were
established. In the meantime the English relief force was
placed under the command of Sir John Norris, but even before

he could leave for the Provinces, Antwerp had fallen. Marnix St Aldegonde, the governor of the city, signed a treaty with Parma allowing for the payment of a fine of 400,000 guilders, to which the Spanish responded by releasing all prisoners and granting a general amnesty. The result was that many of the Protestant inhabitants of the city removed themselves to Holland, taking their commercial skills with them.

These developments naturally hastened the signing of the main treaty between England and the Provinces, and the ampliation pact signed in August. For the next thirteen years it was to remain 'the basis of relations between England and the Netherlands'.[14] Elizabeth now agreed to support 5,000 infantry and 1,000 cavalry, as well as to provide garrisons for Flushing and Brill, making a total commitment of 6,150 men. However, what was not made clear was whether the main strand of support ran from after 22 November, or whether the provisional agreement was nullified by the replacement treaty.[15] The decision was made, however, that the English forces should be commanded by a 'gentleman of quality' who, together with two English aides, would sit on the Dutch Council of State. Both he and his officials would take oaths of loyalty jointly to the Queen and the States-General. Unfortunately for the whole conduct of this campaign there was no agreement on the role of the governor-general. In Elizabeth's eyes he was not a viceroy, yet for the Dutch viceroy and governor-general 'were virtually synonymous . . . far into the 20th century'.[16]

Although Leicester's name did not appear in the treaty designated as the governor-general, few people can have doubted that he would be chosen. Only Burghley and at first Elizabeth seem to have resisted the idea. Since Leicester worked for Anglo-Dutch solidarity for some ten years, and was highly respected by the Dutch of all classes, it would have been virtually impossible to send anyone other than him. It is true that in the autumn of 1585 Elizabeth veered towards Lord Grey de Wilton, but he was too poor and little known. As a correspondent of Walsingham's wrote in September: 'The coming of the Earl of Leicester into these countries is as much wished for as the death of the Prince of Orange was lamented.'

At this time there were twenty-three companies of English troops in the Provinces: 2,000 infantry raised in consultation with the privy council, and some 1,200 to 1,500 raised for the draft arranged by Norris, who was in command until Leicester arrived.[17] Considerable confusion was caused then (as it is today) by the fact that there were English companies paid for by Elizabeth and others paid for by the States-General. The recruiting and transportation costs were partly met by Elizabeth and partly by Norris himself, although it was expected that these would be paid back by the States. Perhaps the most peculiar and disrupting burden was that which fell on the soldiers themselves, for they had to pay for their own equipment, clothing and food. This was to reduce the burden on the Exchequer at a time when the cost of living in the Provinces was higher than in England. Because of the complexities of the arrangements and the anxiety of both sides to avoid as much of the financial burden as they could, it is no surprise that payment of the English auxiliaries ran into trouble from the beginning.[18]

Leicester's pay as governor-general began on 22 October, and, according to Elizabeth's interpretation of the treaties, payments were to be made by the States-General. She took the same view of payments to Lord Grey, the High Marshal, Errington, Master of Ordnance, and other senior English officers. The Dutch disagreed, claiming that no decision had been made on this point in the treaties, and that salaries were therefore Elizabeth's concern. It was Leicester's anxiety to be doing something constructive that persuaded Sir Roger Williams, the commander of Bergen op Zoom (where the town governor and his Walloon troops were actually pro-Spanish), that the earl's appointment was the occasion for real satisfaction. Certainly the States-General felt relieved when it became clear that the earl had been selected and would arrive later in the year. But there was also some deeply held anxiety that Elizabeth's restricted notion of the governor-general's powers was unworkable. They wanted Leicester to have absolute power in regard to war, and Jacques Rossel pressed this point in letters to Walsingham. In one he wrote: '. . . if the nobleman from her Majesty does not command absolutely, I do not think things will succeed'.[19] It was a prophetic statement.

In November Leicester was still waiting to depart. The situation in the Provinces drifted, with many in Zeeland and Holland now inclining to the view that Philip II would eventually be victorious. Roels, the Pensionary of Zeeland, tried to counter this strain of defeatism by a strong advocacy of English protection, and he wrote to Davison with the hope that Leicester might soon arrive before the propaganda campaign on his behalf petered out. But it was Philip Sidney, now Governor of Flushing, who arrive first. Forced to disembark near Rammekens fort, he then had a three-mile trek across the watery flats that lay between the town and the fort. Sidney's links with the Provinces were so close (through his mentor, Hubert Languet), that it was only Elizabeth's strong opposition which prevented his marriage to the daughter of William of Orange – 'a match that would have made him Lord of Holland and Zeeland'.[20]

With Elizabeth still cavilling about his rank and powers, Leicester wrote to Walsingham on 3 December, just prior to leaving, that he would as soon be dead as go without the necessary authority which the Queen seemed to intend. Yet by now the real pressure of events was too great and on the 5th he wrote more stoically that he would go to do his duty, but that if Elizabeth continued in the same vein she would fatally undermine all that she wanted to achieve. There can be no doubt that Leicester knew her view of the necessary restraints on the English commander, but he still allowed a conjunction of circumstances to push him in the direction he had once so ardently sought. Now he wrote:

> I have taken upon me this voyage not as a desperate and forlorn man, but as one well contented with his place at home and calling as any subject ever was, and my cause was not nor is other than the Lord and the queen. If the queen fail, yet must I trust in the Lord, and on Him I see I am wholly to depend.[21]

The composition of Leicester's army is of particular interest. Already, of course, English forces were serving under Norris. Leicester's reinforcements of 6,150 infantry and 1,000 cavalry were a heterogeneous collection of volunteers, levied men and others drawn in substantial numbers from North Wales and the earl's vast landholdings there. South Wales was represented by the company of conscripts assigned to

Flushing and conducted there by Richard Gwynne, a follower of the Sidneys.[22] Two other Welsh companies were commanded by followers of the earl. Captain William Thomas
had been High Sheriff of Caernarvonshire, as well as an
MP. He and John Nuthall, one of the earl's lawyers, and
an Inner Templar, had made advantageous purchases of
Bardsey Abbey lands, which had been passed on to Leicester.
There was a sad end for the loyal captain and his brother-
in-law, Edward Griffith: both died in the campaign in the
Provinces (Thomas in the clash that eventually killed Philip
Sidney).[23] The Cymric strain in Leicester's forces was rein-
forced by the fact that many of the English officers had
connections with Leicester's Welsh lands, and Leicester could
draw on this reservoir of power and patronage confident that
the Council of the Marches in Wales would defend his
interests. Sir Henry Sidney was President of the Council until
1586, and it has been shown that 'almost all the M.P.'s for
North Wales in the 1584–85 Parliament' served in the
expedition. Few of them were as intellectually committed to
the cause as their leader; they were essentially conservative
and feudal in their service.[24]

Chapter 18

Governor and Captain-General

For the military expedition to the United Provinces Leicester called on all his allies for financial and political aid. Among the large retinue of gentlemen volunteers who accompanied him were his stepson, the Earl of Essex, Lord North, Lord Audley, Sir William Russell, Sir Thomas Sherley, Sir Arthur Bassett, Sir Walter Waller, Sir Gervais Clifton and many more. He also had servants and attendants: two chaplains; a secretary for English correspondence and one for French; two surgeons; and two trumpeters, a drummer and fife-player. On 6 December 1585 he and his closest friends dined with Sir Thomas Lucas at his family home of St John's Abbey near Colchester. While there he told the Vice-Admiral of the Fleet, one of the Borough brothers, that they would sail on the evening of 8 December from Harwich. But arriving early in the morning at the port, he decided to board the incongruously named *Amity* that afternoon to sail for Brill. This led to arguments and the sort of irritation that was to become routine throughout the expedition. Borough for his part believed the destination to be Flushing and hence had provided only one pilot for a routine sailing. Brill, as knowledgeable sailors pointed out, was a very different business altogether, and not a safe anchorage, but Leicester persisted in the face of this expert advice. As he bristled at the delay, towns like Ipswich were scoured for pilots, until he eventually abandoned Brill and accepted Borough's advice.

The fleet of some hundred vessels now sailed on a tide of relief, cheered on by crowds at the quayside. On reaching Flushing during the afternoon of 10 December, Leicester landed to yet more gunfire and ovations. Here he was greeted by Dutch leaders and also Philip Sidney before making a slow, watery progress to Middelburg. The town gave him another enthusiastic welcome with a military parade, and the next day there was a church service in the English church. Later that week the Middelburgers held a celebratory dinner for the earl, to which Louise de Coligny, the widow of William of Orange, had been invited. The civic organizers made it a lavish affair, but chose to hold it in a smaller chamber than could accommodate all the guests. With only one table for the earl and his retinue, the astonished hosts were treated to an unseemly scramble for places by the English. Only after Leicester had ordered many of his countrymen out, could the town dignitaries take their seats.[1]

From Middelburg he sailed to Dordrecht on 17 December; a supposedly brief transfer that was halted for days by fog. Provisions became short and the fleet would have been rather distressed but for local people sending provisions aboard. From the town, and until his eventual arrival in The Hague, Leicester's presence was noted by elaborate ceremonies, some of them very costly. In Delft the whole entertainment, plus the charge for breaking the ice to allow the ships to leave, cost some £5,000.[2] Since by English reckoning Christmas was spent in the town, there was a service for the army, followed by a speech from Leicester to boost their morale.

Early in 1586 Leicester was welcomed to The Hague on behalf of the States-General by Elbertus Leonius.[3] Yet at the same time the States of Holland, probably egged on by Paulus Buys, decided to cut costs by reducing to the minimum the amount to be spent on Leicester's reception. The attack of parsimony was so cramping that they set up a committee to find out what could be bought most cheaply, whereas the townspeople arranged an entry that sat better with the earl's dignity. Indeed, despite the somewhat grudging response of the States of Holland, the earl's arrival was generally regarded with interested relief, because for a decade after the death of Charles IX of France the Dutch had been unable to win over any great power to their cause. The Palatinate had sent an army in 1578, the French Huguenots another. In 1581 another French army arrived with the Duke of Anjou, but all these interventions had failed, as had his lamentable attempt at a coup.[4] Many of the

Dutch leaders now hoped that the treaty terms between England and the Provinces, under which Leicester served, could be broadened very significantly. They felt especially that his powers needed to be increased, whatever the anticipated response from Elizabeth. Even before he arrived, the States-General had declared their intention in a letter sent to all provinces. They very soon carried it out after Leicester's arrival in The Hague: what he was offered was the chance to govern the Provinces and to deal with its civil and military requirements, together with a subsidy of 200,000 florins per month. There is some evidence that this proposal came as no surprise to the earl, although Lord North wrote to Burghley that Leicester was not yet ready to accept it. It seems likely that Burghley and Walsingham were privy to his secret intentions, for as the former wrote to Leicester of Elizabeth: 'I am greatly discouraged with her lack of resolutions.'

After the submission of the draft act of authority which suggested that 'Leicester should be given title and commission as governor and captain-general of the United Provinces', there was widespread agreement in the States-General that Leicester was to have absolute powers in military affairs and the same authority in other matters as his Habsburg predecessors.[5] As it was, Leicester knew precisely what Elizabeth had laid down as to the extent of his powers, but the temptation to expand them at the behest of the Dutch was simply too great. When approached by a delegation that seemed to be proposing to turn him into a Burgundian prince, he moved to Leiden for several weeks of negotiation with Sidney, North, Davison and Dr Bartholomew Clerk, expressing his views. Predictably he objected to the weight given to the Council of State, and he was to be 'absolute' in matters of war. Yet 'in matters of peace and war' (and in the raising of new taxes) he had to seek the approval of the States.[6] The most bizarre clause affirmed that he could not interpret anything in the Treaty of Nonsuch in a way that would infringe the privileges of the Provinces.

Dutch historians have claimed, notwithstanding this last item, that Leicester's powers surpassed those of William of Orange through the title 'Algemeen Landvoogd en Kapitein-Generaal'. As it was, after fasting and prayers in Leiden, he accepted the new agreement. The oath of office was taken before the States-General, Prince Maurice, the younger son of William (his elder brother being held hostage by Philip II), and numerous other dignitaries. Leicester, uneasily conscious of the momentous step he had taken, immediately wrote to Burghley and Walsingham of the pressure under which he had been, which was taken only in view of the peril of the country. Leicester surely felt that as a man on the spot he was a better judge of what was necessary than was the Queen isolated in London. We may say that for perhaps the first time since his pursuit of Mary Tudor, he gambled. His instinct was that Elizabeth would hardly risk the whole enterprise through pique.

He was perhaps fortunate that it was an envoy, William Davison, who had the unenviable task of informing the Queen of Leicester's change in status. The States-General also wrote to her in flattering terms; but this was not to deflect her. Davison was held up by adverse winds and did not in fact sail to England until 14 February. Moreover, since breaking the news to her was so acutely disagreeable, he wanted to do it piecemeal. But he was already too late, for on 5 February someone at the English court had revealed all to a queen noted for her fierce temper at the expense of those who flouted her wishes in domestic and political matters. There now followed a magisterial explosion of wrath that was intensified by her embarrassment that she had already had issued a multilingual pamphlet explaining her motives for intervening in the United Provinces, and disclaiming any territory or authority in the country. Leicester's action now seemed to brand her a liar, and to cap her fury she discovered that Lettice Dudley was preparing to join her husband in his moment of triumph. To indicate her rage the Queen decided to send Sir Thomas Heneage as her messenger to the earl and the States-General, with the famous letter of 14 February:

How contemptuously we conceive ourselves to have been used by you, [for] we could never have imagined . . . that a man raised up by ourself, and extraordinarily favoured by us above any other subject in this land, would have in so contemptible a sort broken our commandment, in a cause that so greatly toucheth us in honour; whereof, although you have showed yourself to make but little accompt, in most undutiful a sort, you may not therefore think that we have so little care of the reparation thereof as we mind to pass so great a wrong in silence unredressed. . . .[7]

Her letter to the States-General was in the same tone, even though Burghley and Walsingham tried to modify its acerbity. They did not know that Elizabeth was trying to formulate a peace, even at this stage, and that the power Leicester had taken severely hampered her efforts.

Perhaps the mortification of Leicester's emissary would have been less keen if the earl himself had wooed Elizabeth for approval, adding some jewelled token to the harsh truth. As it was, her anger scarcely abated over several meetings, despite all the efforts of her ministers to soothe her. Their first material success came when Elizabeth issued a second set of instructions to Heneage, which tempered her immoderate tone. Without this change there is little doubt that Leicester's mission would have collapsed. A bout of bad weather also delayed Heneage; and when he delivered a speech to the States-General, he risked a great deal by altering her tone 'and strained his instructions even further by saying that the English would make no peace with the King of Spain without the consent of the Dutch'.[8] In the circumstances of the moment this was a bold move and, being an honourable man, Heneage revealed what he had done. But his candour was not well received by Elizabeth: 'Do that you are bidden, and leave your considerations for your own affairs . . . think you I will be bound by your speech to make no peace of mine own matters, without their consent. . . .'[9] The tone of outraged incredulity has survived the centuries.

Leicester's state of mind was not helped by Anglo-Dutch arguments on a variety of matters, and he became fiercely concerned about the growing antipathy between Paulus Buys and himself. The new Advocate of Holland, he wrote to Walsingham, 'is a very villain, a dissembler, an atheist, and a practiser to make himself rich and great'. But whatever the protests and counter-protests, the most serious damage to Leicester's position had been caused by the attitude of the Queen. Her response shocked and astounded the States-General. Both that body and Leicester wondered for a time if she had any intention of continuing to support the insurgents, and on 9 March the earl wrote to Walsingham to express his distress at the sufferings of the English soldiers: 'There was no soldier yet able to buy himself a pair of hose, and it is too great shame to see how they go.' A week later he wrote to Burghley of his personal distress, but above all to induce some action to ease the burdens of his men: 'There came no penny of treasure over since my coming hither. That which then came was most part due before it came. There is much due to them. They cannot get a penny; their credit is spent; they perish for want of victuals and clothing in great numbers.'[10]

In England in the meantime Burghley realized that the whole enterprise would very likely collapse if Leicester did not receive support. He therefore defended him by threatening to resign if the current veering in the Queen's policy was not rectified. Leicester's family and friends also rallied round, and even the Countess of Warwick raised a company of soldiers to send. Sidney, then Richard Cavendish, wrote to the Lord Treasurer: 'I find . . . it is a thing almost incredible that the care and diligence of any one man living could in so small a time have so repaired so disjointed and loose estate as my lord found these countries in.'[11] Above all, Cavendish was dismayed by the rumour assiduously put about by the brother of Cardinal Granvelle that Elizabeth was still covertly seeking a peace. The Englishman thought this would be the ruin not only of the Dutch, but of the English as well: he was eloquent in describing the wealth, shipping and commercial prosperity of the Dutch, and the ruin for English commerce if it fell under the complete sway of Spain. Leicester was himself acutely conscious of the necessity of a painful reduction in the continuing trade relations between the Provinces and Spain, but he could do little until the contentious issue of his position had been resolved. In March, in an attempt to pacify his irate monarch, he sent as emissary to London Thomas Vavasour, and Vavasour seems to have contrived a more favourable impression of his master, so that when Ralegh wrote to Leicester on 29 March he was able to report that the earl was her 'sweet Robin' again.

Even so, Hereage and Leicester found that their trials were not quite over, for at the end of April Elizabeth's indignation was reignited. She wrote:

We find it very strange that having received three several letters from you, we heard nothing what had been done touching the matter of most special charge committed unto yourself and to our servant, Sir Thomas Heneage, concerning the qualification in point of title of your late accepted government, knowing how greatly it toucheth us in honour.[12]

At this point Leicester's credit was as stretched as his credibility. Before leaving for the United Provinces he had sold individual estates in Essex to Horatio Palavicino for £2,043, sought a huge loan from the same source, and raised £9,000 by mortgages. Even Palavicino, a highly successful banker and merchant who had come as an immigrant from Genoa, could not of his own resources safely raise more than £5,000, but he promised the earl to organize a syndicate for the remainder. Through his agent, Emanuel van Meteren, various wealthy merchants were approached, and when the London money-market heard of Leicester's needs there was something of a stampede to avoid him. In the end Palavicino had to use all his fiscal muscle to raise £16,000, subscribed by thirty-two individual shares of £500 each, with the Denbigh estates of over 6,000 acres as security.[13] With so much at stake Leicester regarded the food exports by the Hollanders to Parma's armies with bemused incredulity. In his view, the clamour of the Zeelanders against the trade was entirely reasonable.

As an indication of the disfavour into which the Hollanders had fallen with their allies, Leicester now settled his government in Utrecht, the spiritual home of the resistance, entering the town on 1 April. Later, on St George's Day, he wore his Garter robes for a service in the cathedral, attended by the leading citizens as well as fifty halberdiers in scarlet cloaks decorated with purple and white velvet. The prayers were led by John Knewstub using the Book of Common Prayer. It had been suggested that the English should adopt for the time being the form of service customary in the country, but Adrianus Saravia had advised Leicester to retain English usage.[14] After the display of piety Leicester gave a banquet, followed by dancing and exhibitions of vaulting and tumbling. The citizens of the town began to feed him with optimistic thoughts that the situation could be saved, and from the anti-Holland refugees he selected a number of aides, including Jacques Reingould, Daniel de Borchgrave, Gerard Prouninck and Adolf van Meetkerke. Of this clique de Borchgrave was a rarity among the Dutch in that he could speak good English, and Prouninck (confusingly called Deventer) was to become 'the undisputed leader not only of the Leicesterian faction of Utrecht, but of the centralist and pro-English movement in the Netherlands as a whole'.[15] Leicester could defend his unusual choices, even the slippery Reingould, by saying that as administrators and officials they had the sort of experience he required. But this contention was not likely to soothe the northerners, who were far from convinced that these were suitable men.

Despite clandestine diplomatic activity by Elizabeth, Leicester clung to the view that the best way to achieve a peace was by a hard war. To 'set the French King and the King of Spain together by the ears' had long been his ambition, and the first step he took to realize it was to try to relieve the besieged town of Grave in Brabant. Grave, the key to defending the northern provinces, had been successfully relieved before, but now Leicester was forced to borrow extra monies from the Merchant Adventurers in Middelburg before he could begin the task again. At the same time Parma launched a concerted attack on the town, and, although the earl tried diversionary attacks elsewhere, it transpired that he was wasting his time, for Parma ignored these efforts and so secured the surrender of the town. Leicester was dismayed and early in June wrote to Elizabeth to blame 'the lewd villainous dealing of van Hemert, governor of Grave' and some of his captains. More impartial observers blamed Leicester and his military advisers for being outwitted by Parma's tactical sense and his diplomatic skill, for the town surrendered, like so many others, on very favourable terms.[16] Despite cooler counsel Leicester was determined to punish the young nobleman, and van Hemert and two of his captains were found guilty of treason and beheaded.

After this defeat Leicester continued to whistle in the dark, seeking more money from the States-General while declaring that, if he were given the necessary support, he could still win the war quickly. But negotiations for an extraordinary grant of 1.4 million florins dragged on into the summer of 1586, and it was not until 7 July that the Act of Consent was prepared. Even then, payment was delayed and the total contribution of the States, 2.9 million florins, did not solve the financial crisis. Leicester's bold pronouncements sat uneasily with the reality of continuing successes for Parma, the capture of Venloo and Neuss, after which the earl complained peevishly of the poor quality of Dutch soldiers. Now his only thought was to stiffen the resolve of towns like Arnheim, Amersfoort and Rhineberg by placing English garrisons in them. This, however, wasted his numerical advantage over Parma, who had only some 9,000 infantrymen and 3,000 cavalry in the field. It was also a duty the men found so boring and demoralizing that Thomas Digges said that all orders to behave as disciplined soldiers were contemptuously shrugged aside by them.

It is far from certain that the privy council was writing from conviction when they sent Leicester a letter saying that they could not consider the earl's recall during the summer campaign, though they sympathized with his predicament. This was aggravated by Parma, who now laid siege to Rhineberg, where his opponent was the brave and ubiquitous Martin Schenk. Yet Leicester, who was at last in the field with supposedly 3,000 cavalry and 10,000 foot, still felt the army was too ill-prepared for a pitched battle. As Norris bitterly remarked, of the 800 cavalry he was supposed to command, only 200 arrived, and they were poorly equipped. So Leicester tried his luring tactic again by marching on Duisburg, which he captured and which his undisciplined men promptly sacked. Then he pushed on north with a view to capturing Zutphen. It was this move, combined with the sturdy efforts of Schenk, that induced Parma to go to the aid of Zutphen.

The skirmish that took place in autumn fogs from the river was between, on the one side, 550 Englishmen and Welshmen, and some 3,000 Spanish infantry and 1,500 cavalry, on the other. Leicester hesitated to commit all the rest of his force because Parma might have been in the immediate vicinity, and the result was that the Spanish convoy slowly moved towards Zutphen until the gates opened for reinforcements which emerged to drive off the English. The dismay of the English and Welsh soldiers was considerable, especially when it became known that Philip Sidney had taken a musket-ball above the knee, which had shattered his femur. It was a fearful wound and the gallant Sir William Russell broke down in tears on seeing his stricken friend. Leicester now ordered that his nephew should be taken to Arnheim for more complete medical care by Dr John James, his own physician, and nursing by Sidney's wife. Leicester remained hopeful, at least rather fitfully, that not only would Sidney recover but that Zutphen would fall as some sort of compensation. Writing to Heneage of his anguish, the earl said: 'Albeit I must say it was too much loss for me, for this young man was my greatest comfort, next her Majesty, of all the world, and if I could buy his life with all I have to my shirt, I would give it.' But though the fortress commanding the Veleuve was taken, by Edward Stanley, in the last engagement of that year's campaign, Leicester's other passionate hope was not fulfilled. Philip Sidney rallied and then declined, finally dying of gangrene, and it was Lord North who was chosen to accompany the body home to England, where it was laid to rest in the Minories before a State funeral on 16 February the following year. We may note that North had also been shot, but had survived the injury to his knee sustained the night before the battle at Warnsfeld. North had gone out to fight in one boot on hearing that his own son was distinguishing himself in the fray, and both were honoured by Leicester for their bravery. As for the lamenting earl, his only consolation for the terrible loss of a nephew he admired so deeply was a stream of letters of condolence, even Philip II noting with sadness the death of England's marvel and greatest gentleman.

Chapter 19

A Judicial Loving Prince

Within a short time of his arrival in Utrecht 'Leicester found himself, perhaps before he realized what had happened, at the head of a political and religious faction. This was in direct contrast to the manner of his predecessor, William, who had conducted himself as head of the Dutch State.'[1] Having had no hereditary involvement with the Dutch before he was invited to lead the Provinces in war, he lacked the political insights necessary to be a successful leader. Certainly his greatest error was to alienate the powerful burgher regents of Holland and Zeeland whose interests were extravagantly sectional and needed to be modified. His attempts to do so by poorly defined government actions with the support of the Utrecht Populist Party were bound to fail. As it was, the privileged merchant aristocrats began to realize that their choice of a leader had disturbing implications for their own power, and their problem became how to neutralize him without bringing to an end English involvement in the struggle against Spain.

Leicester, on the other hand, did not believe that merchants who beat their breasts and wailed about ruin were necessarily telling the truth. His dissatisfaction with the class was so great that he had wanted to keep them off the Council of State even before he arrived in the Provinces. He gained confidence in his view from the approaches of ordinary people whose antipathy to the rich merchant class equalled his own. Leicester's trade decree banning business with the enemy was a major act of policy, and it was one that provoked fierce and sustained opposition from the rich burghers. Those in Holland and Zeeland saw their prosperity cut off at a stroke, while they argued that the war could be continued only if they financed it from their profits. They were also uneasy at the thought of the ban failing to curb English, French or German traders who would benefit accordingly. The trade decree was submitted to the States of Holland for comments, but before they could make any reply Leicester had decided to enforce it. Legally he could ignore them and the Council of State as well if he chose, but the 'trade decree did more to alienate the governmental leaders of Holland and Zeeland than did anything else'.[2]

If Leicester's ban on trade had worked efficiently the revenue for continuing the war would have come from sacrificed resources, especially those of the rich. To co-ordinate financial administration he wanted a Council of Finance, and this was established in July 1586. One of the reasons that expenditure on the war exceeded revenue, and the rich stayed rich at the expense of Leicester and his famished army, was that so much revenue stuck to the fingers of those who collected it; general funds were scandalously ill-administered by Holland.[3] Leicester and his advisers wanted to take the radical step of replacing tax farming by direct taxation, and they also wanted to reform government landholdings as well as to set up an inspection system for the accounts of agents and merchants. To put this bold strategy into operation the Council of State had to be relieved of these duties by a Council of Finance.

If he was somewhat dilatory in the field, Leicester was quite swift-moving when it came to these reforms. The result was that he antagonized the Dutch members of the Council of State, notably Buys and Valcke, and also William Bardesius. After preliminary discussions, the earl decided to ignore their views and went ahead with choosing the members for the Council of Finance: the Count of Nieuwenaar, Sir Henry Killigrew and the Lord of Brakel from the Utrecht Populist Party. Reingould became the treasurer and de Borchgrave the auditor, with Buys, Joust Tielinck and Sebastian van Loosen as its clerks. Unfortunately the mixture was combustible, for Buys disliked and distrusted Reingould so fervently that he refused to work as an underling. From England Walsingham wrote cautioning his colleague against Reingould, and Leicester's brother wrote of the need to 'heed whom you trust, for you have some false boys about you'. The man who caused such unease had once served

Requesens, and had then proposed centralized finances for the Provinces – a view that the Spanish governor had rejected as too contentious.[4]

Reingould's fall from power was the result of indiscretions by one of his associates, Stephen Paret, who was arrested in August 1586 for making unflattering statements about the government. When Paret's private papers were seized, it became clear that he and Reingould were organizing a system whereby State revenues were filched, and they were also auctioning off public appointments. Since Leicester was in the field, both accused and accusers raced to him to state their respective cases, the delegation from the States of Holland arriving first. This was not necessarily an advantage, for, like many stubborn men working under great strain, Leicester was inclined to listen to those who got his ear last, rather than those who possessed clear facts. The representatives of Holland claimed that the activities of Paret and Reingould threatened not only the security of the Provinces, but could mutilate the Anglo-Dutch accords. Their actions seemed treasonable. Leicester's response was to temporize, for in attacking Reingould and Paret they seemed to be attacking him, and he promised to investigate the matter thoroughly.[5] Reingould's ploy was to deny all, and to throw himself on the mercy of a 'judicial loving Prince'.[6] He certainly knew his man, for despite substantial confirmatory evidence of Reingould's guilt, the earl refused to act, and the sometime treasurer retired to Flushing ready for a fast escape if this should become necessary. In the event, he was never brought to trial, though Paret spent some time in prison before being released the following year.

Like many men beset with problems Leicester was inclined to transfer blame for failure on to a convenient scapegoat, in this case the States-General. He had written to Burghley: 'The people I still find best devoted to her Majesty. . . . They still pray God that her Majesty will be their sovereign . . . but to the States they will never return . . . there is such mislike against the States universally.' Yet it was during this period that the States-General increased their powers, though Leicester argued that as delegates from the Provinces they were not representative of anyone but themselves. He saw them as standing for a small, self-renewing oligarchy with aristocratic attachments. Nor was he pleased when, on 22 July, they submitted a list of grievances: musters were not accurately kept; the captains of towns usurped the jurisdiction of the magistrates; the chamber of finances was 'addressed of some odious and evil persons'. Nor was it only the Dutch enemies of Reingould who regarded him with contempt. Sir Thomas Wilkes, a lawyer whom Elizabeth had sent to the Provinces as her independent observer, and who had then joined the Council of State at Leicester's insistence, was at one with Oldenbarnevelt's view of the man. At the same time Oldenbarnevelt was concerned that a commander like Leicester, assailed on all sides, might suddenly round up all those who criticized him and have them executed. Already during the summer Buys had been arrested and imprisoned by the Utrecht militia, and Leicester's participation in the action was generally assumed, although he denied it.

On 27 August the earl invited Oldenbarnevelt to Utrecht for talks on financing the autumn campaign, which was to cost Philip Sidney his life. There was as ever a calamitous shortage of money, for Wilkes did not return from England with £30,000 until the end of October. In the interim funds could come only from the Dutch and even Leicester could not risk arresting Oldenbarnevelt. But with the example of Buys to ponder, the Dutch lawyer was deeply suspicious, and in fairness to Leicester it needs to be recalled that neither Oldenbarnevelt nor for that matter the States of Holland had absolute authority to speak for the great mass of ordinary people. They were trying to live through a time of dislocation, and while Leicester's actions alienated many, others continued to see him as a bulwark against collaborators and the very successful armies of Parma. Leicester's adherents in Utrecht and Friesland were notably loyal, and even pressed him in November 1586 to be more authoritarian in an attempt to curb the rash sectionalism of Holland and Zeeland. They were also dismayed when the States of Holland sought the exclusion of Prouninck (Deventer), the delegate of Utrecht, from the States-General. In mid-November, the States of Holland, now his most persistent corporate critic, presented a long list of grievances to Leicester while he was in The Hague. Interestingly the earl did not brush aside the fifteen items as he might have done six months before, and on 12 November he met representatives of the States of Holland,

Zeeland and Friesland, including Oldenbarnevelt.

By now, of course, Leicester longed to return to England, having reiterated so often his view that nothing was to be achieved if his army remained as badly equipped and paid as it was, with frequent desertions because the enemy offered better conditions and treatment. Apparently, when he did finally announce that he would be returning to England, the Council of State scarcely bothered with an expression of polite regret. By a curious irony it was the representatives of the States-General who expressed their dismay and asked that he should overlook any past hints of incivility. Did they really mean him to stay? Or were they simply terrified that he might angrily denounce them to Elizabeth, and that she, relieved, might leave them to their fate? Shortly after his return to England, the States-General wrote to the Queen in praise of her support for their struggle, and the active involvement of her personal representative who had hazarded life and fortune. It seems they simply could not envisage a successful conclusion to the war without English aid. Evidently Leicester's view now was that the best solution would be for England to annex the Provinces and henceforth take on a greater load.[7]

When Elizabeth agreed to his return to England, Leicester moved from The Hague to Flushing with an alacrity he had rarely shown in the field. He sailed on 4 December and arrived in time to dine with Elizabeth the following day. In the absence of Leicester, which was meant to be temporary, Oldenbarnevelt decided to make moves that would significantly reduce Leicester's power, and he was helped by the arrangements the earl had made for government. With hindsight it seems that the earl had opted for a plan of government almost guaranteed to cause dissension, for he chose to delegate most of his power to the Council of State, leaving Count Hohenlohe to command the Dutch forces and Sir John Norris the English armies. Furthermore, he instructed the Council of State to do nothing that infringed his previous decisions, which soon led to the discovery that effective government was wellnigh impossible in his absence. The absurd situation created by these provisions became apparent so quickly that the Council actually asked Elizabeth that he should return quickly because they lacked the power to act and govern. Some members of the Council cast about for a replacement and wondered if Hohenlohe would be suitable, and Wilkes wrote to Leicester to indicate how much he too wanted to be recalled. Odenbarnevelt's option was to promote the position of Prince Maurice of Orange, and his bodyguard was now raised beyond the figure laid down by Leicester. He was also named Captain-General of Holland and Zeeland.[8]

Not surprisingly the invitation that Leicester sent to Prince Maurice to visit England was spurned by Oldenbarnevelt, who wanted the young man firmly under his tutelage as the woeful condition of the country became obvious to all. Early in 1587 the Council of State wrote to Leicester saying that 'respect and obedience are much diminished by the act restraining our authority'. Worse was to come with the betrayal of the town of Deventer by Sir William Stanley and the fortifications at Zutphen by Sir Rowland Yorke. Both were apparently now Catholic sympathizers who were induced to sell their honour, and late in January 1587 Wilkes wrote to all the leading councillors at home of the opprobrium heaped on loyal Englishmen for these mercenary acts: 'By this dishonour we are all grown hateful to this people. . . . Unless her Majesty sends better succours and a person to command with better method and discretion, they must be wholly lost or seek to the Spaniard for peace.'[9]

The sense of betrayal was perhaps greatest amongst those who had looked on Leicester as a potential saviour, for it was surely his lofty refusal to listen to advice that left the renegades in positions of some authority. The view spread among the Dutch that all Englishmen were venal rogues, and for some time English troops found it uncomfortable to appear in the streets or in markets. At the same time, Leicester, despite his dismay at the betrayals, was still recording his fury at the attitude of the States-General. On 21 January he wrote to Jean Hotman:

I understand how badly the States have dealt with me since my departure thence in giving out such reports of my returning home with so great riches from them, as they themselves cannot but know to be most untrue. For they know that I never received of them but £3,400, neither have I had yet that which was due to me by them. And I spent there of mine own purse above £35,000, and it is very well known that I brought not away £300 with me from Flushing at my coming thence. . . . And this you may boldly justify to be true in all places whatsoever you shall hear the contrary . . . that their ingrate dealing with me may be known and reported openly.[10]

Yet for all the symptoms of an irreversible alienation, much of the animosity was fleeting, and Wilkes reported on the loyalty of the ordinary people to Elizabeth. Indeed, shortly after the loss of Deventer, an embassy came from the Provinces to London for talks, intending to press the view that all might be redeemed if, as Leicester advised, the Queen assumed direct responsiblity for her allies. Their first meeting with the Queen took place on 5 February, but soon after this she was able to respond by showing them a letter of such unflattering opinions instigated by Oldenbarnevelt that the envoys could only show red faces. Their requests for more money were given a chilly response, and by mid-February they knew she had no intention of doling out more cash. Leicester managed to persuade them to remain in England a little longer in the hope of parliamentary intervention following the long sought execution of Mary Queen of Scots. But they regretted their lingering when Sir Roger Williams reported on the unsatisfactory behaviour of the States-General in Leicester's absence. The envoys retreated into diplomatic evasions, and Elizabeth now decided to send an opponent of the war, Thomas, Lord Buckhurst, secretly to test the Dutch about peace negotiations.

Leicester again wrote to Hotman on 10 March: 'My Lord of Buckhurst doth presently come over [and] I do send Atye over with my lord, by whom ye shall understand further, and do ye also inform him of all things fit for this service.'[11] Even as the issues were probed again on both sides Leicester was preparing himself to return to the Provinces, although he was acutely uncomfortable from a bout of the 'stone'. He stated modestly that, if he were required, he would go 'to adventure for God and his prince what he would not for any earthly good'. In the meantime it was Wilkes and Oldenbarnevelt who clashed, the former defending Leicester against the claim that the sovereign power resided with the States-General. In rebuttal, Oldenbarnevelt and Francken, the Pensionary of Gouda, prepared a memorandum, but before the States of Holland could consider it, on 3 April Buckhurst arrived at Flushing. He had been preceded by the Dutch envoys who had raced back from London to report to the States-General at The Hague before favouring the Council of State with a declaration on what they had achieved in their talks.

Chapter 20

My Poor Estate

While the statesmen exchanged various constitutional analyses the war continued in its spasmodic and muffled way. As always it was money that caused the greatest dissension, and both Wilkes and Norris protested vigorously when the States-General made the extraordinary decision to reduce expenditure. This could be done only by disbanding some of their forces, and so twelve companies of cavalry and forty-eight of infantry were paid off as they unilaterally decided to halve the English companies in their pay. It was fortunate that Parma was also hard pressed and it was winter, so that a substantial part of his army had been sent to quarters in Bimburg and Luxemburg, where they stayed for lack of forage until May 1587.

Sir John Conway wrote to Burghley with a vivid clarity: 'This country is subject to much sickness. If a hundred soldiers fall sick, there doth not forty escape. It is impossible for a sickness or a hurt of danger to be healed with no diet but hard cheese.' Wilkes was quite convinced that the lack of pay was as crucial as the quite dreadful quality of the officers 'who for the most part are either such as never served before and have no judgement of how to rule themselves, and such as make their profit of the poor soldier, so extremely are they hateful to the companies.[1] Leicester himself had known the truth behind the little aphorism of Barnaby Rich that 'A hungry man can neither observe discipline, nor perform any great enterprise.'[2] He had also wisely realized 'that the delay of one month's pay loses her Majesty little less than half a month's pay, which with due pay at every month might be saved'.[3] He was given sterling support for his efforts by Thomas Digges, who was execrated by certain of Leicester's officers when they were not able to pocket the wages of the runaways or the dead.

Buckhurst was well aware of the scale of the problems even before he arrived in the Provinces. Moreover, although he seems to have thought that Leicester should have done more to remedy the situation, he was now required by his queen to prepare for the return of the man in whom he had little confidence. His secret instructions dealt with the possibility of luring the Dutch into peace negotiations, and while on a progress of the country he delivered a set speech outlining the loving concern of Elizabeth for the Dutch cause. His skill at dissimulation seems to have been successful and Wilkes wrote to London along those lines, with perhaps at the back of his mind the thought that at last here was a possible successor to Leicester. Certainly it was on Wilkes's advice that Buckhurst became friendly with Buys, who had been released from prison after Leicester's departure for England. Therefore it was not to the envoy's liking when he had to deliver to the States-General a list in Latin of the injuries done to the Queen's subjects, and above all to Leicester. This was read aloud on 14 April to the assembled representatives, and Arthur Atey accompanied Buckhurst.

Elizabeth would tolerate nothing less than the reading of the entire forty-two grievances, but Buckhurst set to work to soften Tudor asperities, and swiftly accepted the counter-views put forward by Menijn, affirming his 'complete satisfaction, in respect of her Majesty, his Excellency and the English nation'.[4] While this may have soothed the States, Buckhurst now managed to anger the Queen when he boldly suggested a loan of £50,000 to the Provinces rather than the payment of two-thirds of the extraordinary cost of the war which the States had requested. On 3 May he received a pointed reply from Elizabeth: '. . . we marvel at your preferring such a request, being not ignorant how greatly we stand charged otherwise, and how unable we are to furnish such a sum, over and above our ordinary contribution, for your duty was to dissuade them from propounding so unreasonable a demand. . . .'[5]

Buckhurst's most particular preoccupation was to make light of Elizabeth's obsessive interest in peace negotiations. But Parma's difficulties and his hints about the desirability of a respite made her eager to rush forward a compromise – that

Philip II's subjects in the Provinces would remain Calvinists but would disguise their doctrinal differences with the Catholic Church. Buckhurst was extremely sceptical about the practicality of this proposal, and even as he revealed the peace moves he undermined them by urging the rebels to maintain a high level of military action with a field army, to be maintained for three months. This earned him another rebuke from Elizabeth.

Leicester's attitude at this time fluctuated as he talked to colleagues and read the correspondence between London and the Provinces. But he was quite clear that Buckhurst, Wilkes, Norris and the reconstructed Council of State were neglecting his interests and dignity. Added to which he was suffering from a depletion of his physical powers, for he was now overweight and short of breath, symptoms that even spa waters at Bath and Buxton could not reverse. By late May Walsingham felt that the Queen was inclining towards Norris as the replacement for the earl, while the latter stated firmly that he was ready to do what she wanted but that he flatly refused to return if money and troops were not available in greater quantities. Leicester's own financial resources were shrinking, for in the same month he begged the Queen to release him from his burden of debt to five mortgagees who had loaned him some £5,800.

Other privy councillors also pressed the Queen to increase the sums spent on the war. Walsingham in a letter to Buckhurst seemed to feel that Leicester was beginning to achieve some change by his show of reluctance, and his disinclination to return was modified when the Queen agreed to limit his service to three months. From Wanstead Leicester wrote to Walsingham: 'I pray you, help me to know her Majesty's full resolution and pleasure for my going over, because it doth greatly concern my poor estate.'[6] The final decision seems to have been made at the end of May, though the news did not reach The Hague until several weeks later. Burghley and Walsingham seem to have played a significant part in the discussions, for whatever their reservations about their colleague's military and political aptitudes, they saw that Anglo-Dutch resistance needed a leader, and he was a useful catalyst in holding the squabbling allies together in a rather ramshackle way.

Since Leicester had stated so fiercely his determination never to serve again with Norris, the latter was conveniently shifted to another colonial war – the one in Ireland. Now Buckhurst and Wilkes also became superfluous, and the former returned to England with a letter from Oldenbarnevelt to the Dutch legation in London which was bitterly critical of the earl, probably in an attempt to curtail his return. But return he did, with the key question unanswered: was he now subordinate to the States-General? He did invite them to a meeting but they made no effort to accommodate him, and on top of this spiralling political ambivalence he had a military crisis on his hands. It was imperative that Sluys be relieved, while at the same time Elizabeth expected some advance on the peace front and the participation of the States-General. The earl might have been able to achieve something significant had his secretary Francis du Jon (Junius) not revealed to everyone in the Provinces Leicester's confident expectation that he would be received back on terms that did not diminish his authority. Oldenbarnevelt seized upon this with something akin to joy and, with the connivance of the other members of the States of Holland, Junius was arrested. The papers containing Leicester's secret instructions to his secretary showed that the governor-general would still be a populist. The Dutch complained as speedily as possible to Buckhurst, who before his own return to London thoughtfully chose Wilkes as his emissary when the latter showed his nervous disinclination to meet the earl face to face.

The military situation in the Provinces when Leicester returned was as bad as ever. Like everyone else's, Parma's armies had virtually starved during the winter of 1586-7, and Parma now began an offensive aimed to capture towns and their vital food supplies. He also benefited from Leicester's absence, as a number of ports remained open and supplies were shipped from France, Holland and Zeeland. On 12 June Parma began the siege of Sluys, and Sir Roger Williams moved from Ostend to aid the town. What he faced was Parma's forces of some 6,000 infantry and 2,000 cavalry as well as the famous battering train of thirty heavy guns. These last Parma very nearly lost when raiders came out from Sluys, catching the guns on the river and driving off the escort; only the arrival of Spanish reinforcements prevented a notable (and much needed) victory. Then, although Williams squeezed into Sluys, he must have found it distinctly uncomfortable, for by late June Parma had captured a fort that allowed him to bombard the town.

Leicester had arrived in Zeeland on 6 July with 4,500 new recruits, of whom 1,500 were meant to be at the States' charge. But his immediate problem was to provide for the pathetically untrained and ill-equipped recruits. Even before sailing he had written to the States-General to have ready food and armour, and this they failed to provide. Consequently he now had to send back to England for pikes, spades, shovels and billhooks; weeks later his companies were only sketchily armed. The airy indifference of the Dutch to the fate of Sluys was merely increased by the recall of Norris and, having saved 200,000 florins in extraordinary contributions, they chose to pay the German cavalry of Count Mors. Only on 13 July did they vote 100,000 florins for the relief of Sluys, of which a fraction was handed over. Leicester wrote to Walsingham that 'nothing is to be gotten but for money, how little money we have and how little assistance that States as yet afford us. I hope you will use all your furtherance for the speedy sending of money'.[7] The postscript in Leicester's own hand says: 'Ye must make the more haste for to send money; for I have dealt with our merchants here and by no means can they, as they say, furnish the treasurer with £3,000. It is high time to look to ye trade, if your merchants decay and others also.'[8]

Leicester had two options left: to make a direct attack on Parma's trenches, or a relief attack from the sea. Parma had foreseen this last possibility and had done his best to make it impossible, but the sea defences were not strong and a gallant Dutch sailor called van Trappen actually swam into Sluys to gather the latest information. He returned safely from this admirable exploit and gave the news that the defenders of the town had a safe spot prepared for relief ships. This was vehemently denied by another sailor called Drogue, who, less the first letter of his name, would have been accurately designated. As it was, the relieving Dutch ships gathered before the town on 20 July and then dispersed when bad weather threatened. Six days later the demoralized town, short on powder, had surrendered, and van Trappen's story was confirmed.

The English regarded the loss of the town as a calamity, and

Leicester brooded on the event in a bout of aggrieved dismay, not hesitating to blame the Dutch. He was probably correct to do so because it does seem that the States-General sacrificed the town in order to prompt Elizabeth to be more generous with subsidies. The cynical argument was that a port in Spanish hands would be an excellent guarantee of continued English involvement in the struggle. Leicester's agitation was increased by the fact that the accumulation of disasters reduced his power and prestige in England as his opponents exploited his absence. His ire was exacerbated when Dutch officers from Sluys blamed the Zeeland naval command and the regent burghers of Holland. They wanted Leicester to attempt a coup and rule directly; but, with the knowledge that Anjou had failed, Leicester sagely put that idea aside and instead called for a meeting at Dort between himself and the States-General. But because he could not coerce them into attending, his visit to the town with a huge retinue proved a waste of time. The States-General strongly suspected that he had a coup in mind, but more accurately we may say that with his patience and money scattered over the land he longed again to return to England. The more conciliatory members of the States, like Menijn, were aware of his feelings, and the Dutch politican contrived the so-called 'Act of Satisfaction', which was passed to the earl on 6 August. Leicester was promised their high regard 'that it may please you to unite your Excellency with the said States-General and to keep them in mutual love and unbreakable accord'.[9] Even if this pronouncement was genuine, Leicester was not in the right frame of mind to use it to his advantage. On 12 August he wrote again to Walsingham: 'Ye may see what case we poor men are in that serve in such absent places. We had need of friends, when we travail day and night, hazard honour, life and all and yet subject to hard conceits. . . .'[10]

Under pressure from Elizabeth to promote peace talks, and from Oldenbarnevelt as well as Parma, who exploited these divisions, Leicester wrote miserably to the privy council on 22 August that 'our soldiers come away daily to the enemy; he giveth them passports, wherewith they go to Calais and so into England'.[11] No wonder that on 27 August he recorded that 'this place hath almost brought me into sickness'.[12]

On 2 September Menijn and Valcke, two of Leicester's

faction, delivered an important message to the States of Holland from the earl. It had something of the flavour of an ultimatum, for Leicester said that as things stood, without money and equipment, it was impossible to continue the struggle against Spain. No further subsidy from England could be expected, and he declared that in the circumstances, however distasteful it might be to him personally, perhaps they should begin peace negotiations. Here was a reversal indeed! The effect was to galvanize the States-General at last and on 8 September they passed a resolution to confirm his authority, while promising more aid to stem the deteriorating military situation.

Although he could achieve nothing by it, Leicester began another tour of the country. The whole effort seemed a pathetic parody of his triumphant tour made some eighteen months earlier, and by redeploying his ravaged army at the same time he created ripples of panic amongst allies and enemies alike. When his troops arrived in Dordrecht all the deputies of Zeeland and Gouda fled, while the placing of his new recruits at Delfshaven and Maashuis created such a storm in Holland that a revolt against him seemed imminent. Oldenbarnevelt intervened at this point and sent two henchmen to meet the earl whose resentment and wrath boiled over; he would find his authority in the will of the people of the Provinces, for the States-General were their servants. Nothing illustrates Leicester's pained, exasperated state of mind better than a letter he wrote to Walsingham from The Hague on 16 September:

> I have received by Page the post a letter from you and withall a safe conduct for ye King of Denmark's commissioners but you neither write why or wherefore you send it to me, nor any word of it more than that you send me such a safe conduct; I am utterly ignorant of anything intended to the King of Denmark; and if it be about any treaty with ye duke of Parma I trust it is not meant to use me as any commissioner; for it is most true there is no man more unfit, as is well known to both our counsellors here, that they have me in ye greatest jealousy in the world. . . . For my own part I am even heartily weary of my generalship, for there is no comfort in taking charge where the poor soldier is not more certainly provided for. . . . [13]

Meanwhile the stir caused by his army's movements continued, and the day after his meeting with Oldenbarnevelt's representatives, the earl published an explanation that seemed to contain a threat. If the States-General would not sanction the powers that he had held from 1585 to 1586, 'I shall need to preserve the honour of her Majesty and myself, again to protest, if any loss or hardship occurs, that the blame and shame should not be given to her Majesty nor to me, but to those who are showing such dishonour, and discourtesy to her Majesty.'[14] Warned by his agents Oldenbarnevelt fled from The Hague to Delft, and he also manoeuvred to keep Prince Maurice out of Leicester's fold as the earl's forces threatened to disintegrate. The States-General now acted to withdraw from his command all their forces in Holland and Zeeland as well as discharging any English companies in their pay.[15]

The final embarrassment for Leicester came from Leiden. Early in October Colonel Cosmo de Pescarengis, a Piedmontese former pawnbroker in the town, who was in charge of a company of disaffected veterans from the siege of Sluys, made plans with various prominent figures, including Adrianus Saravia, professor of theology at the university, Christian van der Wouve, and Nicolas de Maulde, who commanded another company, to seize the town. It cannot be proved that Leicester was directly involved, yet like everything else associated with his time in the Provinces it failed when betrayed to the Leiden magistrates by Andrew Schott. Pescarengis was arrested, but Leicester's great supporter Saravia managed to escape to England, where he obtained various preferments in the Church. The young de Maulde was also seized, and the States of Holland meeting in Delft required Leicester to keep out of Leiden. Conviction for the conspirators was certain, since Prince Maurice, Oldenbarnevelt and his brother were among the judges. The executions having been carried out, Oldenbarnevelt returned to The Hague, another positive sign that Leicester's rule was ending.

At this point Elizabeth decided to send her Master of Requests, John Herbert, on a mission to advocate the cause of peace. Leicester meanwhile moved from Utrecht to Dordrecht and then to Flushing to await recall. Herbert reached Flushing on 16 November, and Leicester's military command, which had been such a torment to him, passed to Lord Willoughby. Even now, Leicester practised one small face-saving exercise: he decided to hold back, without reference to anyone, Willoughby's patent of office until he himself had returned to English soil. Thus Leicester's involvement in the struggle for freedom of the Dutch people ended on the quibbling sort of note that had been the hallmark of the wretchedly misconceived venture.

With hindsight we can see that Leicester was woefully ill-chosen for the task of reconciling a queen who wanted peace with factious rebels who harried her greatest enemy. Age and life at court had taken the edge from Leicester's bellicosity, and he had not fought in battle for some thirty years. In addition, he was not used to individual command and the multiplicity of problems that the special circumstances of the Provinces presented. He was also singularly unfortunate in his choice of associates; at home in the administration of his affairs he was so much better served. In the English army, however, there were those who were courageous and loyal, like Sir William Pelham who died late in 1587 as a result of a wound sustained in the trenches before Duisburg. He was shot in the stomach as Leicester stood immediately behind him and thus saved the earl from the musket-ball. The earl also had the ungrudging aid of Lord North, who first served under Captain Reade as a private soldier; the same captain whom Leicester thought 'worth his weight in pearl'. When the governorship of Brill fell vacant, Leicester wanted it to be given to North, yet he was overruled and the appointment went to Lord Burgh.[16]

Yet for all the individual gallantry of its officers and men, Leicester's army seems to have been permanently on the brink of disintegration, assailed by sickness, starvation and desertion. Like all commanders of the time the earl adopted the tactic of executing several deserters to discourage others, and he wrote to the privy council pressing them to demand vigilance from the coastal authorities so that stragglers who actually reached England could be severely punished. It has been said that Leicester's disciplinary code was 'one of the most comprehensive of the reign'.[17] Apart from the peroration on the virtues of justice and discipline, together with a number of military articles, there was also a section to cover the spiritual life of the army, since many viewed this as a kind of crusade against Catholicism. To establish the tone it was stated 'that all men will proceed to divine service when summoned by the sound of trumpet or drum, unless they are sick or on special duty'.

Lacking wide and continuous experience in the field, Leicester overestimated Spanish strength. A number of his contemporaries like Bingham and Williams were far less impressed, having had more recent service in the armies against which they now fought. Williams believed in the superiority of the English and the Dutch, given the right leaders or leader. Although he supported Leicester at first, his disillusionment with his commander's military and diplomatic tactics grew. Yet however inadequate Leicester was as a general, the fact remains that Parma, despite his tactical brilliance, could not finish the task of defeating the squabbling allies. The crowning irony is that Leicester did effect one piece of organization in marine matters that was highly beneficial to the Dutch. For a cumbersome administrative policy that had served hitherto he substituted three marine bodies: at Hoorn in Zeeland, Rotterdam in Holland and Veere in West Friesland. They were made directly responsible to the supreme commander, and, despite some criticism of this centralization, the move does seem to have been useful and practical.[18]

Leicester returned to England acutely aware that his public reputation and influence had plummeted. He left the United Provinces with only a rueful medal struck on his own orders to mark his departure; it showed a mastiff guarding sheep and bore the motto *Non gregem sed ingratos invitus desero*. Stung, the Dutch responded with a medal showing an ape in the act of smothering her young; the reverse shows a man falling into a fire as he resists the smoke, and the motto reads *Fugiens fumum, incidit in ignum*. Now in his mid-fifties, periodically ailing and emotionally stunned, Leicester was too sluggish to respond to devious allies and aggressive enemies. Only Buckhurst seems to have contemplated one move that might have brought benefits to the allies: the employment of Leicester as political governor, the command of the army being left to Williams or Norris. Even they might have been swamped when what the English army required was the reorganizing genius of an Oliver Cromwell.

Chapter 21

Sudden Hurly-burlies

Returning chastened to England, Leicester slipped back into his familiar roles of courtier and councillor. His overriding concerns were for the coming war and his finances, for he was desperate to restore some strength to his private fortune. One plan was for the Queen to confiscate Church land for him valued at £2,000 per annum, to be abstracted from vacant sees. But when this failed he put forward a modified scheme, which lapsed only when he died.[1] In the meantime he battled gamely with Burghley for the wardship of the late Earl of Rutland's children, both being supervisors of the earl's will, but as Master of the Court of Wards Burghley held him off.[2]

Leicester surely viewed with contempt a conciliar commission formed in January 1588 to treat with Philip II's representatives at Bourbourg, especially if he read Sir James Croft's hope for 'a most honourable and firm peace'. But then Croft seems to have been prepared to antagonize the earl by scornfully noting the seizure of Spanish treasure by Drake, who was an ally of Leicester. (A Spanish bribe to Croft probably encouraged him.) But his ardour for peace earned him a reproof from Elizabeth when, late in April, he left his colleagues for an independent mission to Bruges to meet Parma. This solo effort was disavowed by the Queen, who generously attributed it to 'some over zeal'. However, when Croft returned to England he was commanded to appear before the privy council to explain his actions, despite assurances Elizabeth had given that he had her forgiveness. And when he ended up in the Tower, informed opinion held that Leicester was certainly behind it.[3]

As lord lieutenant of a number of counties, Leicester was at this time perusing returns on the horse musters, which provided facts of particular interest to the ex-Master of the Horse who had relinquished this cherished office to his stepson. The privy council was not impressed by many of those submitted, so officers of the bands were pressed to have men trained and prepared. The problem was as usual that errors and discrepancies had to be corrected by individuals who, too weighed down with administrative burdens, tended to get trapped by minutiae. Thus, as the great crisis of the summer of 1588 gathered momentum, the justices of the peace of Staffordshire wrote to the Earl of Essex requesting him to ask Leicester if they could supply oxen rather than sheep to the household. In April the justices in Dorset wrote to Leicester to complain of the activities of purveyors, and they even sent two representatives to treat with him, saying they would rather pay cash than supply provisions. As late as July, the justices of Huntingdon, rather distant from the great alarms of the south-east of England, wrote complaining of the difficulties of supplying sheep and cattle and asking that they should be allowed to substitute fowls.

As the Armada gathered at Corunna, Sir Henry Gray and Sir Thomas Mildmay wrote to Leicester that the forces of Essex had been assembled, with gentlemen of the county supplying thirty-eight horseman and ninety-four foot soldiers. They requested an allowance for Mr Twiddy, the Provost-Marshal, and also advice on the raising of 2,000 men of the trained bands to act as the Queen's bodyguard. On 24 July Leicester wrote to Walsingham of the problem of reducing the trained bands to manageable proportions so that the bodyguard could be created. By this time, as fragmentary news came in of the engagement of the Armada fleet and the English fleet off Portland, Leicester was Lieutenant and Captain-General of the Queen's Armies and Companies. A resounding title, but one that left him free to organize the great Tilbury camp, and to oversee defence in the south-east of England. On 22 July he had written from his London home to Walsingham of a conversation he had had with Peter Pett about lighters, and a chain on the Thames at the camp which he thought needed strengthening with masts. The finished boom of masts, chains and cables cost £305. 19*s*. 5*d*. The earl and Pett had gone down the river to view the preparations, and on 23 July he wrote again to his friend and ally about the vulnerability of these estuary defences, and requested more powder, ordnance and shovels. The next day he was in Tilbury, which he judged more vulnerable than Gravesend, and he scribbled a note to the council that he intended to send someone to put the south coast in arms. Furthermore, he was dissatisfied that he held only the commission of lieutenant for Essex, which he thought inadequate, especially if there was a landing in Kent or Suffolk, and his commission was then modified and forwarded to him at Gravesend.

On the evening of 24 July Leicester wrote again to Walsingham that they had received news of English advantages in the sea battle which was spasmodically raging at this time. He did not recommend that the 4,000 infantry in the Tilbury camp should yet be disbanded, and he was now anxious to see the return to the camp of Norris and Williams, who did in fact arrive back from Dover on the 26th. Only now did it become clear that the camp itself was desperately under-provided with food and drink, especially beer and bread. Leicester, ever concerned about the fighting man, was incensed. 'I did two whole days before the coming of these make proclamation in all market towns for victuals to come to the place where the soldiers should encamp and to receive ready money for it, and there is not one victualler come in to this hour.' The men in the camp were 'forward and willing men as ever I saw', so the earl ordered 100 tuns of beer and sent notice that reinforcements marching from London should stop where they were unless they carried provisions of their own. As he noted, 'great dilatory wants are found upon all sudden hurly-burlies', and then supplies began to arrive, but only at excessive prices. A proclamation was made on 7 August, fixing the rates. It was this schedule that laid down that every man who was paid 8*d*. per day should have a meal costing 3*d*. – dinner or supper of bread and beer, and on fish days, salt fish or ling, eggs and butter peas or beans.

After 27 July, when 'the Spaniards went always before the English . . . like sheep', there were constant arrivals in the camp until the maximum numbers were reached on 1 August. The statement of account of pay shows that there were twenty-seven companies of horse and fifty companies of infantry, totalling some 11,000 men, and to the grand total of 13,504 we can add a contingent of 700 from Flushing, so that with other men detailed to the camp an overall figure of 15,000 is suggested. The cost, including the defence works at Gravesend constructed by Federico Gianibelli and Thomas Ridwell, and the transport costs of the Flushing men, came to £23,356. 4s. 5d. When the problem of feeding them had been solved, Leicester felt confident enough to invite Elizabeth to visit Camp Royal in preference to Dover, which was altogether too close to the Armada fleet lying in Calais Roads and Parma's armies. The Queen's particular concern at this time was not simply the peril from Spain, but the appalling cost of defending her throne, for her reserve fund was disappearing at a frightening rate. Even before the final flight north of the mangled Armada was known, the privy council was considering dismissing the camp and Sir Thomas Sherley was sent to Tilbury to ask Leicester's opinion. Having worked so strenuously for the whole event, however, Leicester was in no mood for it to be dispersed without something to raise the morale of the men in miserably wet weather. Moreover, *he* was being paid £6 per day.

The decision that Elizabeth should visit the camp evolved over several days, Leicester originally suggesting that she should stay in her palace at Havering. In a later letter he omitted this arrangement and the Queen sailed down the Thames in the royal barge accompanied by her ladies, rowed by forty brawny river-men in white shirts 'with trumpets sounding and dubbing drums'. In the gilded cabin she and her ladies sat in comfort, and ahead of the little flotilla on that 8 August went a wind band playing fanfares to rouse the people on the banks of the river and in small boats. Arriving at Tilbury at about midday, she took refreshments with Leicester and, when a salute had been fired, flags and emblems were hoisted all over the camp, which she reached by coach.

Camp Royal was a colourful and deeply impressive piece of Elizabethan propaganda. The site was well chosen, being on a hill at West Tilbury, some two miles from the river, and on sandy, easily draining soil in an area surrounded by unhealthy marshes. Leicester, Essex and the other courtiers had spacious multicoloured tents, while the ordinary soldiers lived in huts made from willow and thatch, their floors strewn with rushes or straw. There were even tables and seats fashioned from turf to make living in the huts a little easier.[4] So, together with

Leicester and Lord Grey, the Lord Marshal, the Queen and her guard now rode to the camp enclosure between soldiers assembled along the way. As she passed they fell on their knees and called out blessings to her in an unabashed gesture of love and obeisance.[5] Then, having been shown round the camp, she went to Ardern Hall, about three miles farther up the road in Horndon-on-the-Hill. The house, which was rented from William Poley by Thomas Rich, the son of Lord Rich, had been inspected by Leicester and Richard Brackenbury, a gentleman usher of the court who held Leicester in high esteem.[6] Several days before the Queen's arrival the earl had written solicitously to her as follows: 'Your usher also liketh your lodging, a proper sweet cleanly house.'[7]

The following day, 9 August, Elizabeth rode back to the camp with the procession led by the sergeant trumpeter with mace, and nine trumpeters in scarlet attire. They were followed by the King of Heralds in blue and crimson velvet embroidered with gold thread. He was followed by the Queen's two sergeants in velvet coats and carrying gold maces, after whom came Leicester and Grey, followed by the Queen, her ladies and four footmen. Marching behind was the personal detachment of her bodyguard dressed in scarlet, and carrying bows and arrows. As they entered the camp Leicester and Essex walked on their sovereign's right and left, in armour but bare-headed. The Queen, seated on a white gelding, was dressed in white velvet, with a silver breastplate engraved with mythological allusions; her red wig was strewn with pearls and she carried a small silver staff tipped with gold. The assembled men now adopted battle order for the inspection and the royal party toured the lines. Then came the march past and finally the clarion call of the legendary speech, which few beyond the front lines could have heard, but which was later printed for those who could read.[8] This ringing piece of oratory was cheered with tumultuous acclaim, even before the news that the Armada had scattered, a broken force.

After this moving expression of the Queen's fierce and indomitable will to serve her country, even if it were to cost her her life, Leicester entertained the royal party and his officers in his marquee. Then with superb timing, which even the earl could not have anticipated, the Earl of Cumberland arrived

from Harwich with confirmation in dispatches that the English
fleet was sailing to port short of food, powder and shot, but that
the Armada of the King of Spain had disintegrated as a result of
fire, shot and storm. The only remaining anxiety was that
Parma seemed determined to come out on the most advantageous
tide, and there was still some agitation about where he might
land.

After supper, the Queen, her ladies and escort moved to Erith
to spend the night. The following morning she was rowed to
Greenwich, and from there went via Deptford to Lambeth
Stairs for the river crossing to Westminster. As Strype wrote,
when it was clear to the country that the threat was eliminated,
'the kingdom was filled with a sense of gratitude to God for this
wonderful deliverance'. The same day the order was given to
discharge the English fleet, save for the squadron of the Narrow
Seas.

Leicester, elated at the victory and the affectionate esteem
which Elizabeth had shown him, remained behind at Tilbury to
oversee the dismantling of the camp. On 15 August he wrote to
the Earl of Shrewsbury:

> I must most earnestly entreat you not to think me forgetful
> that I have not written to you of late; the true cause I trust you
> hear and conceive, which is indeed the continual toil and
> business I have been in since my coming to this camp. But
> now, God be thanked, the most difficulties are past, which lay
> most upon my own hand, and our gracious Mistress has been
> here with me to see her camp and people, which so enflamed
> the hearts of her good subjects, as I think the weakest person
> amongst them is able to match the proudest Spaniard. . . .

By 19 August most of his work was done, and relieved and tired he
took himself off to his beloved Wanstead for relaxation, before a
triumphal ride through London to St James's Palace. Towards
the end of the month, however, he felt increasingly unwell, and
though generally sceptical of the efficacy of spa waters, he
decided to make a leisurely journey with Lettice to Kenilworth
and then Buxton. Leaving on about 26 August they passed
through Maidenhead and stopped at Cornbury, where the
resident was John Fortescue, Keeper of Wychwood Forest, a

distant cousin of Lettice. Leicester had taken to using this house
since his appointment in 1585 as Chief Justice Itinerant of all
forests south of the Trent.

It was at Cornbury that his physical condition very markedly
declined. He took to his bed, observed by his gentleman of the
bedchamber, William Haynes, and ministered to by Lettice for
his bodily health, and William James, Dean of Christ Church,
Oxford, and Master of University College, for his spiritual
nourishment. On the morning of 4 September 1588 Leicester
died of a malarial fever. The news was carried to Elizabeth,
whereupon she retired to her bedchamber for many hours of
silent grief. His last letter to her became a treasured memento,
which she kept in a casket by her bed long after the whisper of
poison had been forgotten. The doubt did lead the privy council
to investigate a report that Edward Croft, the eldest son of Sir
James Croft, had approached a reputed 'conjuror' called John
Smith to kill the earl by magic, but when Croft was examined
nothing significant was uncovered.

In the court and country the death of this powerful
Renaissance prince attracted less attention than might have
been expected. It was as if the fierce clamour of the summer had
exhausted emotions, and therefore the passing of a dominant
courtier required only a brief acknowledgement. Some made
anonymous and smirking references to him in satirical doggerel:

> Here lies the worthy warrior
> That never bloodied sword.
> Here lies the loyal courtier
> That never kept his word.
> Here lies his noble excellence
> That ruled all the states.
> Here lies the Earl of Leicester
> Whom earth and heaven hates.

But this was not true of everyone, and from the loyal Henry
Killigrew in The Hague came a request to the privy council for a
few weeks' leave to attend the earl's funeral 'that I may yield
him the last service and testimony of my devotions'. It seems that
Lettice was more matter-of-fact about his death, for within a
year she had remarried, this time to Sir Christopher Blount, her

late husband's Master of the Horse. It was a match that ended with Blount's execution in 1601 for his part in his own stepson's rebellion against the Queen, an event that was doubly unfortunate for Lettice, since her son Essex was also executed. However, her concern at the moment was Leicester's will and his funeral, which was held with great pomp and expense despite the decline of the family's fortune in the last decade.

Leicester's will was dated 1 August 1587 and had been written in Middelburg, designating Lettice as executrix, and that his brother and certain friends should assist her. Lettice and Warwick were the immediate chief beneficiaries, and when they died it was intended that much of the properties and land would devolve to Leicester's illegitimate son, Robert Dudley, now aged about fourteen. If the latter died without heirs, the great mansion in London would pass to his stepson Essex, and meantime Lettice inherited half the contents. Other properties also passed to her, including Wanstead and its contents. To Warwick went Kenilworth, and the manors of Denbigh and Chirk, which at his demise would pass to Robert Dudley, whom some thought Leicester had intended for marriage to Arabella Stuart. Taken together the Kenilworth inventory and the probate inventory instigated by the Queen, so that some of Leicester's huge debt to her might be paid from the estate, show a representative and astonishing accumulation of goods, domestic and otherwise. The 1588 inventory valued the contents of Leicester House alone at over £3,000, and if the contents of Wanstead and Kenilworth are added, the total is some £8,000.[9] Moreover, there was a twenty-room property at Benington in Hertfordshire whose contents were valued at £117. 13s. 4d. Yet by 1590 when the goods in these houses were reassessed under a writ of *diem clausit extremum* in the hope of satisfying the Queen as Leicester's chief creditor, the value of the contents calculated by her agents had fallen dramatically. Doubtless Lettice had used the intervening two years to good effect, removing a great deal that was valuable, and the Leicester House total in particular is striking, having fallen from over £3,000 to just under £500; perhaps not so surprising when plate and armour previously listed at £1,040 and £436 respectively were reduced by the Queen's agents in 1590 to 40s. and nothing. The quantities of both are fascinating: the plate in Leicester House amounted to over 4,000 ounces in 1588; while the list of arms and armour noted 57 corselets, nearly 400 morions, 76 muskets, 372 calivers, 100 cuirasses, 442 black bills and 280 bows with arrows, thus nearly matching the collection at Kenilworth where arms and armour were valued at £478. 4s. Even six of Leicester's horses were noted: three bays valued at £32 including Bay Ley; two piebalds valued at £17. 13s. 4d., and a grey at £2. 13s. 4d. It is not clear what was sold at auction and how much money was raised, but by the end of Elizabeth's reign Lettice had paid out £22,000 to the Crown, and in the reign of James I added another £3,000 to that very substantial total.

There are a number of items that give us further clues to aspects of Leicester's conspicuous consumption. There was an expensive Thames barge, the banqueting tent, valued at £160, and even the *Galleon Leicester*, which after her service against the Armada was valued at £250. Alderman Richard Martin, the goldsmith, was owed £3,500, while over fifty other suppliers were owed many hundreds of pounds for groceries, timber, oats, hay, jewellery, furs, velvets and lace. There were also debts for plate, beer, trumpets and strings.

Leicester when he made his will had no illusions about the general state of his finances, for as a consequence he felt his bequests of items could not be very substantial. 'I have not dissembled with the world my estate, but have lived always above any living I had (for which I am heartily sorry) lest that through my many debts, from time to time, some men have taken loss of me.' His posthumous gift to Elizabeth was a jewel of emeralds and diamonds as well as a rope of 600 pearls. To Sir Christopher Hatton, 'mine old dear friend', he gave a basin and ewer in gilt 'with my best George and Garter'. Warwick, 'my dear and noble brother', received a gold cup and a George emblem: but 'my last and best token to him shall be to present a faithful sister [in-law] and handmaid to him, whilest you both live, which I pray God may be many years'. (For Lettice this wish was granted, for she died at the grand old age of ninety-two. Warwick, however, died in 1590.) The Lords Howard of Effingham and North, as well as Sir Thomas Heneage, received gifts, as did Burgane, his secretary during the last years.

Charitable bequests included provision of certain lands in Wales which were set aside to provide an income to maintain two scholars at University College, Oxford. Leicester also intended that if the income of the Leycester Hospital, Warwick, did not reach £200 per annum, it should be made up out of the profits from the manor of Great Hampton in Worcestershire, which had reverted to Ambrose Dudley. The £200 of ready money he left the hospital Lettice was far from inclined to disgorge, and several years later the Master, Thomas Cartwright, was forced to complain to Burghley that he was supporting the hospital out of his own pocket.

As for a political inheritance, there was none, although his stepson became Master of the Horse and for a time also won the affection of the ageing Queen. But the court career of Essex was a matter of fits and starts compared with that of Leicester; he never learned to curb his tongue or his instincts, even when they earned the violent disapproval of Elizabeth. In contrast, although he was detested by many from all social levels, Leicester did build a political power base as the bold leader of the Puritan courtiers, notwithstanding that his Puritanism was not primarily a matter of theology. It is also true that the merchant class, notably in London, regarded him as a friend at court, and to a certain extent Essex inherited some of this esteem. But when he fell into the trap of a rising in 1601, these were the very people who remained soberly and responsibly at home.[10] The rebellion of Essex was essentially personal, the whim of a thwarted aristocrat; unlike his stepson, and indeed his own father, Leicester sagely avoided the lure of the great adventure that led to the block. His loyalty to Elizabeth was too great for him even to envisage it.

Leicester has been called 'the first great English art collector'.[11] Through his patronage he also influenced the growth of technical and scientific knowledge, leading to its spreading among 'a wider and more broad-based social group'. He was, in addition, a patron of translators of classical literature 'which put the republican ideas of Greece and Rome into the hands of the lower and middle classes'.[12] As Geoffrey Whitney stated in his dedication in the *Choice of Emblems*: '. . . divers, who are now famous men, had been through poverty long since discouraged from their studies if they had not found your honour so prone to be their patron'. Little wonder that Leicester was called an 'Earl of Excellence' by John Florio in his *Worlds of Words* published a decade after Leicester's death. The earl was a proud man, sometimes uneasily conscious of his dignity as a Dudley, but withal loyal, witty, intelligent, conscientious, stylish and vigorously patriotic. It was from a volatile mixture of vanity and high motives that he allowed himself to be drawn into the annihilating tangle of the Dutch struggle, from which he emerged with lamentably little to his credit. Appropriately it was Lord North who found the words to express the gratitude of many for his life and their sorrow at his death:

> The untimely death . . . of that noble earl of Leicester, is a great and general loss to the whole land, and cannot but be generally and greatly lamented of the good and best sort. In his life he had advanced the glory of God, and loyally served his sovereign; he lived and died with honour, in special grace and favour of her Majesty and the good subject.[13]

Appendix A

Giordano Bruno arrived in England in the late spring of 1583 to lodge in the London residence of the ageing French ambassador Mauvissière. Beaumont House stood in Butchers Row, a narrow lane running into the Strand near St Clement Danes, and thus very close to Leicester House.[1] The fact that the ambassador and the earl were close neighbours was surely useful to the quixotic Bruno, especially since Philip Sidney lived at Leicester House and was to become a patron of the Italian. Mauvissière himself certainly helped his lodger, perhaps because his visitor was also undertaking a covert political mission for Henri III.

The visit of Albrecht Łaski to Oxford in June 1583, and the disputations that Leicester had organized for him, gave Bruno a grand opportunity to expound his view of the cosmos, and especially to promote the cause of Copernicus, in whom Leicester's protégé Thomas Digges had shown such a passionate interest, publishing his *Parfit Description of the Celestiall Orbes* in 1576. Yet Bruno's vibrant, dogmatic personality led him astray, for he was rarely able to argue calmly on controversial matters, and his pungent criticism led to a bitter clash with the Oxonian 'pedants'. Moreover, he compounded his error there by talking not so much about Copernicus as about Hermetic religion, and one of the 'pedants' soon discovered that lengthy sections in Bruno's presentation had been plagiarized.[2] His public response to this humiliating exposure was the publication in 1584 of *La Cena de le Ceneri* (The Ash Wednesday Supper). It was written in London, where the author was stranded in the French embassy, an embarrassing and expensive lodger for Mauvissière who was suffering from irregular royal payments of his funds. Bruno's intention was to rebuke uncouth, insolent Oxford where the dons he claimed knew more about beer than Greek, and generally England, which made him thoroughly uncomfortable. Individuals in and around the court, which Bruno often attended with Mauvissière, seem to have been scorned or praised according to their social standing (and perhaps their treatment of the author). His countryman, Tommaso di Vicenzo Sassetti, the ex-mercenary soldier who now served Leicester as a bodyguard, is obliquely sneered at in the text. However, the Queen and a handful of English courtiers – Leicester himself, Walsingham, Sidney and Fulke Greville – were all praised. Yet it is difficult to believe that the earl, for all his 'most generous humanity', would have been pleased with Bruno's acid comments on the university, and some strain seems to have crept into the philosopher's relationship with Greville, perhaps because the Nolan (as Bruno calls himself in the book) set the 'Cena' in Greville's town house, which he reached, apparently in reality, only after wading through mud. (The Strand was a notorious quagmire.)

Despite the anger that reverberated round Oxford's colleges after his eruption, Bruno did manage to make friends with men he respected: Tobie Matthew, Dean of Christ Church; Alberico Gentili; Dr Matthew Gwynne, who later helped John Florio translate Montaigne; and Alexander Dicson, who became a disciple of the Italian, and who dedicated his own books to Leicester.[3] Then in October 1585 Mauvissière was recalled to Paris and Bruno went with him, presumably relieved at quitting a city which he compared so unfavourably (and probably unfairly) with others in Europe; a derisive comparison he was able to make from his own frequent travels in search of an audience and patronage – travels that eventually led to his capture by the papal Inquisition and death by burning in 1600.

Appendix B

Robert Dudley's prayer from the Arundel Harington manuscript at Arundel Castle:

O mightie Lorde to whome/ all vengeance doth belonge
and iust revendge for their desertes/ whiche do oppresse by
                                                    wronge
Thye praid for presence shew/ thow iudge and rightuouse guyde
And pay them with a due rewarde/ that swell in hatefull pryde
ffor Lorde yf thow forbeare/ and suffer suche to raigne
How longe shall then those hawltie men/ so lordlye vs disdayne
Which do dispyse thye flocke/ and vse with threates the iuste
And widowes withe the faultles men/ they order as they luste
And eke the helpless babes/ whiche fatherless remayne
They spare not in their guiltlesse blood/ their cruell handes to
                                                    stayne
And thus amonge them selves/ they holde the Lord is blynde
And deeme his powre to farr to short/ their cloked faultes to fynde
But yet in tyme beware/ you froward bloddie band
What thinges against the Lord your god/ you seeke to take in hand
ffor whoe can hyde from hym/ one deede or secreat thought
Syns cares and eyes with eache good gifte/ alone by hym weare
                                                    wrought
Or whoe can hym restrayne/ to ponishe at his will
Syns that his Rodd cloth rule bothe sortes/ as well the good as yll
And eke the Lord doth know/ no thought in man doth raigne
That framed ys by natures worke/ but is bothe fraile and vayne
But blessid is that man/ whom Lord thow doste correct
And by those pathes thow doste appoint/ his wayes aye to dyrecte
And in his trobled state/ dothe graunt him patient mynde
till wasteful graves shall swallow vpp/ the vyle and wicked kynde
ffor from the faithfull flock/ the Lord will never swarve

But garde them with his mightie shyeld/ and safelye them presarve
And eke restore agayne/ true iudgement to his seate
Tyll rightuousnesse may guyd the iust/ and vanquyshe all disceate
Wheare, when the wicked rulde/ and bare the swaye by might
No one wolde preace to take my parte/ or once defend my right
So that for want of helpp/ I had bene sore opprest
Yf that the Lorde had not with speede/ my wofull plight redrest
Whoe, when he heard me crye/ and for his goodness call
With mercye streight he staide my foote/ and sav'de me from the fall
And eke from carefull thoughtes/ that did consume my brest
His endlesse powre hath cleane discharg'de/ and fild my soule with
rest

He hates the cruell kynde/ that wresteth iustice still
and makes their lawes obaye their lustes/ as good men do gods will
And shameless wayes conspyre/ the wicked to preserve
And searche by powre to sheede the blood/ of suche as least desarve
But sure the Lorde my god/ myne ayde and only strengthe
Will them rewarde and sharplye scordge/ with endlesse payne at
lengthe
And them destroye eache one/ that waytes not others woe
That they shulde know the mightie Lord/ hath powre to plague
them so./

ffinis Ro. Dudley

Appendix C

THE DUDLEY–LISLE FAMILY LINEAGE 1400–1620

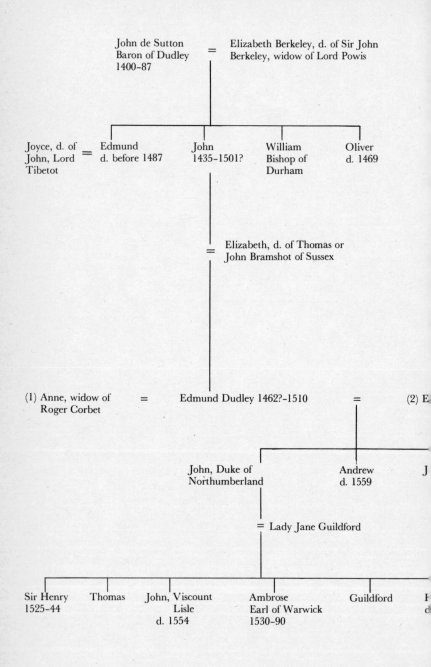

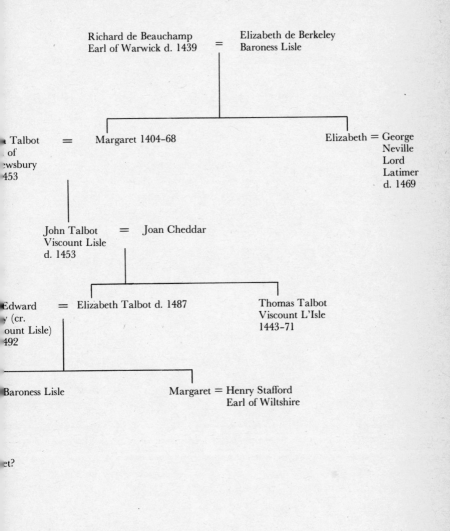

Richard de Beauchamp
Earl of Warwick d. 1439 = Elizabeth de Berkeley
Baroness Lisle

␣ Talbot
␣ of
␣wsbury
␣453 = Margaret 1404–68

Elizabeth = George
Neville
Lord
Latimer
d. 1469

John Talbot
Viscount Lisle
d. 1453 = Joan Cheddar

␣Edward
␣y (cr.
␣ount Lisle)
␣492 = Elizabeth Talbot d. 1487

Thomas Talbot
Viscount L'Isle
1443–71

␣Baroness Lisle

Margaret = Henry Stafford
Earl of Wiltshire

␣et?

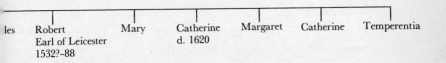

␣les Robert
Earl of Leicester
1532?–88

Mary

Catherine
d. 1620

Margaret

Catherine

Temperentia

Abbreviations in Notes and Bibliography

APC	Acts of the Privy Council
AQ	Army Quarterly
BAJ	Berkshire Archaeological Journal
BBCS	Bulletin of the Board of Celtic Studies
BIHR	Bulletin of the Institute of Historical Research
BM	Burlington Magazine
BMQ	British Museum Quarterly
BUSE	Boston University Studies in English
CJH	Canadian Journal of History
CPR	Calendar of Patent Rolls
CQR	Church Quarterly Review
CS	Camden Society
CSP	Calendar of State Papers (various)
DHST	Denbighshire Historical Society Transactions
DUJ	Durham University Journal
EC	Essex Countryside
EcHR	Economic History Review
EHR	English History Review
EJ	Essex Journal
ELR	English Literary Renaissance
EM	English Miscellany
HJ	Historical Journal
HLB	Huntington Library Bulletin
HLQ	Huntington Library Quarterly
HT	History Today
HS	Hakluyt Society Publications
HSNP	Harvard Studies and Notes in Philology

JAAHSCNW	*Journal of the Architectural, Archaeological and Historical Society of Chester and North Wales*
JAAS	*Journal of the Arms and Armour Society*
JBAA	*Journal of the British Archaeological Association*
JEH	*Journal of Ecclesiastical History*
JHI	*Journal of the History of Ideas*
JWCI	*Journal of the Warburg and Courtauld Institute*
LQ	*Library Quarterly*
LRS	London Record Society
MM	*Mariner's Mirror*
MP	*Modern Philology*
NA	*Norfolk Archaeology*
N&Q	*Notes and Queries*
PMLA	*Publications of the Modern Language Association*
PQ	*Philological Quarterly*
QR	*Quarterly Review*
RD	*Renaissance Drama*
RHS	Royal Historical Society
SANHS	Shropshire Archaeological and Natural History Society
SB	*Studies in Bibliography*
SEL	*Studies in English Literature*
SR	*Studies in the Renaissance*
TA	*The Athenaeum*
TAPS	*Transactions of the American Philosophical Society*
TBAS	*Transactions of the Birmingham Archaeological Society*
TCBS	*Transactions of the Cambridge Bibliographical Society*
TCHS	*Transactions of the Caernarvonshire Historical Society*
TCWAAS	*Transactions of the Cumberland and Westmorland Antiquarian and Archaeological Society*
TGBAS	*Transactions of the Gloucester and Bristol Archaeological Society*
TI	*Terrae Incognitae*
TM	*The Monthly*
TRHS	*Transactions of the Royal Historical Society*
TvG	*Tijdschrift voor Geschiednis*
WANHM	*Wiltshire Archaeological and Natural History Magazine*
WHistR	*Welsh Historical Review*
WHR	*Western Humanities Review*

Notes and References

INTRODUCTION

1 E. Rosenberg, *Leicester, Patron of Letters* (1955).

CHAPTER 1

1 D.M. Brodie, 'Edmund Dudley, Minister of Henry VII', *TRHS*, 4th ser., 15 (1932), 135-6.

2 B.L. Beer, *Northumberland: The Political Career of John Dudley, Earl of Warwick and Duke of Northumberland* (1973), p. 8.

3 Ibid., p. 48.

4 R.C. McCoy, 'From the Tower to the Tiltyard: Robert Dudley's Return to Glory', *HJ*, 27, 2 (1984), 431.

5 D. Hoak, 'Rehabilitating the Duke of Northumberland: Politics and Political Control, 1549-53' in J. Loach and R. Tittler (eds), *The Mid-Tudor Polity, c. 1540-1560* (1980), pp. 30-1.

6 H. Trevor-Roper (Lord Dacre), 'The Bishopric of Durham and the Capitalist Reformation', *DUJ*, 38, new ser., VII, 2 (1946), 48.

7 Beer, op. cit., p. 142.

8 Ibid.

9 R. Tittler and S.L. Battley, 'The Local Community and the Crown in 1553: The Accession of Mary Tudor Revisited', *BIHR*, LVII, 136 (1984), 132-3.

10 J. Bellamy, *The Tudor Law of Treason* (1979), p. 54.

11 Beer, op. cit., p. 197.

12 Ibid., pp. 168-9.

13 McCoy, 'From the Tower', op. cit., 425.

14 Ibid., 430.

15 Ibid.

16 D.M. Loades, *The Reign of Mary Tudor* (1979), p. 461.

17 McCoy, 'From the Tower', op. cit., 432-3.

18 Ibid., 426.

19 R. Tighe and J. Davis (eds), *Annals of Windsor*, vol. 1 (1858), p. 612.

CHAPTER 2

1 The Leycester Hospital, Warwick, has an example attributed to her.
2 J.E. Jackson (Canon), 'Amye Robsart', *WANHM*, XVII (1878), 47–93.
3 Ibid., 64.
4 B. Frere (Sir Bartle Frere), *Amy Robsart of Wymondham* (1937), pp. 37–8.
5 W. MacCaffery, *The Shaping of the Elizabeth Regime* (1969), p. 138.
6 I. Aird, 'The Death of Amy Robsart', *EHR*, 71 (1956), 69–79.
7 Jackson, 'Robsart', op. cit., 75–6.
8 H.L. Thompson, *The Church of St. Mary the Virgin, Oxford* (1903), p. 164.
9 At this time Appleyard was married to Margaret, the widow of Dudley's dead brother Henry.
10 A. Lang, *The Mystery of Amy Robsart* (1903), p. 180.
11 D.C. Peck, *Leicester's Commonwealth, 1584* (1985), p. 246.

CHAPTER 3

1 M. Hume, *The Courtships of Queen Elizabeth* (1904), p. 54.
2 R.C. Christie (ed.), *Letters of Sir Thomas Copley* (1897), xxiii.
3 Ibid.
4 Hume, op. cit., pp. 56–7.
5 Ibid., p. 59.
6 Ibid., p. 63.
7 C.G. Bayne, *Anglo-Roman Relations, 1558–65*, vol. II (1913), p. 209.
8 S.L. Greenslade, 'William Whittingham, Dean of Durham, 1524–79', *DUJ*, 39, new ser., VIII (1946), 29.

CHAPTER 4

1 M. Axton, 'Robert Dudley and the Inner Temple Revels', *HJ*, 13, 3 (1970), 365.
2 Ibid., 367.
3 Ibid., 375.
4 He eventually married the daughter of Albrecht V of Bavaria.
5 *CSP (Spanish, Simancas), 1558–67*, vol. 1, p. 492.

CHAPTER 5

1 F.G. Emmison, *Elizabethan Life (Disorder), Mainly from Essex Sessions and Assize Records* (1970), p. 42.
2 J. Osborn, *Young Philip Sidney* (1972), pp. 72–3.
3 C. Read, 'Walsingham and Burghley in Queen Elizabeth's Privy Council', *EHR*, XXVIII (1913), p. 38.
4 M. Waldman, *Elizabeth and Leicester* (1946), p. 160.
5 *CPR (Elizabeth), 1569–72*, vol. 5, pp. 376, 448.

CHAPTER 6

1 H.G. Owen, 'Family Politics in Elizabethan Merionethshire', *BBCS*, 18, 1 (1958), 187–8.

2 S.L. Adams, 'The Composition of 1564 and the Earl of Leicester's Tenurial Reformation in the Lordship of Denbigh', *BBCS*, 26, 4 (1976), 492.

3 Ibid., 495.

4 Ibid.

5 C.A. Gresham, 'The Forest of Snowdon in Its Relation to Eifionydd', *TCHS*, 21 (1960), 54.

6 C.A. Gresham, *Eifionydd* (1973), p. 224.

7 Adams, 'Composition', op. cit., 505.

8 P.H. Williams, *The Council of the Marches in Wales under Elizabeth I* (1958), p. 261.

9 Ibid.

10 Ibid., p. 264.

11 Ibid., pp. 269–70.

12 J.H.E. Bennett, 'Two Elizabethan Chamberlains of the Palatinate of Chester', *JAAHSCNW*, new ser., XX, (1914), 196.

13 J.E. Neale, *The Elizabethan House of Commons* (1949), pp. 153–4.

14 S.L. Adams, 'The Gentry of North Wales and the Earl of Leicester's Expedition to the Netherlands, 1585–6', *WHistR*, 7 (1974–5), 144–5.

15 Tighe and Davis, *Annals*, vol. 1, p. 636.

16 Neale, op. cit., pp. 210–11.

17 Adams, 'Gentry', op. cit., 145.

18 A.L. Merson (ed.), *The Third Book of Remembrance of Southampton, 1514–1602* (1952), p. 34.

19 Adams, 'Gentry', op. cit., p. 145.

CHAPTER 7

1 C.M. Dent, *Protestant Reformers in Elizabethan Oxford* (1983), p. 29.

2 E. Rose, *Cases of Conscience: Alternatives Open to Recusants and Puritans under Elizabeth I and James I* (1975), pp. 214–15.

3 J.H. Primus, *The Vestments Controversy* (1960), p. 73.

4 A.G. Kinder, *Casiodoro de Reina: Spanish Reformer of the Sixteenth Century* (1975), p. 24.

5 Delemus was a victim of the plague which Ambrose Dudley's forces brought back from France.

6 Kinder, op. cit., p. 28.

7 P. Collinson (ed.), 'Letters of Thomas Wood, Puritan, 1566–77', *BIHR*, spec. supp., 5 (1960), xi.

8 Primus, op. cit., p. 76 n. 5.

9   Ibid., p. 75.

10 Ibid., p. 87.

11 Greenslade, 'William Whittingham', op. cit. (ch. 3), p. 33.

12 P. Collinson, *The Elizabethan Puritan Movement* (1967), p. 73.

13 Primus, op. cit., p. 102.

14 Collinson, 'Letters', op. cit., xxiv.

15 Bridgewater later became a Catholic apologist for the executed Mary Queen of Scots.

16 Rosenberg, *Leicester*, pp.124–8.

17 Collinson, 'Letters', op. cit., xxv.

18 S. Cassan, *The Lives of the Bishops of Winchester* (1827), pp. 32 ff.

19 Collinson, 'Letters', op. cit., xxxiii.

20 Ibid., xxxiv.

21 Ibid., xxvii.

22 F.M. Butler, ' "The Erle of Leycester and his friendes" and Ecclesiastical Patronage in the Elizabethan Era' (unpublished M. Phil. thesis, London University, 1979), p. 131.

CHAPTER 8

1   Rosenberg, *Leicester*, pp. 209–10.

2   Ibid., pp. 217–18.

3   A.C. Southern, ' "The Best Wits out of England": University Men in Exile under Elizabeth', *TM*, 7, 1 (1952), 20.

4   B.W. Beckingsale, *Burghley: Tudor Statesman* (1967), pp. 246–7.

5   P. Lake, *Moderate Puritans and the Elizabethan Church* (1982), p. 180.

6   Ibid.

7   A.J. Haynes, 'The English in Padua, 1222–1660', *HT*, 27 (1977), 109.

8   Dent, *Protestant Reformers*, p. 126.

9   Ibid.

10 Ibid., p. 127.

11 W. Prest, *The Inns of Court under Elizabeth I and the Early Stuarts, 1590–1640* (1972), pp. 190–2.

12 Dent, *Protestant Reformers*, p. 124.

13 R.J.W. Evans, *Rudolf II and His World: A Study in Intellectual History, 1576–1612* (1973), p. 122.

14 P. French, *John Dee: The World of an Elizabethan Magus* (1972), p. 154.

15 Ibid., p. 119.

16 C. Hill, *The Intellectual Origins of the English Revolution* (1966), p. 22.

CHAPTER 9

1   Beckingsale, *Burghley*, p. 271.

2   P.N. Siegel, *Shakespearean Tragedy and the Elizabethan Compromise* (1957), p. 194 n. 26.

3   Ibid., pp. 23-4.

4   E. Hughes, 'The English Monopoly of Salt in the Years 1563-71', *EHR*, 40 (1925), 334-50.

5   P. Croft, *The Spanish Company* (1973), x.

6   H. Trevor-Roper (Lord Dacre), 'The Bishopric of Durham', op. cit. (ch. 1), 55.

7   N. Shipley, 'Thomas Sutton and His Landed Interest in Essex', *EJ*, 8, 4 (1973), 113.

8   E.A. Bond (ed.), *Russia at the Close of the Sixteenth Century*, HS, vol. XX (1856), p. 215.

9   Ibid.

10 H. Brown, untitled article on Venice, *QR*, 230 (1918), 264-5.

11 Merson, *Third Book of Remembrance*, app. V, pp. 70-6.

12 Ibid., p. 72.

CHAPTER 10

1   A. Laroui, *The History of the Maghrib* (1977), p. 252.

2   E.W. Bovill, 'Queen Elizabeth's Gunpowder', *MM*, 33, 3 (1947), 182.

3   R. Hakluyt, *Principle Navigations, 1598-1600*, vol. 6 (1904), pp. 285-93.

4   A death lamented in Thomas Heywood's *If You Know Not Me, You Know Nobody*, I. viii.

5   T.S. Willan, *Studies in Elizabethan Foreign Trade* (1959), p. 164.

6   Ibid., p. 166.

7   Ibid., p. 167.

8   Ibid., p. 241.

9   Ibid., p. 255.

CHAPTER 11

1   C. Leech and T.W. Craik (eds), *The Revels History of Drama in English*, vol. 3 (1975), p. 8.

2   Ibid., pp. 10-11.

3   T. Lennam, *Sebastian Westcott, the Children of St. Paul's and the Marriage of Wit and Science* (1975), p. 53.

4   M. Shapiro, *Children of the Revels: The Boy Companies of Shakespeare's Time and Their Plays* (1977), p. 14.

5   C.C. Stopes, 'William Hunnis, the Dramatist', *TA* (1900), 410-12.

6   Rosenberg, *Patron of Letters*, p. 298.

7   H.M. Nixon, 'Elizabethan Gold-tooled Bindings' in D.E. Rhodes (ed.), *Essays in Honour of Victor Scholderer* (1970), pp. 224-44.

8   J. Nichols (ed.), *The Progresses and Public Processions of Queen Elizabeth*, vol. 1 (1823), p. 380.

9 Jackson, 'Amye Robsart', op. cit. (ch. 2), 92.

10 L. Stone, *The Crisis of the Aristocracy, 1558–1641* (1965), p. 276.

11 M. Girouard, *Robert Smythson and the Architecture of the Elizabethan Era* (1966), p. 54.

12 L.E. Pearson, *Elizabethans at Home* (1957), pp. 63–5.

13 J. Clark, 'The Buildings and Art Collections of Robert Dudley, Earl of Leicester' (unpublished MA report, London University, 1981), p. 6.

14 J. Nichols (ed.), *History and Antiquities of Leicestershire* (1815), vol. II, pt 1, p. 633.

15 H.M. Colvin (ed.), *History of the King's Works, 1485–1660*, vol. III, pt 1 (1975), p. 326.

16 E.J. Buxton, *Elizabethan Taste* (1963), p. 101.

17 J. Clark, 'Eliseus Libaerts and His English Connections', *JAAS*, XI, 2 (1983), 45 n. 12.

18 R. Strong (Sir Roy Strong), 'Federigo Zuccaro's Visit to England in 1575', *JWCI*, XXII (1959), 359–60.

19 R. Strong (Sir Roy Strong), 'The Leicester House Miniatures: Robert Sidney, 1st Earl of Leicester and His Circle', *BM*, CXXVII, 991 (1985), 694–701.

20 Clark, 'Libaerts', op. cit., 45 n. 8.

21 Ibid., 42.

22 H.M. Dillon, (Viscount Dillon), 'Tilting in Tudor Times', *AJ*, LV, 2nd ser., V (1898), 338–9.

CHAPTER 12

1 E.G. Tibbitts, 'The Hospital of Robert, Earl of Leicester in Warwick', *TBAS 1936*, LX (1940), 122.

2 I. Morgan, *The Godly Preachers of the Elizabethan Church* (1965), p. 57.

3 L. Butler, 'Leicester's Church, Denbigh: An Experiment in Puritan Worship', *JBAA*, 3rd ser., XXXVII (1974), 45.

4 J.C. Cox, 'An Elizabethan Clergy List of the Diocese of Lichfield', *SANHS*, 2nd ser., V (1893), 253.

5 Bishop Morgan was born of humble parents in about 1540 in Ty Mawr, near Bettwys-y-Coed, Caernarvonshire.

6 Butler, 'Leicester's Church', op. cit., 62.

7 Collinson, 'Letters', op. cit. (ch. 7), 22–3.

8 Ibid., 14.

9 A.J. Haynes, 'The English Earthquake of 1580', *HT*, 29 (1979), 542.

CHAPTER 13

1 B. Hill, 'Trinity College, Cambridge MS. B.14.52 and William Patten', *TCBS*, 4, 3 (1966), 196.

2 B. O'Kill, 'The Printed Works of William Patten' (*c*. 1510–1600), *TCBS*, 7, 1 (1977), 35–9.

3 D. Scott, 'William Patten and the Authorship of Robert Laneham's "Letter" (1575)', *ELR*, 7, 3 (1977), 297–305.

4 K. Thomas, *Religion and the Decline of Magic* (1971), p. 231.

5 M. Axton, *The Queen's Two Bodies: Drama and the Elizabethan Succession* (1977), p. 66.

6 A.J. Collins, *Jewels and Plate of Queen Elizabeth I: The Inventory of 1574* (1955), pp. 161–2.

7 P. Johnson, *Elizabeth I: A Study in Power and Intellect* (1974), p. 229.

8 Ibid.

CHAPTER 14

1 Waldman, *Elizabeth and Leicester*, p. 162.

2 Anon., untitled article, *Home Counties Magazine*, 9 (1907), 48–9.

3 *CSP (Domestic, Addenda), 1566–79*, p. 523.

4 Rosenberg, *Leicester*, p. 279.

5 Butler, '"The Erle of Leycester"', p. 16 n. 20.

6 *CPR (Elizabeth), 1569–72*, vol. 5, p. 340.

7 M.B. Pulman, *The Elizabethan Privy Council in the 1570's* (1970), p. 245.

8 J. Hurstfield, *The Queen's Wards* (1958), pp. 121–4.

9 W.A. Evans, 'The Salusburys of Llewenni near Denbigh', *DHST*, 4 (1955), 16.

10 V.J. Watney, *Cornbury and the Forest of Wychwood* (1910), p. 85.

11 R.A. Houlbrooke (ed.), *The Letter Book of John Parkhurst, Bishop of Norwich* (1974–5), p. 148.

12 F.F. Foster, *The Politics of Stability: A Portrait of the Rulers in Elizabethan London* (1977), p. 139.

13 Rosenberg, *Leicester*, p. 326.

14 G.F. Lytle, 'Patronage Patterns in Oxford' in L. Stone (ed.), *The University in Society* (1975), vol. I, p. 115.

15 V.F. Stern, *Gabriel Harvey* (1979), pp. 54, 69.

16 Rosenberg, *Leicester*, p. 344.

17 H. Dick, 'Thomas Blundeville's "The true order and methods of wryting and reading Hystories" (1574)', *HLQ*, 3, 2 (1939–40), 152–3.

CHAPTER 15

1 R. Strong (Sir Roy Strong) and J.A. van Dorsten, *Leicester's Triumph* (1964), p. 10.

2 Hume, *Courtships*, p. 198.

3 R. Kimbrough and P. Murphy, 'The Helmingham Hall MS. of Sidney's "The Lady of May"', *RD*, new ser., 1 (1968), 104–7.

4 Hume, *Courtships*, p. 216.

5 K. Duncan-Jones and J.A. van Dorsten (eds), *Miscellaneous Prose of Sir Philip Sidney* (1973), p. 36.

6 A.L. Rowse, *The Elizabethan Renaissance: The Life of the Society* (1971), p. 160.

7 D.C. Peck, 'Raleigh, Sidney, Oxford and the Catholics, 1579', *N&Q*, new ser., 25, 5 (1978), 428.

8 Ibid., 429.

9 N. Council, ' "O Dea Certe": The Allegory of "The Fortress of Perfect Beauty"', *HLQ*, 39, 4 (1976), 331.

10 Ibid., 332.

11 *CSP (Spanish, Simancas), 1580–6*, vol. 3, p. 217.

12 Ibid., p. 211.

13 W.T. MacCaffery, 'The Anjou Match and Elizabethan Foreign Policy' in P. Clark, A.G.T. Smith and N. Tyacke (eds), *The English Commonwealth, 1547–1640* (1979), p. 73.

14 E.S. Donno (ed.), *An Elizabethan in 1582: The Diary of Richard Madox, Fellow of All Souls*, HS, 2nd ser., vol. 147 (1974), p. 87 n. 6.

15 MacCaffery, 'The Anjou Match', op. cit., p. 74.

CHAPTER 16

1 A. Wagner (Sir Anthony Wagner), *English Genealogy* (1972), p. 362.

2 Colvin, *History*, vol. III, pt 1, pp. 79–80.

3 A. Woodward, 'Purveyance for the Royal Household in the Reign of Elizabeth I', *TAPS*, new ser., XXXV, 1 (1945–6), 8.

4 Ibid., 12.

5 Nichols, *History*, vol. II, pt 1, p. 533.

6 Woodward, 'Purveyance', op. cit., 58.

7 *CSP (Spanish Simancas), 1580–6*, vol. 3, p. 2.

8 Ibid., p. 19.

9 Donno, *An Elizabethan*, p. 120 n. 3.

10 Ibid., p. 20 n. 7.

11 D. Fischer, 'Merchants, Courtiers and the Sea Route to the Indies: The Case of Elizabethan England', *TI*, 4 (1972), 114.

12 Ibid.

13 Ibid., p. 112.

CHAPTER 17

1 *CSP (Domestic, Addenda), 1580–1625*, pp. 136–8.

2 Peck, *Leicester's Commonwealth*, p. 36.

3 D.C. Peck, 'Government Suppression of Elizabethan Catholic Books: The Case of Leicester's Commonwealth"', *LQ*, 47, 2 (1977), 169–71.

4 Ibid., 165.

5   R. Lloyd, *Dorset Elizabethans* (1967), p. 72.

6   Peck, 'Government Suppression', op. cit., 165.

7   Duncan-Jones and van Dorsten, *Miscellaneous Prose*, p. 123.

8   D.C. Peck, ' "News from Heaven and Hell": A Defamatory Narrative of the Earl of Leicester', *ELR*, 8, 2 (1978), 141–58.

9   Ibid., 158.

10 Ibid., 142.

11 W.S. Maltby, *The Black Legend in England: The Development of Anti-Spanish Sentiment, 1558–1660* (1971), p. 71.

12 G. de Jong, 'The Earl of Leicester's Administration of the Netherlands, 1585–6' (unpublished Ph.D. thesis, Wisconsin University, 1956), p. 42.

13 J. Bruce (ed.), *Correspondence of Robert Dudley, Earl of Leicester, 1585–6*, CS, old ser. (1844), p. 27.

14 J. den Tex, *Oldenbarnevelt* (1973), vol. 1, p. 38.

15 A.M. van der Woude, 'De Staten, Leicester en Elizabeth in Financiele Verwikkelingen', *TvG*, 74 (1961), 65.

16 den Tex, *Oldenbarnevelt*, vol. 1, pp. 38–9.

17 van der Woude, 'De Staten', op. cit., 66.

18 Ibid., 65.

19 *CSP (Foreign), 1582–6*, vol. 20, p. 76.

20 G. Kipling, *The Triumph of Honour: Burgundian Origins of the Elizabethan Renaissance* (1977), p. 169.

21 *CSP (Foreign), 1585–6*, vol. 20, p. 197.

22 Adams, 'Gentry', op. cit. (ch. 6), 132–3.

23 Ibid., 134.

24 Ibid., 145.

CHAPTER 18

1   Strong and van Dorsten, *Leicester's Triumph*, p. 36.

2   Ibid., p. 41.

3   R. Holinshed, *Chronicles* (ed. Henry Ellis), vol. 6 (1807–8), p. 642.

4   G. Parker, 'The Dutch Revolt and the Polarization of International Politics', *TvG*, 88, 3 (1976), 3.

5   F. Oosterhoff, 'The Earl of Leicester's Governorship of the Netherlands, 1586–87' (unpublished Ph.D. thesis, London University, 1967), p. 99.

6   de Jong, 'Leicester's Administration', p. 81.

7   Bruce, *Correspondence*, p. 110.

8   de Jong, 'Leicester's Administration', p. 90.

9   Bruce, *Correspondence*, p. 243.

10 *CSP (Foreign), 1585–6*, vol. 20, pp. 446–7.

11 Ibid., p. 459.

12 Ibid., pp. 585–6.

13 L. Stone, *An Elizabethan: Sir Horatio Palavicino* (1956), pp. 191–2.

14 W. Nijenhuis, *Adrianus Saravia* (1980), pp. 97–8.

15 Oosterhoff, 'Leicester's Governorship', pp. 216–17.

CHAPTER 19

1 de Jong, 'Leicester's Administration', p. 111.

2 Ibid., p. 127.

3 Ibid., p. 133.

4 Ibid., p. 138.

5 Ibid., p. 142.

6 Ibid., p. 145.

7 Oosterhoff, 'Leicester's Governorship', p. 216.

8 den Tex, *Oldenbarnevelt*, p. 87.

9 *CSP (Foreign), 1586–7*, vol. 21, p. 333.

10 R. Broersma and G. Huet, *Letters of Leicester Found in the Papers of Jean Hotman* (1913), vol. 34, p. 134.

11 Ibid., pp. 172–3.

CHAPTER 20

1 H. Brugmans (ed.), *Correspondentie van Robert Dudley, Graaf van Leycester en andere documenten betreffende zijn . . . 1585–88* (1931), vol. II, p. 47.

2 C.G. Cruikshank, *Elizabeth's Army* (1966), p. 76.

3 *CSP (Foreign), 1585–6*, vol. 20, pp. 446–7.

4 den Tex, *Oldenbarnevelt*, vol. 1, p. 103.

5 *CSP (Foreign), 1587*, vol. 21, pt 3, p. 49.

6 Brugmans, *Correspondentie*, vol. III, p. 275.

7 Ibid., vol. III, pp. 4–5.

8 Ibid., p. 6.

9 den Tex, *Oldenbarnevelt*, p. 113.

10 Brugmans, *Correspondentie*, vol. II, pp. 59–61.

11 Ibid., p. 78.

12 Ibid., p. 98.

13 Ibid., pp. 128–30.

14 den Tex, *Oldenbarnevelt*, vol. 1, p. 117.

15 *CSP (Foreign), 1587*, vol. 21, p. 401.

16 F. Bushby, *Three Men of the Tudor Times* (1911), pp. 114–15.

17 Cruikshank, *Elizabeth's Army*, p. 161.

18 de Jong, 'Leicester's Administration', p. 177.

CHAPTER 21

1   C. Cross, *The Royal Supremacy in the Elizabethan Church* (1969), p. 79.
2   L. Stone, *Family and Fortune: Studies in Aristocratic Finance in the Sixteenth and Seventeenth Centuries* (1973), p. 176.
3   O.G.S. Crofts, *The House of Croft of Croft Castle* (1949), p. 67.
4   T.A. Baker, '"Camp Royal" at Tilbury', *EC*, 25 (1977), 246.
5   M. Christy, 'Queen Elizabeth's Visit to Tilbury in 1588', *EHR*, 34 (1919), 50.
6   L.C. John, 'Elizabethan Letter Writer', *PQ*, 24 (1945), 108.
7   Christy, 'Queen Elizabeth's Visit', op. cit., 47.
8   Ibid., 53.
9   C.L. Kingford, 'Essex House', *Archaeologia*, 73 (1922–3), 51.
10 Siegel, *Shakespearean Tragedy*, p. 194 n. 6.
11 Buxton, *Elizabethan Taste*, pp. 99–102.
12 Hill, *Intellectual Origins*, p. 276.
13 Bushby, *Three Men*, p. 133.

APPENDIX A

1   G. Bruno, *Cause, Principle and Unity: Five Dialogues by Giordano Bruno* (trans. from the Italian by J. Lindsay) (1962), p. 7.
2   G. Bruno, *The Ash Wednesday Supper* (trans. from the Italian, *La Cena de le Ceneri*, by Stanley L. Jaki) (1975), p. 14.
3   Hill, *Intellectual Origins*, p. 135 n. 7.

Bibliography

All books, etc., listed were published in London unless otherwise stated.

BOOKS

Addison, W., *Audley End*. 1953.

Adlard, G. *The Sutton-Dudleys of England*. 1862.

——. *Amye Robsart and the Earl of Leicester*. 1870.

Airs, M. *The Making of the English Country House*. 1975.

Axton, M. *The Queen's Two Bodies: Drama and the Elizabethan Succession*. RHS, 1977.

Bayne, C.G. *Anglo-Roman Relations, 1558–65*. Oxford, 2 vols., 1913.

Beckingsale, B.W. *Burghley: Tudor Statesman*. 1967.

Beer, B. *Northumberland: The Political Career of John Dudley, Earl of Warwick and Duke of Northumberland*. Kent, Ohio, 1973.

Bellamy, J. *The Tudor Law of Treason*. 1979.

Bickley, F. *Kings' Favourites*. 1910.

Boas, F. *Queen Elizabeth in Drama and Related Studies*. 1950.

Bond, E.A. (ed.). *Russia at the Close of the Sixteenth Century*. HS, vol. XX. Cambridge, 1856.

Boynton, L. *The Elizabethan Militia, 1558–1638*. 1971.

Bradbrook, M. *The Rise of the Common Player*. 1962.

Broderick, G. *A History of the University of Oxford*. 1886.

Bruno, G. *Cause, Principle and Unity: Five Dialogues by Giordano Bruno*. Trans. from the Italian by J. Lindsay. 1962.

——. *The Ash Wednesday Supper*. Trans. from the Italian, *La Cena de le Ceneri*, by Stanley L. Jaki. 1975.

Bushby, F. *Three Men of the Tudor Times.* 1911.

Buxton, E.J. *Sir Philip Sidney and the English Renaissance.* 1954.

——. *Elizabethan Taste.* 1963.

Cassan, S. *The Lives of the Bishops of Winchester.* 1827.

Castries, H. de. *Les sources inédites de l'histoire du Maroc,* 1st ser., vol. 1. Paris, 1918–25.

Chambers, E.K. *The Elizabethan Stage,* vol. IV. 1923.

Clark, P., Smith, A.G.T. and Tyacke, N. (eds). *The English Commonwealth, 1547–1640.* 1979.

Colligan, J.H. *The Honourable William Whittingham of Chester.* 1934.

Collins, A.J. *Jewels and Plate of Queen Elizabeth I: The Inventory of 1574.* 1955.

Collinson, P. *The Elizabethan Puritan Movement.* 1967.

Colvin, H.M. (ed.). *History of the King's Works, 1485–1660.* 6 vols, 1963–.

Crofts, O.G.S. *The House of Croft of Croft Castle.* Hereford, 1949.

Cross, C. *The Royal Supremacy in the Elizabethan Church.* 1969.

Cruikshank, C.G. *Elizabeth's Army.* Oxford, 1966.

Dent, C.M. *Protestant Reformers in Elizabethan Oxford.* 1983.

Deventer, M.L. van. *Gedenkstukken van Johan van Oldenbarnevelt en zijn tijd,* vol. I. The Hague, 1860.

Dorsten, J.A. van. *Poets, Patrons and Professors: Sir Philip Sidney, Daniel Rogers and the Leiden Humanists.* Leiden: Sir Thomas Browne Institute, 1962.

——. *The Radical Arts: First Decade of an Elizabethan Renaissance.* Leiden: Sir Thomas Browne Institute, 1973.

Duncan-Jones, K. and Dorsten, J.A. van (eds). *Miscellaneous Prose of Sir Philip Sidney.* 1973.

Durant, D. *Bess of Hardwick.* 1977.

Emmison, F.G. *Elizabethan Life (Disorder), Mainly from Essex Sessions and Assize Records.* Chelmsford, 1970.

Evans, R.J.W. *Rudolf II and His World: A Study in Intellectual History, 1576–1612.* Oxford, 1973.

Foster, F.F. *The Politics of Stability: A Portrait of the Rulers in Elizabethan London.* RHS, 1977.

French, P. *John Dee: The World of an Elizabethan Magus.* 1972.

Frere, B. (Sir). *Amy Robsart of Wymondham.* Norwich, 1937.

Girouard, M. *Robert Smythson and the Architecture of the Elizabethan Era.* 1966.

Godfrey, E.S. *The Development of English Glass-making, 1560-1640.* 1975.

Golding, L.T. *An Elizabethan Puritan: Arthur Golding.* New York, 1937.

Gresham, C.A. *Eifionydd.* Cardiff, 1973.

Hakluyt, R. *Principal Navigations, 1598-1600.* 12 vols, 1903-5.

Heal, F. *Of Prelates and Princes: A Study of the Economic and Social Position of the Tudor Episcopate.* 1980.

Hembry, P. *The Bishops of Bath and Wells, 1540-1640.* 1967.

Hill, C. *The Intellectual Origins of the English Revolution.* 1966.

Hopkins, S. *The Puritans during the Reigns of Edward VI and Queen Elizabeth.* Boston, Mass., 3 vols, 1860.

Hore, J.P. *History of the Royal Buckhounds.* 1892.

Howell, R. *Sir Philip Sidney: The Shepherd Knight.* 1968.

Hume, M. *The Courtships of Queen Elizabeth.* 1904.

Hurstfield, J. *The Queen's Wards.* 1958.

James, M. *Family, Lineage and Civil Society, 1500-1640.* 1974.

Jebb, S. *The Life of Robert, Earl of Leicester.* 1727.

Johnson, P. *Elizabeth: A Study in Power and Intellect.* 1974.

Kenny, R.W. *Elizabeth's Admiral: The Political Career of Charles Howard, Earl of Nottingham.* 1970.

Kinder, A.G. *Casiodoro de Reina: Spanish Reformer of the Sixteenth Century.* 1975.

Kipling, G. *The Triumph of Honour: Burgundian Origins of the English Renaissance.* Leiden, 1977.

Knappen, M.M. *Tudor Puritanism.* Chicago, Ill., 1939.

Lake, P. *Moderate Puritans and the Elizabethan Church.* Cambridge, 1982.

Lang, A. *The Mystery of Amy Robsart.* 1903.

Lapsley, G.T. *The County Palatine of Durham.* Cambridge, Mass., 1896.

Laroui, A. *The History of the Maghrib.* Princeton, N.J., 1977.

Lathrop, H.B. *Translations from the Classics into English.* Madison, Wis., 1933.

Leech, C. and Craik, T.W. (eds). *The Revels History of Drama in English.* 1975.

Lees-Milne, J. *Tudor Renaissance.* 1951.

Lennam, T. *Sebastian Westcott, the Children of St. Paul's and the Marriage of Wit and Science.* Toronto, Ont., 1975.

Lindeboom, J. *Austin Friars: History of the Dutch Reformed Church in London, 1550–1950.* The Hague, 1950.

Lloyd, R. *Dorset Elizabethans.* 1967.

Loach, J. and Tittler, R. (eds). *The Mid-Tudor Polity, c. 1540–1560.* 1980.

Loades, D.M. *The Reign of Mary Tudor.* 1979.

Lowers, J.K. *Mirror for Rebels.* 1953.

MacCaffery, W. *The Shaping of the Elizabethan Regime.* 1969.

Maltby, W.S. *The Black Legend in England: The Development of Anti-Spanish Sentiment, 1558–1660.* Durham, N.C., 1971.

Morgan, I. *The Godly Preachers of the Elizabethan Church.* 1965.

Motley, J.L. *History of the United Netherlands.* 4 vols, 1869.

Neale, J.E. *The Elizabethan House of Commons.* 1949.

——. *Elizabeth I and Her Parliaments.* 2 vols: *1559–81; 1584–1601.* 1949–57.

Nijenhuis, W. *Adrianus Saravia (c.* 1532–1613). Leiden, 1980.

Osborn, J. *Young Philip Sidney.* New Haven, Conn., 1972.

Pearson, L.E. *Elizabethans at Home.* Stanford, Calif., 1957.

Phillips, J.E. *Images of a Queen: Mary Stuart in Sixteenth Century Literature.* 1964.

Prest, W. *The Inns of Court under Elizabeth I and the Early Stuarts, 1590–1640.* 1972.

Primus, J.H. *The Vestments Controversy.* Kampen, 1960.

Pulman, M.B. *The Elizabethan Privy Council in the 1570's.* Berkeley, Calif., 1971.

Raab, F. *The English Face of Machiavelli.* 1964.

Read, C. *Mr. Secretary Walsingham and the Policy of Queen Elizabeth.* Oxford, 3 vols, 1925.

——. *Mr. Secretary Cecil and Queen Elizabeth.* 1955.

——. *Lord Burghley and Queen Elizabeth.* 1960.

Rebholz. R. *The Life of Fulke Greville, First Lord Brooke.* Oxford, 1971.

Reese, M.M. *The Royal Office of Master of the Horse.* 1976.

Rhodes, D.E. (ed.). *Essays in Honour of Victor Scholderer.* Mainz, 1970.

Rose, E. *Cases of Conscience: Alternatives Open to Recusants and Puritans under Elizabeth I and James I.* 1975.

Rosenberg, E. *Leicester, Patron of Letters.* New York, 1955.

Rowse, A.L. *The Elizabethan Renaissance: The Life of the Society.* 1971.

Salmon, J.H.M. *Society in Crisis: France in the Sixteenth Century.* 1975.

Sargent, R.M. *At the Court of Queen Elizabeth: The Life and Lyrics of Edward Dyer.* 1935.

Shapiro, M. *Children of the Revels: The Boy Companies of Shakespeare's Time and Their Plays.* New York, 1977.

Siegel, P.N. *Shakespearean Tragedy and the Elizabeth Compromise.* New York, 1957.

Simon, J. *Education and Society in Tudor England.* 1966.

Singer, D.W. *Giordano Bruno: His Life and Thought.* 1950.

Smith, A.G.R. *Servant of the Cecils: The Life of Sir Michael Hickes, 1543-1612.* 1977.

Smith, L.P. *Tudor Prelates and Politics.* Princeton, N.J., 1953.

Stern, V.F. *Gabriel Harvey.* 1979.

Stevenson, W.H. and Salter, H.E. *The Early History of St. John's College.* Oxford, 1939.

Stone, L. *An Elizabethan: Sir Horatio Palavicino.* 1956.

——. *The Crisis of the Aristocracy, 1558-1641.* 1965.

——. *Family and Fortune: Studies in Aristocratic Finance in the Sixteenth and Seventeenth Centuries.* 1973.

Strong, R. (Sir Roy Strong) and Dorsten, J.A. van. *Leicester's Triumph.* Leiden/Oxford, 1964.

Strong, R. (Sir Roy Strong). *The English Icon.* 1969.

Strype, J. *Annals of the Reformation under Elizabeth.* 7 vols, 1824.

Swart, J. *Thomas Sackville.* Groningen, 1949.

Tex, J. den. *Oldenbarnevelt.* Cambridge, 2 vols, 1973.

Thomas, K. *Religion and the Decline of Magic.* 1971.

Thompson, C.J. *Poisons and Poisoners.* 1949.

Thompson, H.L. *The Church of St. Mary the Virgin, Oxford.* 1903.

Tittler, R. *Nicholas Bacon: The Making of a Tudor Statesman.* 1976.

Ungerer, G. *Anglo-Spanish Relations in Tudor Literature.* Madrid, 1956.

——. *A Spaniard in Elizabethan England: The Correspondence of Antonio Perez's Exile.* 2 vols, 1974-6.

Venezky, A.S. *Pageantry on the Elizabethan Stage*. New York, 1951.

Wagner, A. (Sir Anthony Wagner). *English Genealogy*. Oxford, 1972.

Waldman, M. *Elizabeth and Leicester*. 1946.

Watney, V.J. *Cornbury and the Forest of Wychwood*. 1910.

Webb, H.J. *Elizabethan Military Science*. Madison, Wis., 1965.

Wernham, R. *Before the Armada*. 1966.

Willan, T.S. *The Early History of the Russia Company, 1553–1603*. Manchester, 1956.

——. *Studies in Elizabethan Foreign Trade*. Manchester, 1959.

Williams, P.H. *The Council of the Marches in Wales under Elizabeth I*. Cardiff, 1958.

——. *The Tudor Regime*. Oxford, 1979.

Wilson, C. *Queen Elizabeth and the Revolt of the Netherlands*. 1970.

Wilson, D. *Sweet Robin: A Biography of Robert Dudley, Earl of Leicester*. 1981.

ARTICLES AND ESSAYS

Adams, S.L. 'The Gentry of North Wales and the Earl of Leicester's Expedition to the Netherlands, 1585–6', *WHistR*, 7, 1974–5.

——. 'The Composition of 1564 and the Earl of Leicester's Tenurial Reformation in the Lordship of Denbigh', *BBCS*, 26, 4, 1976.

Aird, I. 'The Death of Amy Robsart', *EHR*, 71, 1956.

Axton, M. 'Robert Dudley and the Inner Temple Revels', *HJ*, 13, 3, 1970.

Backus, I. 'Laurence Tomson (1539–1608) and English Puritanism', *JEH*, 28, 1, 1977.

Baker, T.A. ' "Camp Royal" at Tilbury', *EC*, 25 (1977), 246.

Beeching, H.C. 'The Library of the Cathedral Church of Norwich', *NA*, XIX, 1917.

Bellorini, M. 'Un medico italiano alla corte di Elisabetta, Giulio Borgarucci', *EM*, 19, 196.

Bennett, J.H.E. 'Two Elizabethan Chamberlains of the Palatinate of Chester', *JAAHSCNW*, new ser., XX, 1914.

Bovill, E.W. 'Queen Elizabeth's Gunpowder', *MM*, 33, 3, 1947.

Bradbrook, M. 'Princely Pleasures at Kenilworth', Rice Institute pamphlet, 46, 1959–60.

Brodie, D.M. 'Edmund Dudley, Minister of Henry VII', *TRHS*, 4th ser., 15, 1932.

Brown, H. Untitled article on Venice, *QR*, 230, 1918.

Butler, L. 'Leicester's Church in Denbigh: An Experiment in Puritan Worship', *JBAA*, 3rd ser., XXXVII, 1974.

Christy, M. 'Queen Elizabeth's Visit to Tilbury in 1588', *EHR*, 34, 1919.

Clark, J. 'Eliseus Libaerts and His English Connections', *JAAS*, XI, 2, 1983.

Collingwood, W.G. 'Elizabethan Keswick', *TCWAAS*, tract ser., 8, 1912.

Collins, A.J. 'The Progress of Queen Elizabeth to Tilbury, 1588', *BMQ*, 10, 1936.

Cooke, J.H. 'The Great Berkeley Lawsuit of the Fifteenth and Sixteenth Centuries', *TGBAS*, 1878-9.

Council, N. ' "O Dea Certe": The Allegory of "The Fortress of Perfect Beauty" ', *HLQ*, 39, 4, 1976.

Cox, J.C. 'An Elizabethan Clergy List of the Diocese of Lichfield', *SANHS*, 2nd ser., V, 1893.

Demolen, R. 'Richard Mulcaster and Elizabethan Pageantry', *SEL*, 14, 1974.

Dick, H.C. 'Thomas Blundeville's "The true order and methods of wryting and reading Hystories" (1574)', *HLQ*, 3, 2, 1939-40.

Dillon, H.M. (Viscount Dillon). 'Tilting in Tudor Times', *AJ*, LV, 2nd ser., V, 1898.

Dormer, E.W. 'Lettice Knollys', *BAJ*, 39, 1, 1935.

Evans, W.A. 'The Salusburys of Llewenni near Denbigh', *DHST*, 4, 1955.

Fischer, D. 'Merchants, Courtiers and the Sea Route to the Indies: The Case of Elizabethan England', *TI*, 4, 1972.

Gavin, J. 'Politics in the Elizabethan Church: The Appointment of Bishop Matthew, 1582-96', *CJH*, 9, 2, 1974.

Greenlaw, E.A. 'Spenser and the Earl of Leicester', *PMLA*, 25, new ser., 18, 1910.

——. 'Spenser and British Imperialism', *MP*, 9, 1911-12.

Greenslade, S.L. 'William Whittingham, Dean of Durham (1524-79)', *DUJ*, 39, new ser., VIII, 1946-7.

Gresham, C. 'The Forest of Snowdon and Its Relation to Eifionydd', *TCHS*, 21, 1960.

Hall, E.V. 'Lettice's Will', *N&Q*, CLXVIII, Jan. 1935.

Haynes, A.J. 'The English in Padua, 1222-1660', *HT*, 27, 1977.

——. 'The English Earthquake of 1580', *HT*, 29, 1979.

Hill, B. 'Trinity College, Cambridge MS. B.14.52 and William Patten', *TCBS*, 4, 3, 1966.

Hintz, E.W. 'The Elizabethan Entertainment and "The Faerie Queene"', *PQ*, 14, 1935.

Hughes, E. 'The English Monopoly of Salt in the Years 1563-71', *EHR*, 40, 1925.

Jackson, J.E. (Canon). 'Amye Robsart', *WANHM*, XVII, 1878.

John, L.C. 'Elizabethan Letter Writer', *PQ*, 24, 1945.

Jones, J.E. 'The Parliamentary Representation of Berkshire and Its Boroughs during the Reign of Elizabeth I', *BAJ*, 63, 1967-8.

Jordan, W.K. and Gleason, M.R. 'The Saying of John Late Duke of Northumberland upon the Scaffold, 1553', *HLB*, 23, 1, 1975.

Kimbrough, R. and Murphy, P. 'The Helmingham Hall MS. of Sidney's "The Lady of May"', *RD*, new ser., 1, 1968.

Kingford, C.L. 'Essex House', *Archaeologia*, 73, 1922-3.

Lytle, G.F. 'Patronage Patterns in Oxford' in L. Stone (ed.), *The University in Society*, vol. 1, 1975.

McCoy, R.C. 'From the Tower to the Tiltyard: Robert Dudley's Return to Glory', *HJ*, 27, 2, 1984.

May, S.W. 'William Hunnis and the 1577 "Paradise of Dainty Devices"', *SB*, 28, 1975.

Nevinson, J.L. 'New Year's Gifts to Queen Elizabeth I, 1584', *Costume*, 9, 1975.

Newton, A.P. 'The Establishment of the Great Farm of the English Customs', *TRHS*, 4th ser., 1, 1918.

O'Kill, B. 'The Printed Works of William Patten (*c.* 1510-1600)', *TCBS*, 7, 1, 1977.

Owen, H.G. 'Family Politics in Elizabethan Merionethshire', *BBCS*, 18, 1, 1958.

——. 'Lectures and Lectureships in Tudor London', *CQR*, CLXII, 1961.

Owen, L.V.D. 'Sir Roger Williams and the Spanish Power in the Netherlands', *AQ*, 34, 1937.

Parker, G. 'The Dutch Revolt and the Polarization of International Politics', *TvG*, 88, 3, 1976.

Parks, G.B. 'The First Italianate Englishman', *SR*, 8, 1961.

Pearce, B. 'English Food Policy and the Armed Forces', *EcHR*, 12, 1912.

Peck, D.C. 'Government Suppression of English Catholic Books: The Case of "Leicester's Commonwealth"', *LQ*, 47, 2, 1977.

——. ' "News from Heaven and Hell": A Defamatory Narrative of the Earl of Leicester', *ELR*, 8, 2, 1978.

——. 'Raleigh, Sidney, Oxford and the Catholics', 1579, *N&Q*, new ser., 25, 5, 1978.

Read, C. 'Walsingham and Burghley in Queen Elizabeth's Privy Council', *EHR*, XXVIII, 1913.

Scott, D. 'William Patten and the Authorship of Robert Laneham's "Letter" (1575)', *ELR*, 7, 3, 1977.

Shipley, N. 'Thomas Sutton and His Landed Interest in Essex', *EJ*, 8, 4, 1973.

Southern, A.C. ' "The Best Wits out of England": University Men in Exile under Elizabeth', *TM*, 7, 1, 1952.

Stopes, C.C. 'William Hunnis, the Dramatist', *TA*, 1900.

Strong, R. (Sir Roy Strong). 'Federigo Zuccaro's Visit to England in 1575', *JWCI*, XXII, 1959.

——. 'The Leicester House Miniatures: Robert Sidney, 1st Earl of Leicester and His Circle', *BM*, CXXVII, 991, 1985.

Tibbits, E.G. 'The Hospital of Robert, Earl of Leicester in Warwick', *TBAS 1936*, LX, 1940.

Tittler, R. and Battley, S.L. 'The Local Community and the Crown in 1553: The Accession of Mary Tudor Revisited', *BIHR*, LVII, 136, 1984.

Trevor-Roper, H. (Lord Dacre). 'The Bishopric of Durham and the Capitalist Reformation', *DUJ*, 38, new ser., VII, 2, 1946.

Waller, G.F. 'Bruno, Calvin and the Sidney Circle', *Neophilologus*, 55, 1972.

Webb, H.J. 'Elizabethan Soldiers', *WHR*, 4, 2, 1949-50.

Williams, F.B. 'Leicester's Ghost', *HSNP*, 18, 1935.

Woodward, A. 'Purveyance for the Royal Household in the Reign of Elizabeth I', *TAPS*, new ser., XXXV, 1, 1945-6.

Woude, A.M. van der. Der Staten, Leicester en Elizabeth in Financiele Verwikkelingen', *TvG*, 74, 1961.

Wright, C.T. 'The Queen's Husbands: Some Renaissance Views', *BUSE*, 3, 1957.

PRINTED CALENDARS AND REPORTS

Acts of the Privy Council, 1571-5, 1577-8, 1581-2, 1586-7, 1587-8.

Calendar of Patent Rolls (Elizabeth), 1569-72.

Calendar of the Register of the . . . Council in . . . Wales and the Marches of the Same, 1569-91, Cymmrodorion Record Society, series 8, 1916.

Calendar of State Papers (Domestic), 12 vols.

Calendar of State Papers (Foreign), 23 vols.

Calendar of State Papers (Spanish/Elizabethan), *1558-67*, *1568-79*, *1580-6*.

Calendar of State Papers (Venetian), *1558-80*.

State Papers (Foreign Series/Elizabeth I), *1589-90*.

PRINTED DOCUMENTS AND TEXTS

Broersma, R. and Huet, G. (eds). *Letters of Leicester Found in the Papers of Jean Hotman, Bijdragen en Mededeelingen van het Historisch Genootschap*, vol. 34, 1913.

Bruce, J. (ed.). *The Correspondence of Robert Dudley, Earl of Leicester, 1585-86*, Camden Society, old ser., 27, 1844.

Brugmans, H. (ed.). *Correspondentie van Robert Dudley, Graaf van Leycester en andere documenten betreffende zijn gouvernement generaal in der Nederlanden, 1585-88*, 3 vols, 1931.

Christie, R.C. (ed.). *Letters of Sir Thomas Copley*, 1897.

Collins, A. (ed.). *Letters and Memorials of State, Collected by Sir Henry Sydney . . .*, 2 vols, 1746.

Collinson, P. (ed.). 'Letters of Thomas Wood, Puritan, 1566-77', *BIHR*, spec. supp., 5, 1960.

Croft, P. *The Spanish Company*, LRS, 1973.

Davies, D.W. (ed.). *The Actions of the Low Countries by Sir Roger Williams* (Folger Documents of Tudor and Stuart Civilization), Cornell, N.Y., 1964.

Donno, E.S. (ed.). *An Elizabethan in 1582: The Diary of Richard Madox, Fellow of All Souls*, Hakluyt Society, 2nd ser., vol. 147, Cambridge, 1974.

Holinshed, R. *Chronicles* (ed. Henry Ellis). 6 vols, 1807-8.

Houlbrooke, R.A. (ed.). *The Letter Book of John Parkhurst, Bishop of Norwich*, Norfolk Record Society, 1974-5.

Kemp, T. (ed.). *The Black Book of Warwick*, 1898.

Lodge, E. *Illustrations of British History*, 2 vols, 1791.

Merson, A.L. (ed.). *The Third Book of Remembrance of Southampton, 1514-1602*, 1952.

Murdin, W. (ed.). *Burghley State Papers*, 1759.

Nichols, J. (ed.). *History and Antiquities of Leicestershire*, vol. II, 1815.

——. *The Progresses and Public Processions of Queen Elizabeth*, 3 vols, 1823.

O'Malley, C.D. *Satan's Stratagems: Jacopo Aconcio*, San Francisco, Calif., 1940.

Peck, D.C. *Leicester's Commonwealth, 1584*, Athens, Ohio, 1985.

Quinn, D.B. and Cheshire, N. *The New Found Land of Stephen Parmenius*, 1972.

Taylor, E.G.R. (ed.). *The Troublesome Voyage of Captain Edward Fenton, 1582–83*, Hakluyt Society, Cambridge, 1959.

Tighe, R. and Davis, J. (eds). *Annals of Windsor*, vol. 1, 1858.

UNPUBLISHED THESES

Butler, F.M. '"The Erle of Leycester and his friendes" and Ecclesiastical Patronage in the Elizabethan Era', M.Phil., London University, 1979.

Clark, J. 'The Buildings and Art Collections of Robert Dudley, Earl of Leicester', MA, London University, 1981.

Hodgkinson, L.A. 'The Administration of the Earl of Leicester in the United Provinces', MA, Liverpool University, 1925.

Jong, G. de. 'The Earl of Leicester's Administration of the Netherlands, 1585–86', Wisconsin University, Wis., 1956.

Oosterhoff, F.G. 'The Earl of Leicester's Governorship of the Netherlands, 1586–87', London University, 1967.

Index